W9-BRZ-440

AMERICAN CIVIL WAR NAVIES:

A Bibliography

by

Myron J. Smith, Jr.

American Naval Bibliography, Vol. III

The Scarecrow Press, Inc.

Metuchen, N.J. 1972

Library of Congress Cataloging in Publication Data

Smith, Myron J
American Civil War navies.

(American naval bibliography, v. 3)
1. United States--History--Civil War--Naval operations--Bibliography. I. Title. II. Series.
Z1242.S63 016.9737'5 72-6063
ISBN 0-8108-0509-X

CONTENTS

PUBLISHER'S NOTE

The present work, the first of the American Naval Bibliography series to be completed and published, was originally conceived of by the compiler as a one-volume venture. It was not until numerous friends and colleagues commented on the potential value of the *American Civil War Navies: A Bibliography* that he elected to attempt the up-dating of the grand endeavors of Messers. Harbeck and Neeser, completed over 60 years ago. This volume, number III of the series, represents the beginning of that up-dating project.

The other volumes of the series are in various stages of preparation and will appear subsequently. Back on course, the next volume, *Navies in the American Revolution: A Bibliography*, will apear in Winter 1972/73. It will be followed by volume II, *The American Navy, 1789-1860: A Bibliography*; (volume III); volume IV, *The American Navy, 1865-1940: A Bibliography*; and volume V, *The American Navy, 1941-1970's: A Bibliography*.

PREFACE

After the fall of Vicksburg in 1863, Abraham Lincoln wrote to a friend, "nor must Uncle Sam's web-feet be forgotten." The President was, of course, referring to the Northern Navy, but his words might have applied just as well to the Southern. Unfortunately over the years, his words have largely gone unheeded. For most Americans, knowledge of the huge role played by Union and Confederate sea forces in the Civil War has been clouded or overlooked.

The neglected war of the "web-feet" is nowhere more fully illuminated than in the bibliographical control of Rebellion literature. While literally tons of copy have poured forth about the conflict, not a single bibliography has ever been devoted exclusively to those printed materials demonstrating the achievements of sailors and marines North and South. The present volume is designed to fill this gap.

The effort to provide scholars or buffs with as many leads as possible has led the compiler to a policy of comprehensive inclusion. In using this tool, students will note some references which would appear upon a surface inspection to be wholly non-naval. These are provided for the insight they may lend to naval or combined operations, particularly on the Western waters.

In choosing references, it was necessary to develop some criteria. To this end, the following types of materials are represented by citations: books; scholarly papers; periodical or magazine articles; documents of an American or English language origin; important general works; and important doctoral and masters' degree papers. The following types of materials are not represented: poetry; childrens works; newspaper articles (unless reprinted by a periodical); fiction; and book reviews. Annotations of a non-critical nature are supplied wherever their application might improve the value of citations.

The 2, 800-plus numbered entries of the bibliography span the period between the 1850's and 1970's. The whole is arranged alphabetically by authors and titles. Joint-author, compiler, and editor cross references are provided within the body of the text, each receiving an entry number. The appendix and a subject index complete the work.

While the Civil War continues to attract talented chroniclers, no tool of this nature can hope to remain the final word. Inevitable omissions will, of course, be noted, and for these apology is offered. In an area where little bibliographic control has previously existed, it is hoped that this volume will prove a worthy starting point and guide to further exploration.

For their advice and assistance in the formulation, research, and completion of this project, the following persons and libraries are gratefully and alphabetically acknowledged: Prof. Alwyn Barr, Texas Tech. University; Dr. Benjamin F. Cooling, U.S. Army Military History Research Collection; The Enoch Pratt Free Library; Mr. William E. Geoghegan, Museum Specialist, Smithsonian Institution; The Gettysburg College Library; Prof. Benjamin F. Gilbert, San Jose State College; Mr. W. Bart Greenwood, Librarian, Navy Department Library; Rear Admiral John D. Hayes, USN (ret.); Mr. Robert H. Land, Chief, General Reference Section, Library of Congress; The Louisiana State University Library; Dr. Philip K. Lundeberg, Curator of Naval History, Smithsonian Institution; Prof. James M. Merrill, University of Delaware; Prof. John D. Milligan, State University of New York at Buffalo; Dr. William J. Morgan, Head Research Section, Naval History Division, Navy Department; The Richmond (Va.) Public Library; Dr. Charles Schultz, former Librarian, Mystic Seaport; Prof. H. Ray Stevens, Western Maryland College; Prof. William N. Still, East Carolina University; The University of Delaware Library; The University of Maryland Library; The United States Naval Academy Library; and The Virginia State Library.

For her aid in all the preparation, grateful thanks are given to my wife Susan.

This work is dedicated to the memory of all those departed souls who might once have served in the Union or Confederate Navy or Marine Corps. May those "web-feet" be no longer forgotten.

Myron J. Smith, Jr.

FOREWORD

Scarcely more than a decade ago the United States entered upon the Centennial commemoration of our most traumatic national experience, the American Civil War. Much was learned during that prolonged experience in collective reminiscence and re-evaluation, including directions not to take on similar future occasions. The avalanche of publications generated by the Centennial covered military and naval operations exhaustively, yet it failed rather surprisingly to include a series of comprehensive bibliographic studies that might accurately have established the dimensions of the vast literature of this many-faceted conflict. In retrospect, the harvest was wisely delayed. For in achieving, one decade later, a more definitive survey of the naval bibliography of the Civil War, Myron J. Smith has fashioned a tool of enduring value to future historians, be they teachers, writers, librarians, archivists or, indeed, museum curators.

An historical bibliography endowed with such deepened perspective affords substantially greater insight into the degree of thoroughness with which areas of the broad maritime panorama have been examined. By their serried achievements, major contributors to our Civil War naval historiography stand sharply identified, offering a challenge for new approaches to seemingly exhausted themes or suggesting, often indirectly, some rather exciting lacunae. Indications may be found that much remains to be evaluated in major areas of naval technology--notably in ordnance and warship construction--provided that contemporary plans, models and other production data, as well as photographs and museum survivals, are imaginatively re-examined in relation to the men and institutions that created these weapons systems. That the author's index offers no entry on convoy operations is understandable in terms of Federal naval policy; that it contains numerous entries on blockade running but none on fleet logistics or sea-borne supply suggests an attractive challenge to the practitioners of modern quantitative analysis. While the aura of the lost cause has served to immortalize through biography a number of notable leaders of the Confederate Navy, it is apparent that important figures in Union ranks still await adequate appraisal.

The author has carefully delimited his survey in several regards, perhaps most notably in restricting it to English-language publications. As has been strongly suggested by Professor Jay Luvaas in *The Military Legacy of the Civil War: The European Inheritance*, joint operations during that conflict received searching professional appraisal both by contemporary European observers and by later British and Continental historians, important sources for the mature student. Ultimately one must also consider scores of unpublished observers' reports long forgotten in European archives, numerous articles in such professional journals as the remarkably rewarding Russian naval publication *Morskoi Sbornik*, and a number of restricted technical studies by *ad hoc* military commissions. It is clearly indicated that *much* yet remains to be discovered, analyzed and synthesized on the technological and institutional aspects of Civil War naval history, a fact abundantly evident from an analysis of the publication at hand.

Philip Karl Lundeberg
Smithsonian Institution

ABBREVIATIONS

Annals of the War	*The Annals of the War. Written by Leading Participants North and South.* Philadelphia; the Times Publishing Company, 1879. 800p.
George M. Vickers, ed. *Under Both Flags*	Vickers, George M., ed. *Under Both Flags: Tales of the Civil War as Told by the Veterans.* Philadelphia: People's Publishing, 1896. 592p.
Lewis R. Hamersly, ed. *A Naval Encyclopedia*	Hamersly, Lewis R. *A Naval Encyclopedia, Comprising a Dictionary of Nautical Words and Phrases; Biographical Notices and Records of Naval Officers; Special Articles on Naval Art and Science, Written Expressly for this Work by Officers and Others of Recognized Authority in the Branches Treated by Them, Together with Descriptions of the Principal Naval Stations and Seaports of the World.* Philadelphia: Hamersly, 1884. 872p.
Robert U. Johnson and Clarence C. Buell, eds. *B & L*	Johnson, Robert U. and Clarence C. Buell, eds. *Battles and Leaders of the Civil War: Being for the Most Part Contributions by Union and Confederate Officers.* 4 vols. New York: Century, 1887.

BIBLIOGRAPHY

1. Abbot, Henry C., Joint Author. See Humphreys, Andrew A., no. 1225.

2. Abbot, Willis J. Blue Jackets of '61: A History of the Navy in the War of Secession. New York: Dodd, Mead, 1886. 318p.

3. -----. The Naval History of the United States. New York: Dodd, Mead, 1896. 1,028p.

4. Abbott, John S. C. "Charles Ellet and His Naval Steam Rams." Harper's New Monthly Magazine, XXXII (February 1866), 295-312.

5. -----. "The Civil War in the Wilds of Arkansas." Harper's New Monthly Magazine, XXXIII (October 1866), 581-601

    Includes the Battle of the Post of Arkansas.

6. -----. The History of the Civil War in America. 2 vols. New York: Henry Bell, 1866.

7. -----. "A Military Adventure." Harper's New Monthly Magazine, XXX (December 1864), 3-20.

    Deals in part with action in the waters off North Carolina.

8. -----. "Military Adventures Beyond the Mississippi." Harper's New Monthly Magazine, XXX (April 1865), 575-592.

    Actions on the Western Rivers.

9. -----. "The Navy in the North Carolina Sounds." Harper's New Monthly Magazine, XXXII (April 1866), 567-583.

10. -----. "Opening the Mississippi." Harper's New Monthly Magazine, XXXIII (August 1866), 296-309.

11. -----. "Siege and Capture of Port Hudson." Harper's New Monthly Magazine, XXX (March 1865), 425-439.

12. -----. "Siege of Vicksburg." Harper's New Monthly Magazine, XXX (January 1865), 150-166.

13. -----. "Texas Lost and Won." Harper's New Monthly Magazine, XXXIII (September 1866), 444-463.
Includes the 1 January 1863 Battle of Galveston.

14. -----. "True Chivalry: Benjamin H. Porter." Harper's New Monthly Magazine, XXXIV (April 1867), 559-571.

15. Abraham Lincoln's Campaign Against the Merrimack. Tales of Old Fort Monroe, no. 9. Fort Monroe, Va.: The Casemate Museum, n.d. 4p.

16. Abrams, Alexander St. Clair. A Full and Detailed History of the Siege of Vicksburg. Atlanta: Georgia Intelligencer Steam Power Presses, 1863. 80p.

17. An Account of the Reception Given by the Citizens of New York to the Survivors of the Officers and Crews of the U.S. Frigates Cumberland and Congress. April 10th, 1862. New York: J.A. Gray & Grim, 1862. 38p.
Destroyed by the Rebel ironclad Virginia.

18. Adams, Charles F. Charles Francis Adams, by his Son.... Boston: Houghton, Mifflin, 1900. 426p.
Biography of the Union Minister to Great Britain, part of whose duties was to prevent the sailing of British-built Confederate cruisers.

19. -----. "The Trent Affair." American Historical Review, XVII (April 1912), 540-562.

20. ----- -----. Magazine of History, XX (March-April 1915), 90-98, 141-157.

21. Adams, F. Colburn. High Old Salts; Stories Intended for the Marines but Told Before an Enlightened Committee of Congress. Washington: Government Printing Office, 1876. 138p.
Highly critical of Admiral David D. Porter.

22. Adams, William H. D. Dewey and Other Great Naval Commanders. London: G. Routledge, 1899. 487p.
Includes Farragut and Porter.

23. Adams, William T. "The Birth of the Aircraft Carrier." United States Naval Institute Proceedings, XCIII (April 1967), 162-165.
The balloon boat George Washington Parke Curtis.

24. -----. "Guns for the Navy." Ordnance, XLV (January-February 1961), 508-511.
Contributions of Admiral John Dahlgren.

25. -----. "The Red Rover: First Hospital Ship of the United States Navy." United States Naval Institute Proceedings, XCIV (November 1968), 149-151.
On the Mississippi.

26. -----. "The Ship-Shore Duel." Ordnance, XLV (May-June, 1961), 798-800.

27. -----. "The Underwater War." Ordnance, XLVII (November-December 1962), 317-319.

28. -----. "The Union Mortar Boats." Ordnance, XLVI (March-April 1961), 659-661.

29. "Admiral Raphael Semmes." Confederate Veteran, XXXV (January-December 1927), 376.

30. "Admiral Raphael Semmes, C.S.N." Confederate Veteran, XXXIX (January-December 1931), 342.

31. Ahmat, Sharom bin. "The Alabama in Singapore Waters." Peninjau Sejarah [Malaya], II (January 1967), 25-29.

32. The Alabama: A Statement of Facts from Official Documents, with the Sections of the Foreign Enlistment Act Violated by Her Equipment. London: J. Snow, 1863. 16p.

33. "The Alabama and Her Doings, and Crew." Nautical Magazine (March 1864), 135-141.

34. "Alabama and Kearsage Armament." Confederate Veteran, IX (January-December 1901), 10.

35. "The Alabama at Capetown." Confederate Veteran, II (January-December 1894), 332-333.

36. Albion, Robert G. "The Administration of the Navy, 1798-1945." Public Administration Review, V (May-June 1945), 293-302.
Includes the Civil War period.

37. -----. "The Naval Affairs Committees, 1816-1917." United States Naval Institute Proceedings, LXXVIII (November 1952), 1227-1237.

38. Albion, Robert G. Naval and Maritime History: An Annotated Bibliography. 3rd ed. Mystic, Conn.: Marine Historical Association, 1963. 230p.
Many Civil War citations.

39. ----- -----. First Supplement, 1963-1965. Mystic, Conn.: Marine Historical Association, 1966. 62p.

40. ----- -----. Second Supplement, 1966-1968. Mystic, Conn.: Marine Historical Association, 1968. 60p.

41. -----. Sea Lanes in Wartime, the American Experience, 1775-1942, by Robert G. Albion and Jennie B. Pope. New York: W. W. Norton, 1942. 367p.
Includes the damages wrought by Rebel cruisers.

42. Alden, Carroll Storrs. George Hamilton Perkins, Commodore, U.S.N.; His Life and Letters. Boston: Houghton, Mifflin, 1914. 302p.

43. -----. The Makers of Naval Tradition. Rev. ed. Boston: Ginn, 1943. 398p.
Includes Farragut and Porter.

44. -----. "The Santee: an Appreciation." United States Naval Institute Proceedings, XXXIX (June 1913), 761-779.

45. -----. "Stephen Bleecker Luce, U.S.N." United States Naval Institute Proceedings, L (December 1924), 2010-2028.

46. -----. The United States Navy: A History, by Carroll S. Alden and Allan Westcott. Philadelphia: Lippincott, 1943. 452p.

47. Alden, John D. "Born Forty Years Too Soon." American Neptune, XXII (October 1962), 252-263.
The U.S.S. Roanoke.

48. Alderson, William T., Jr. "Operation Cairo Salvages Ironclad." History News, XX (April 1965), 70-71.

49. Aldrich, Almy M. History of the United States Marine Corps. From Official Reports and Other Documents. Compiled by Captain Richard S. Collum. Boston: Shepard, 1875. 257p.

50. Alexander, Violet. "The Confederate Navy Yard at Charlotte, North Carolina, 1862-1865." Southern Historical Society Papers, XL (1915), 184-192.

51. Alexander, W. A. "The Confederate Torpedo Boat Hunley." Gulf States Historical Magazine, I (September 1902), 81-91.

52. ----- -----. Southern Historical Society Papers, XXX (1902), 164-174.

53. -----. "Heroes of the Hunley." Munsey Magazine, XXIX (August 1903), 746-749.

54. [Alger, F. S.] "The Congress and the Merrimac: the Story Retold by F. S. Alger." Edited by F. H. Curtis. New England Magazine, XIX (February 1899), 687-693.

54a. Allbaugh, William A., III. Confederate Faces: A Pictorial Review of the Individuals in the Confederate Armed Forces. Solana Beach, Calif.: Verde Publishers, 1970. 229p.
Includes members of the Southern navy and marine corps.

55. Alldredge, J. Haden. et al. A History of Navigation on the Tennessee River System. Washington: U.S. Government Printing Office, 1937.
Includes the action at Fort Henry, 1862.

56. Allen, Charles J. "Some Account and Recollections of the Operations Against the City of Mobile and its Defences, 1864 and 1865." In Glimpses of the Nation's Struggle: A Series of Papers Read Before

the Minnesota Commandry, Military Order of the Loyal Legion of the United States. 6 vols. St. Paul: St. Paul Book and Stationary, 1887-1909. Vol. I, pp. 54-88.

57. Allen, W. "Defence of Charleston Harbor in the Civil War." New Englander, LIII (November 1890), 406-410.

58. Almy, John J. Incidents of the Blockade. District of Columbia Commandery, Military Order of the Loyal Legion of the United States. War Papers, no. 9. Washington: The Commandery, 1892.

59. Ambrose, Stephen E. "Fort Donelson: A 'Disastrous' Blow to the South." Civil War Times Illustrated, V (June 1966), 4-13, 42-49.

60. -----. Halleck, Lincoln's Chief of Staff. Baton Rouge: Louisiana State University Press, 1962. 226 p.
Was in the West with Foote and the gunboats.

61. Ambrose, Stephen E. et al. "Struggle for Vicksburg: The Battles and Siege that Decided the Civil War." Civil War Times Illustrated, VI (July 1967), 1-66.
A special number.

62. -----. "The Union Command System and the Donelson Campaign." Military Affairs, XXIV (Summer 1960), 78-86.

63. -----. ed. See Newton, James K., no. 1785.

64. America: History and Life--a Guide to Periodical Literature. Santa Barbara, Cal., Clio Press, July 1964-. v.1, no. 1-. Quarterly.
Includes abstracts for items on Civil War naval history. Useful for updating Historical Abstracts and Writings on American History.

65. The American Heritage Picture History of the Civil War. Editor in Charge: Richard M. Ketchum. Narrative by Bruce Catton. New York: American Heritage Publishing, 1960. 630p.
Some excellent illustrations of naval craft.

66. American Iron and Steel Association. History of the Manufacture of Armor Plate for the United States

Navy. Philadelphia: The Association, 1899. 33p.
Includes the Civil War period.

67. "The American Monitors." Nautical Magazine (August 1864), 425-431.

68. "The American Navy in the Late War." Edinburgh Review, CXXIV (July 1866), 188-222.
The British view.

69. Ames, Adelbert. The Capture of Fort Fisher, North Carolina, January 15, 1865. n.p., 1870. 24p.

70. ----- -----. In Civil War Papers, Read Before the Commandery of the State of Massachussetts, Military Order of the Loyal Legion of the United States. 2 vols. Boston: The Commandery, 1890. Vol. I, pp. 271-298.

71. Ammen, Daniel. The Atlantic Coast. Vol. II of The Navy in the Civil War. New York: Scribner, 1883. 273p.

72. Ammen, Daniel. "The Career of Commander William B. Cushing." The United Service, II (June 1880), 692-697.

73. -----. "Commander W. B. Cushing, U.S.N." In Lewis R. Hamersly, ed. A Naval Encyclopedia. p. 187-188.

74. -----. "DuPont and the Port Royal Expedition." In Robert U. Johnson and Clarence C. Buell, eds. B & L. Vol. I, pp. 671-690.

75. -----. "Marine Rams." In Lewis R. Hamersly, ed. A Naval Encyclopedia. p. 480-482.

76. -----. The Old Navy and the New. Philadelphia: Lippincott, 1891. 553p.
Includes the author's Civil War adventures aboard the Federal ships Roanoke, Seneca, Sebago, Patapsco, and Mohican.

77. -----. "The Second Bombardment of Fort Fisher." District of Columbia Commandery, Military Order of the Loyal Legion of the United States. War

Papers, no. 4. Washington: The Commandery, 1887.

78. Amory, Charles B. A Brief Record of the Army Life of Charles B. Amory; Written for His Children. [Boston?] Priv. Print., 1902. 43p.
A small account of Carolina coastal operations.

79. Anderson, B. Robert. "The Hollow Victory of the Submarine Hunley." Compass, XL (March-April 1970), 21-25.

80. Anderson, Bern. By Sea and by River; the Naval History of the Civil War. New York: Knopf, 1962. 303p.

81. -----. "The Naval Strategy of the Civil War." Military Affairs, XXVI (Spring 1962), 11-21.
On ocean and river.

82. Anderson, Galusha. The Story of a Border City during the Civil War. Boston: Little, Brown, 1908. 385p.
Useful for an understanding of feelings in St. Louis where numerous gunboats were built or fitted out.

83. Anderson, John Q., ed. See Holmes, Sarah K (Stone), no. 1157.

84. Anderson, William H. "Blockade Life." In War Papers, Read Before the Commandery of the State of Maine, Military Order of the Loyal Legion of the United States. 3 vols. Portland: Thurston, 1898-1908. Vol. II, pp. 1-10.

85. Andrews, Christopher C. History of the Campaign of Mobile; Including the Cooperative Operations of General Wilson's Cavalry in Alabama. New York: D. Van Nostrand, 1867. 276p.

86. Andrews, J. Cutler. The North Reports the Civil War. Pittsburgh: University of Pittsburgh Press, 1955. 813p.
Contains excerpts covering naval matters.

87. -----. The South Reports the Civil War.

Princeton, N. J.: Princeton University Press, 1970. 611p.
Including Confederate efforts afloat.

88. Angle, Paul M. "The End of the Civil War." Chicago History, VII (July 1965), 193-197.
Title misleading; refers to cruise of the C.S.S. Shenandoah.

89. -----. "The Last Years of the Shenandoah." Chicago History, VII (August 1965), 242-245.
The sale and postwar fate of the raider.

90. The Annals of the War. Written by Leading Participants North and South. Philadelphia: The Times Publishing Company, 1879. 800p.

91. An Answer to Misrepresentations (Mr. Gideon Welles and His Writings). Washington: Chronicle Publishing Company, 1872. 28p.
Felt to exist in his journal articles.

92. Aptheker, Herbert. "The Negro in the Union Navy." Journal of Negro History, XXXII (April 1947), 169-200.
The only full-scale study on the subject.

93. "Armor Plate." Confederate Veteran, X (January-December 1902), 20.

94. Armstrong, James. Defence of Commodore James Armstrong, U.S.N. Washington: G. S. Gideon, 1861. 21p.
Courtmartialed for surrendering the Pensacola Navy Yard to Florida's Rebel forces.

95. Armstrong, Warren, pseud. See Bennett, William E., no. 246.

96. The Army and Navy Official Gazette. Containing Reports of Battles; Also, Important Orders of the War Department, Record of Courts-Martial, etc. Washington: J.C. Rives, July 7, 1863-June 27, 1865. v.1-2.
An early source of official materials; often inaccurate with many gaps.

97. Army Times Publishing Company, Editors of, Joint Authors. See Hoehling, Adolph A., no. 1159.

98. Arnold, E. G. Persecution of the Volunteer Naval Officers. Providence: A. Crawford Greene, 1863. 30p.
In the matter of rank, pay, etc.

99. Arthur, Robert. History of Fort Monroe. Fort Monroe, Va.: The Coast Artillery School, 1930. 290p.
Includes the Monitor vs. the Merrimack.

100. Ashcraft, Allan C. "Civil War Naval Weapons That Might Have Been." American Neptune, XXII (October 1962), 280-289.
Some of the ideas peddled by inventors to the Union and Confederate governments.

101. Ashe, Samuel A'Court. "Captain James Iredell Waddell." North Carolina Booklet, XIII (October 1913), 126-142.
Skipper of the Shenandoah, Rebel raider.

102. -----. "Trained in the Old Naval School." Confederate Veteran, XXXVIII (January-December 1930), 8-9.

103. Asprey, Robert B. "The Assault on Fort Fisher." Marine Corps Gazette, XLIX (November 1965), 30-31.

104. Atkins, John B. The Life of Sir William Howard Russell, C.V.O., L.L.D., the First Special Correspondent. London: J. Murray, 1911.
Held a high opinion of Union naval officers.

105. Atkinson, J. H., ed. See Fletcher, Elliot, Jr., no. 868.

106. "The Attack on Helena, July 4, 1863." Southern Historical Society Papers, XXIV (1896), 197-200.
Reprint of a July 1896 New York Sun piece.

107. Avery, Myrta L., Joint Editor. See Chesnut, Mary B., no. 483.

108. Avery, William B. Gun-boat Service on the James River. Personal Narratives of Events in the War of the Rebellion, Being Papers Read Before the Rhode Island Soldiers and Sailors Historical Society. 3rd Series, no. 3. Providence: N. B. Williams, 1884.

109. Bache, R. Meade. "What the Coast Survey Has Done for the War." United States Service Magazine, III (June 1865), 499-511.
Particularly helpful in mapping the Western Rivers.

110. [Bacon, George B.] "The Civil War Letters of Lieutenant-Commander George B. Bacon." Edited by John K. Mahon. American Neptune, XII (October 1952), 271-281.
Saw service in the Battle of New Orleans.

111. -----. "One Night's Work, April 20, 1862: Breaking the Chain for Farragut's Fleet at the Forts Below New Orleans." Magazine of American History, XV (March 1886), 305-307.

112. Bacon, Thomas. "The Fight at Port Hudson: Recollections of an Eye Witness." The Independent, XIII (March 1901), 589-598.

113. Bacot, Clara. "Destruction of a Federal Gunboat." Confederate Veteran, XVI (January-December 1908), 347.
The successful mission of twelve Southern scouts in knocking out a small Federal gunboat running up Warpool Cut and firing on Charleston in the Spring of 1862.

114. Badeau, Adam. The Military History of U. S. Grant, April 1861-April 1865. 3 vols. New York: D. Appleton, 1881.
Written by the General's secretary.

115. Badlam, William H. "The First Cruise of the Kearsarge." In Civil War Papers, Read Before the Commandery of the State of Massachusetts, Military Order of the Loyal Legion of the United States. 2 vols. Boston: The Commandery, 1890. Vol. I, pp. 11-26.

116. -----. The Kearsarge and the Alabama. Personal Narratives of Events in the War of the Rebellion, Being Papers Read Before the Rhode Island Soldiers and Sailors Historical Society. 5th Series, no. 2. Providence: N. B. Williams, 1884.

117. [Bailey, Theodorus]. History Set Right. Attack on New Orleans and its Defenses, by the Fleet under Admiral Farragut, April 24, 1862. New York: Office of the Army and Navy Journal, 1869. 14p.
The Bailey-Farragut correspondence reprinted from the Army and Navy Journal of July 17, 1869.

118. Baker, John W. and Lee C. Dickson. "Army Forces in Riverine Operations." Military Review, XLVII (August 1967), 64-74.
Includes the Civil War period.

119. Baker, Marion A. "Farragut's Demands for the Surrender of New Orleans." In Robert U. Johnson and Clarence C. Buell, eds. B & L. Vol. II, pp. 95-98.

120. Bakewell, Henry P., Jr. "The U.S.S. Sabine." American Neptune, XXIII (October 1963), 261-263.

121. Balch, T. W. "The Removal of Mason and Slidell from the Trent." The Nation, LXXXVIII (February 1911), 137-138.

122. Baldwin, H. D. "Farragut in Mobile Bay, Recollections of One Who Took Part in the Battle." Scribner's Monthly, XIII (February 1877), 542.

123. Ball, Francis K., Joint Author. See Blaisdell, Albert F., no. 276.

124. Ballard, D. M. "What Happened in the Battle of Baton Rouge." Confederate Veteran, XX (January-December 1912), 469-470.
Failure of the Confederate ram Arkansas.

125. Banta, Richard E. The Ohio. Rivers of America. New York: Rinehart, 1949. 592p.
Cruised by Yankee "tinclads."

126. Barbet, Paul. "Naval Encounter between the Kearsarge and Alabama Fought in Sight of Cherbourg, France, on June 19, 1864." United States Naval Institute Proceedings, LII (August 1926), 1681-1686.

127. Barker, Albert S. Everyday Life in the Navy; the Autobiography of Rear Admiral Albert S. Barker. Boston: R. G. Badger, 1928. 422p.
Who served aboard the U. S. S. Mississippi.

128. Barnes, Elinor, Joint Editor. See Boyer, Samuel P., no. 305.

129. Barnes, Frank. Fort Sumter National Monument, South Carolina. National Park Service Historical Handbook Series, no. 12. Rev. ed. Washington: U. S. Government Printing Office, 1962. 47p.

130. Barnes, Horace R. "Rear Admiral William Reynolds: A Distinguished Lancastrain, 1815-1879." Lancaster County Historical Society Papers, XXXVIII (1934), 61-66.
Commanded the Port Royal naval depot for the South Atlantic Blockading Squadron.

131. Barnes, James. David G. Farragut. The Beacon Biographies of Eminent Americans. London: K. Paul, Trench, Trubner, 1899. 132p.

132. -----. "The Port Royal Expedition, 1861." Harper's Weekly, LV (December 23, 1911), 9.
Thoughts fifty years later.

133. -----. "Rear Admiral John G. Walker." Review of Reviews, XVI (September 1897), 298-302.
Skipper of the ironclad Baron de Kalb; Second commander of the Yazoo Pass Expedition, 1863.

134. Barnes, James A., Joint Editor. See Boyer, Samuel P., no. 305.

135. [Barnes, John S]. "The Battle of Port Royal Ferry, South Carolina; With the Entry for New Year's Eve and Day, 1862 from the Journal of John S. Barnes." Edited by John D. Hayes and Lillian

O'Brien. New York Historical Society Quarterly, XLVII (April 1963), 109-136.

136. -----. Submarine Warfare, Offensive, and Defensive. Including a Discussion of the Offensive Torpedo System. New York: D. Van Nostrand. 1869. 233p.
Based largely on Civil War experiences.

137. Barr, Alwyn. "The Battle of Blair's Landing." Louisiana Studies, II (Winter 1963), 204-212.
Between the Yankee monitor Osage and the "timberclad" Lexington for the North and Thomas Green's Southern cavalry during the Red River Expedition of 1864.

138. -----. "The Battle of Calcasieu Pass." Southwest Historical Quarterly, LXVI (July 1962), 59-67.
A Louisiana operation, May 6-7, 1864, involving the U.S. gunboats Granite City, Wave, New London, and the transport Ella Morse.

139. -----. "Confederate Artillery in Arkansas." Arkansas Historical Quarterly, XXII (Fall 1963), 238-272.

140. -----. "Confederate Artillery in the Trans-Mississippi." Military Affairs, XXVII (Summer 1963), 77-84.

141. -----. "Confederate Artillery in Western Louisiana, 1862-1863." Civil War History, IX (March 1963), 74-85.

142. -----. "Confederate Artillery in Western Louisiana, 1864." Louisiana History, V (Winter 1964), 53-73.
The Red River Expedition.

143. -----. Polignac's Texas Brigade. Texas Gulf Coast Historical Association, Publication Series, v. 8, no. 1. Houston: The Association, 1964. 72p.
The Red River Expedition.

144. -----. "Sabine Pass, September, 1863." Texas Military History, II (February 1962), 17-22.

Saw the loss of the Federal gunboats Sachem and Clifton to the Confederates.

145. Barr, Alwyn. "Texas Coastal Defense, 1861-1865." Southwest Historical Quarterly, LXV (July 1961), 1-31.

146. -----. ed. See Smith, N. H., no. 2235.

147. Barrett, Edward. Gunnery Instructions, Simplified for the Volunteer Officers of the United States Navy, with Hints for Executive and Other Officers. New York: D. Van Nostrand, 1863. 88p.

148. Barrett, John G. The Civil War in North Carolina. Chapel Hill: University of North Carolina Press, 1963. 484p.

Includes naval operations.

149. Barthell, Edward E., Jr., ed. The Mystery of the Merrimack. Muskegon, Mich.: Dana, 1959. 54p.

150. Bartlett, John R. "The Brooklyn at the Passage of the Forts." In Robert U. Johnson and Clarence C. Buell, eds. B & L. Vol. II, pp. 56-69.

The Battle of New Orleans, 1862.

151. Bartlett, Samuel J. "A Union Volunteer with the Mississippi Ram Fleet." Edited by L. Moody Sims, Jr. Lincoln Hearld, LXX (Winter 1968), 189-192.

Service aboard the Ellet vessel Monarch.

152. [Bartlett, Stephen C.] "Letters of Stephen Chaulker Bartlett aboard the U.S.S. Lenapee, January-August 1865." Edited by Paul Murray and Stephen R. Bartlett, Jr. North Carolina Historical Review, XXXIII (January 1956), 66-92.

153. Bartlett, Stephen R., Jr., Joint Editor. See Bartlett, Stephen C., no. 152.

154. Bartols, Barnabas H. "Remarks on the Monitor." Journal of the Franklin Institute, LXXIII (1862), 284-285.

155. -----. A Treatise on the Marine Boilers of the

United States. Philadelphia: R. W. Barnard, 1851.
Includes data on the machinery of a number of heavy Union vessels, including the *Mississippi.*

156. Basler, Roy P., Joint Editor. *See* Lincoln, Abraham, no. 1454.

157. Basoco, Richard W., William E. Geoghegan, and Frank J. Merli, eds. "A British View of the Union Navy, 1864; a Report Addressed to Her Majesty's Minister at Washington." *American Neptune*, XXVII (January 1967), 30-45.

158. "The Cruise of 'Savez' Read." *Civil War Times Illustrated*, II (December 1963), 10-15.
Aboard the *Clarence*-*Tacony*-*Archer*, commerce raiders of the Confederacy.

159. Bassett, F. S. "Admiral David Dixon Porter." *United Service*, New Series V (April 1891), 381-384.

160. -----. "Farragut and His Service during the Rebellion." *United Service*, New Series I (February 1889), 128-138.

161. -----. "Rear Admiral Charles Wilkes, U.S.N." *In* Lewis R. Hamersly, ed. *A Naval Encyclopedia.* p. 845.

162. Basso, Hamilton. *Beauregard, the Great Creole.* New York: Scribner, 1933. 333p.

163. Batcheller, Oliver A. "The Battle of Mobile Bay, August 5, 1864." *In War Papers, Read Before the Commandery of the State of Maine, Military Order of the Loyal Legion of the United States.* 3 vols. Portland: Thurston, 1898-1908. Vol. I, pp. 58-72.

164. ----- -----. *Magazine of History*, XIV (December 1911), 217-230.

165. Bates, Alan L. "Will S. Hayes--The Man." *Steamboat Bill*, XVIII (Spring 1961), 3-8.
A Civil War pilot; later River Editor of *The Louisville Courier-Journal.*

166. [Bates, Edward]. The Diary of Edward Bates, 1859-1866. Edited by Howard K. Beale. Washington: U. S. Government Printing Office, 1933. 685p.
A Missourian; Friend of James B. Eads.

167. Bathe, Greville. Ship of Destiny: A Record of the U. S. Steam Frigate Merrimac, 1855-1862. With an Appendix on the Development of U. S. Naval Cannon from 1812-1865. St. Augustine, Fla.: n. p., 1951. 82p.

168. Batten, John M. Random Thoughts. Pittsburgh: The Author, 1896. 320p.

169. -----. Reminiscences of Two Years in the United States Navy. Lancaster, Pa.: Inquirer Press, 1881. 125p.
By a surgeon aboard the Valley City on the Wilmington blockade, April 1864-1866.

170. "The Battle of Belmont." Confederate Veteran, IX (January-December 1901), 116-117.
In which the gunboats Lexington and Tyler helped save General Grant's soldiers.

171. "The Battle of Drewry's Bluff." Marine Corps Gazette, LIV (November 1970), 30-32.
Celebrates the exploits of Cpl. John F. Mackie, U. S. M. C.

172. "The Battle of Helena, Arkansas." Confederate Veteran, XXV (January-December 1917), 403-404.

173. "The Battle of Milliken's Bend." Confederate Veteran, VIII (January-December 1900), 67-68.
In which the gunboats Choctaw and Lexington aided the Black Yankee soldiers to beat off a strong Rebel thrust, June 7, 1863.

174. "The Battle of Sabine Pass." Confederate Veteran, XXV (January-December 1917), 364-365.

175. -----. Confederate Veteran, XXIX (January-December 1921), 303-304.

176. Baty, Thomas. Prize Law and Continuous Voyage. London: Stevens & Haynes, 1915. 134p.
The Springfield Case.

177. Baugh, Virgil E., comp. See U.S. National Archives, no. 2557.

178. Baxter, James P., III. "The British Government and Neutral Rights, 1861-1865." American Historical Review, XXXIV (October 1928), 9-29.
Includes the holding of the Laird rams.

179. -----. The Introduction of the Ironclad Warship. Cambridge, Mass.: Harvard University Press, 1933. 398p.
Chapters 12 to 14 related to the Rebellion.

180. Bayard, T. F. Oration at the Unveiling of the Statue of Rear Admiral DuPont, Washington, D.C., December 20, 1885. Washington: The Author, 1885. 31p.

181. Baylen, Joseph O. and William W. White, eds. "James M. Mason and the Failure of the Confederate Naval Effort in Europe, 1863-1864." Louisiana Studies, II (Fall 1963), 98-108.

182. Beale, Howard K. "Is the Printed Diary of Gideon Welles Reliable?" American Historical Review, XXX (April 1925), 547-552.

183. -----. ed. See Bates, Edward, no. 166.

184. -----. ed. See Welles, Gideon, no. 2726.

185. Bear, Camille N. "Reminiscences of an Old-Timer." United States Naval Institute Proceedings, LXI (December 1935), 1772-1779.
Who first decided upon a naval career in June 1863 when, as a youngster, visited the Hartford to sell turtles and there saw Admiral Farragut.

186. [Bear, Henry C.]. "The Civil War Letters of Henry C. Bear: A Soldier of the 116 Illinois Volunteer Infantry." Edited by Wayne C. Temple. Lincoln Hearld, LXII (Fall 1960), 116-129.
A participant in the Battle of Arkansas Post.

187. Beard, W. M. E. "The Log of the C. S. Submarine." United States Naval Institute Proceedings, XLII (September-October 1916), 1545-1557.
The Hunley.

188. Bearss, Edwin C. "The Battle of Baton Rouge." Louisiana History, III (Spring 1962), 77-128.

189. -----. "The Battle of Chickasaw Bayou." Unpublished paper, Files of the Vicksburg National Military Park, 1958.
Includes the contribution of Porter's flotilla.

190. -----. "The Battle of Dover." Unpublished paper, Files of the Fort Donelson Military Park, 1960.

191. -----. "The Battle of Drewry's Bluff." Unpublished paper, Files of the Eastern District of the National Park Service, 1960.

192. -----. "The Battle of Helena, July 4, 1863." Arkansas Historical Quarterly, XX (Autumn 1961), 256-297.

193. -----. "The Battle of the Post of Arkansas." Arkansas Historical Quarterly, XVIII (Autumn 1959), 237-279.

194. -----. "The Campaign Culminating in the Fall of Vicksburg: March 29-July 4, 1863." Iowa Journal of History, LIX (April 1961), 173-180.
Includes naval activities.

195. -----. "The Civil War Comes to the Lafourche." Louisiana Studies, V (Summer 1966), 97-155.
Union General Weitzel's drive, with naval aid, against Confederate Richard Taylor.

196. -----. "Civil War Operations In and Around Pensacola." Florida Historical Quarterly, XXXVI (October 1957), 125-165; XXXIX (January-April 1961), 231-255, 330-353.

197. -----. "A Construction History of the U.S.S. Cairo." Unpublished paper, Files of the Vicksburg National Military Park, 1959.

198. -----. Decision in Mississippi. Jackson, Miss.: Mississippi Committee on the War Between the States, 1962. 636p.
Much information on the Arkansas.

199. -----. "The Destruction of the Cairo." By Edwin

C. Bearss and Warren E. Grabau. Journal of Mississippi History, XXIII (July 1961), 141-163.

200. -----. "The Fall of Fort Henry." West Tennessee Historical Society Publications, XVII (1963), 85-107.

201. -----. "The Federal Expedition Against St. Mark's Ends at National Bridge." Florida Historical Quarterly, XLV (April 1967), 369-390.

202. -----. "A Federal Raid up the Tennessee River." Alabama Review, XVII (October 1964), 261-270.
By Union gunboats in 1862.

203. -----. "The Fiasco at Head of Passes." Louisiana History, IV (Fall 1963), 301-311.
When the Manassas rammed the Richmond in October 1861.

204. -----. "Fort Henry." By Edwin C. Bearss and Howard P. Nash. Civil War Times Illustrated, IV (November 1965), 9-15.

205. -----. "The Fortifications at Fort Donelson." Unpublished paper, Files of the Fort Donelson Military Park, 1959.

206. -----. "From Millikens Bend to Vicksburg With Private [Charles E.] Affeld." Louisiana Studies, VI (Fall 1967), 203-265.
With some comments on naval activities.

207. -----. "Grand Gulf's Role in the Civil War." Civil War History, V (March 1959), 5-29.
Bombarded by Porter's fleet in April 1863.

208. -----. "Gunboat Operations at Forts Henry and Donelson." Unpublished Paper, Files of the Vicksburg National Military Park, 1959.

209. -----. Hardluck Ironclad: The Sinking and Salvage of the Cairo... Baton Rouge: Louisiana State University Press, 1966. 208p.

210. -----. "How Porter's Flotilla Ran the Gauntlet Past Vicksburg." By Edwin C. Bearss and Warren E. Grabau. Civil War Times Illustrated, I (December

1962), 38-48.
In April 1863.

211. -----. "Military Operations in the St. Johns, September-October 1862: The Union Navy Fails to Drive the Confederates from St. John's Bluff." Florida Historical Quarterly, XLII (January 1964), 232-247.

212. -----. "Private Charles E. Affeld Keeps Action West of the Mississippi." Journal of the Illinois State Historical Society, LX (Autumn 1967), 267-296.

213. -----. Rebel Victory at Vicksburg. Vicksburg: Centennial Commemoration Commission, 1963. 299p.

214. -----. "The Seizure of the Forts and Public Property in Louisiana." Louisiana History, II (Fall 1961), 401-409.

215. -----. "Sherman's Demonstration at Snyder's Bluff." Journal of Mississippi History, XXVII (Spring 1965), 168-186.

216. -----. "The Story of Fort Beauregard." Louisiana Studies, III (Winter 1965), 330-384; IV (Spring 1965), 3-40.
A Confederate fort on the Ouachita River, April 1863 to March 1964.

217. -----. "The Steeles Bayou Expedition." Unpublished paper, Files of the Vicksburg National Military Park, 1960.

218. -----. "The Trans-Mississippi Confederates Attempt to Relive Vicksburg." McNeese Review, XV (1964), 46-70.
Includes the Battle of Millikens Bend.

219. -----. "Unconditional Surrender: The Fall of Fort Donelson." Tennessee Historical Quarterly, XXI (June 1962), 47-62.

220. -----. "The Union Raid Down the Mississippi and Up the Yazoo, August 16-27, 1862." Military

Affairs, XXVII (Fall 1962), 108-119.
By Yankee gunboats.

221. -----. "Vicksburg River Defenses and the Enigma of 'Whistling Dick.' " *Journal of Mississippi History*, XIX (January 1957), 21-30.
Includes the Federal ironclads' bombardment of May 1863.

222. -----. "The White River Expedition, June 10-July 15, 1862." *Arkansas Historical Quarterly*, XXI (Winter 1962), 305-362.
In which the Union ironclad *Mound City* met disaster.

223. Beauregard, Pierre G. T. "The Campaign of Shiloh." In Robert U. Johnson and Clarence C. Buell, eds. *B & L*. Vol. I, pp. 569-593.
In which a pair of "timberclads" took an important part.

224. -----. "The Defense of Charleston." In Robert U. Johnson and Clarence C. Buell, eds. *B & L*. Vol. IV, pp. 1-22.

225. -----. "Note Relative to the Obstructions Designed by Colonel [Pierre] G. T. Beauregard for the Mississippi River at Fort Jackson and Fort St. Philip, La., in Feb'y 1861." *Louisiana Historical Quarterly*, II (October 1919), 451-453.

226. -----. "Torpedo Service in Charleston Harbor." *In Annals of the War*. p. 513-526.

227. -----. "Torpedo Service in the Harbor and Water Defences of Charleston." *Southern Historical Society Papers*, V (1878), 145-161.

228. -----. Author of Report. *See* C.S.A. Army Department of South Carolina, Georgia, and Florida, no. 548.

229. Bedford, H. L. "Fight Between the [Rebel] Batteries and [Union] Gunboats at Fort Donelson." *Southern Historical Society Papers*, XIII (1885), 165-173.

230. Beers, Henry P. "The Bureau of Navigation, 1862-

1864." American Archivist, VI (October 1943), 212-252.
Rear Admiral C. H. Davis, Chief.

231. -----. comp. See U.S. National Archives, nos. 2553-2554.

232. Belcher, Wyatt W. The Economic Rivalry Between St. Louis and Chicago, 1850-1880. New York: Columbia University Press, 1947. 223p.

233. Belknap, George E. "The Home Squadron in the Winter of 1860-61." In Publications of the Military History Society of Massachusetts. 14 vols. Boston: The Society, 1895-1918. Vol. XII, pp. 75-100.

234. -----. "Reminiscences of the New Ironsides off Charleston." United Service, I (January 1879), 63-82.

235. -----. "Reminiscences of the Siege of Charleston." In Publications of the Military History Society of Massachusetts. 14 vols. Boston: The Society, 1895-1918. Vol. XII, pp. 155-208.

236. Bell, John T. Tramps and Triumphs of the Second Iowa Infantry, Briefly Sketched. Omaha: Gibson, Miller, & Richardson, 1886. 32p.
Fort Donelson and Shiloh coverage.

237. Bell, Robert E., comp. A Bibliography of Mobile, Alabama. University of Alabama Studies, no. 11. University: University of Alabama Press, 1956. 96p.

238. Belser, Thomas A. "Military Operations in Missouri and Arkansas, 1861-1865." Unpublished PhD Dissertation, Vanderbilt University, 1961.

239. Benedict, G. G. Vermont in the Civil War: A History of the Part Taken by the Soldiers and Sailors in the War for the Union, 1861-1865. 2 vols. Burlington: The Free Press Association, 1886-1888.

240. Benedict, James B., Jr. "General John Hunt Morgan: the Great Indiana-Ohio Raid." Filson Club Historical Quarterly, XXXI (April 1957), 147-171.

In which the "tinclad" Moose, Lieutenant Commander Leroy Fitch, U.S.N., took an important part in stopping.

241. Benham, Edith W. and Anne M. Hall. Ships of the United States Navy and Their Sponsors, 1797-1913. Norwood, Mass.: Priv. print., 1913. 227p.

242. Benjamin, Judah P., Author of Instructions. See C.S.A. State Department, no. 583.

243. Bennett, Frank M. "The Albemarle in Albermarle Sound." United Service, New Series XI (May 1893), 438-457.

244. -----. The Monitor and the Navy Under Steam. Boston: Houghton, Mifflin, 1900. 369p.

245. -----. The Steam Navy of the United States: A History of the Growth of the Steam Vessel of War in the Navy, and of the Naval Engineer Corps. Pittsburgh: Warren, 1897. 953p.

246. Bennett, William E. Cruise of a Corsair. By Warren Armstrong, pseud. London: Cassell, 1963. 207p.

247. Bernard, Montague. Notes on Some Questions Suggested by the Case of the Trent. London: J. H. and J. Parker, 1862. 39p.

248. Bernath, Stuart L. Squall Across the Atlantic: American Civil War Prize Cases and Diplomacy. Berkeley: University of California Press, 1970. 229p.

249. -----. "Squall Across the Atlantic: The Peterhoff Episode." Journal of Southern History, XXXIV (August 1968), 382-401).

250. Bernett, Muriel, ed. See Welles, Gideon, no. 2733.

251. Berry, Chester D. Loss of the Sultana and Reminiscences of Survivors. Lansing, Mich.: Darius D. Thorp, 1892. 426p.

252. Besse, Sumner B. The C.S. Ironclad Virginia;

With Data and References for a Scale Model. Newport News, Va.: The Mariners Museum, 1937. 47p.

253. -----. The U.S. Ironclad Monitor; With Data and References for a Scale Model. Newport News, Va.: The Mariners Museum, 1936. 24p.

254. Bethel, Edward E., ed. See Semmes, Raphael, no. 2149.

255. Bethel, Elizabeth, ed. See U.S. National Archives, no. 2558.

256. -----. ed. See U.S. National Archives, no. 2562.

257. Bettersworth, John K. Mississippi in the Confederacy. 2 vols. Baton Rouge: Louisiana State University Press, 1961.

258. Betts, Samuel R., Reporter. See U.S. Circuit Court. Southern District of New York, no. 2431.

259. Bevier, Robert S. History of the First and Second Missouri Confederate Brigades, 1861-1865. St. Louis: Bryan, Brand, 1879. 480p.
Whose members often found themselves under fire from Yankee gunboats.

260. Beyer, Walter F., ed. Deeds of Valor; How America's Heroes Won the Medal of Honor; a History of Our Country's Recent Wars in Personal Reminiscences and Records of Officers and Enlisted Men who Were Rewarded by Congress for Most Conspicuous Acts of Bravery on the Battle-Field, on the High Seas, and in Arctic Explorations. 2 vols. Detroit: Perrien-Keydel, 1903.

261. Beymer, W. G. "Mrs. Greenhow, Confederate Spy." Harper's Monthly Magazine, CXXIV (March 1912) 563-576.
Who died in the wreck of a blockade runner.

262. Bigelow, John. France and the Confederate Navy, 1862-1868: An International Episode. New York: Harper, 1888. 274p.

263. Bigelow, Martha M. "The Significance of Milliken's Bend in the Civil War." Journal of Negro History, XLV (July 1960), 156-164.

264. Billias, George A. "Maine Lumbermen Rescue the Red River Fleet." New England Social Studies Bulletin, XVI (January 1958), 5-8.
Dam building in 1864.

265. Bingham, Luther G. The Young Quartermaster: The Life and Death of Lieutenant Luther M. Bingham, of the First South Carolina Volunteers, New York: Reformed Protestant Dutch Church, 1863. 216p.
During the siege of Charleston.

266. "Birth and Death of the Monitor." New York State and the Civil War, I (January 1962), 16-17.

267. "Bishop." "The Battle of Arkansas Post." Confederate Veteran, V (January-December 1897), 151-152.

268. Bissell, J. W. "Sawing Out the Channel Above Island Number Ten." In Robert U. Johnson and Clarence C. Buell, eds. B & L. Vol. I, pp. 460-462.

269. Blackwell, Sarah E. A Military Genius, Anna Ella Carroll of Maryland, ("the Great Unrecognized Member of Lincoln's Cabinet."). 2 vols. Washington: Judd & Detweiler, 1891-1895.
Supports the lady's claim of originating the strategy followed by Grant and Foote on the Tennessee and Cumberland Rivers in 1862. Suggests she be compensated by the Congress for her efforts.

270. [Blades, Henry S.]. The Queen of the West Runs the Blockade, February 3, 1863. Edited by Walter H. Rankins. Frankfort, Ky.: Roberts Printing, 1956.
Of Vicksburg to blockade the Red River.

271. Blair, C. H. M. "Historic Sketch of the Confederate Navy." United Service, 3rd Series IV (May 1903), 1115-1184.

272. Blair, Carvell H. "Submarines of the Confederate

Navy." United States Naval Institute Proceedings, LXXVIII (October 1952), 1114-1121.

273. Blair, Clay. Diving for Pleasure and Treasure. Cleveland: World, 1960. 348p.
Includes the recent search for the hulk of the Monitor.

274. Blair, John L. "Morgan's Ohio Raid." Filson Club Historical Quarterly, XXXVI (July 1962), 242-271.

275. Blair, Montgomery. "Opening the Mississippi." United Service, IV (January 1881), 35-41.

276. Blaisdell, Albert F. and Francis K. Ball. Heroic Deeds of American Sailors. Boston: Little, Brown, 1915. 182p.
Includes William B. Cushing.

277. Blake, W. H. "Coal Barging in War Times, 1861-1865." Gulf States Historical Magazine, I (May 1903), 409-412.

278. Blakeman, A. Noel. "Some Personal Reminiscences of the Naval Service." In Personal Recollections of the War of the Rebellion; Papers Read before the New York Commandery, Military Order of the Loyal Legion of the United States. 4 vols. New York: The Commandery, 1891-1912. Vol. II, pp. 231-239.

279. Blakeney, Jane. Heroes, U.S. Marine Corps. 1861-1955; Armed Forces Awards, Flags. Washington: Guthrie Lithograph, 1957. 621p.

280. Blanding, Stephen F. Recollections of a Sailor Boy; or, The Cruise of the Gunboat Louisiana. Providence: E. A. Johnson, 1886. 330p.

281. Blatchford, Samuel, Reporter. See U.S. Circuit Court. Southern District of New York, no. 2432.

282. Blessington, Joseph P. The Campaigns of [John G.] Walker's Texas Division, by a Private Soldier. New York: Lange, 1875. 314p.
Involved in the 1863 Perkin's Plantation skirmish with the Federal ironclad Carondelet.

283. "Blockade Runners: Pictorial Supplement." *American Neptune*, XXI (January-October 1961), unpaged.
Series of water colors and a few photographs not previously published.

284. "Blockade Runners." *Nautical Magazine*, (January 1865), 37-41.

285. Boatner, Mark M., III. *The Civil War Dictionary*. New York: McKay, 1959. 974p.

286. Bodder, Charles H., pseud. *See* Shepherd, Charles H. B., no. 2162.

287. [Bodman, Albert H.]. " 'In Sight of Vicksburg': the Private Diary of a Northern War Correspondent." Edited by Leo M. Kaiser. *Historical Bulletin*, XXXIV (May 1956), 202-221.
His accounts of the *Queen of the West* in the Red River in 1863 are graphic.

288. Bogle, Robert V. "Defeat Through Default: Confederate Naval Strategy for the Upper Tennessee and Its Tributaries, 1861-1862." *Tennessee Historical Quarterly*, XXVII (Spring 1968), 62-71.

289. Bogle, Victor M. "A Nineteenth Century River Town: A Social-Economic Study of New Albany, Indiana." Unpublished PhD dissertation, Boston University, 1951.
Includes the Civil War period.

290. Bolander, Louis H. "The *Alligator*, First Federal Submarine of the Civil War." *United States Naval Institute Proceedings*, LXIV (June 1938), 845-854.

291. -----. "Better Than Anything We Have." *Shipmate*, XXI (February 1958), 6-8.

292. -----. "Civil War Annapolis." *United States Naval Institute Proceedings*, LXIII (November 1937), 1612-1616.
Based on a four page weekly newspaper, *The Crutch*.

293. -----. "The Introduction of Shells and Shell Guns

in the United States Navy." Mariners Mirror, XVII (April 1931), 105-112.

294. -----. "The Stone Fleet in Charleston Harbor." Confederate Veteran, XXXIX (January-December 1931), 133-134.

295. Bolles, John A. Report Upon the Claims of Lieutenant Samuel Belden and Others Formerly of the Volunteer [Naval] Service. Washington: n. p., 1872. 6p.

296. [Bolles, L., Jr.]. "The Chaplin's Picture of Vicksburg, 1863." Edited by Laurence B. Romaine. Manuscripts, VI (Spring 1954), 170-175.
Under bombardment from the river.

297. Bond, Otto F., ed. See Hopkins, Owen J., no. 1194.

298. Booth, Alan R. "The Alabama at the Cape, 1863." American Neptune, XXVI (April 1966), 96-108.

299. Bourne, John. A Treatise on the Screw Propeller, Screw Vessels, and Screw Engines as Adapted for Purposes of Peace and War. New Edition. London: Longmans, Green, 1867. 428p.

300. Botkin, Benjamin A., ed. A Treasury of Mississippi River Folklore; Stories, Ballads, Traditions, and Folkways of the Mid-American River Country. New York: Crown, 1955. 620p.
Some accounts of the river navies.

301. Bowles, R. C. "The Ship Tennessee." Southern Historical Society Papers, XXI (1893), 290-294.
The Southern ironclad commanded by Admiral Buchanan at the Battle of Mobile Bay.

302. Bowman, Berry. "The Hunley--Ill-Fated Confederate Submarine." Civil War History, V (September 1959), 315-319.

303. Boyd, Charles H. "An Incident on the Coast of Maine in 1861." In War Papers, Read Before the Commandery of the State of Maine, Military Order of the Loyal Legion of the United States. 3 vols. Portland: Thruston, 1898-1908. Vol. I, pp. 318-322.

Capture of a Confederate vessel.

304. Boyd, Mark F. "The Joint Operations of the Federal Army and Navy Near St. Marks, Florida, March 1865." Florida Historical Quarterly, XXIX (October 1950), 96-124.

305. [Boyer, Samuel P.]. Naval Surgeon: The Diary of Dr. Samuel Pellman Boyer. Edited by Elinor and James A. Barnes. 2 vols. Bloomington: Indiana University Press, 1963.
Aboard the U. S. S. Fernandina and Mattabasset, September 1862-May 1865. Useful data on the blockade and shipboard medical exercises.

306. Boykin, Edward C. The Ghost Ship of the Confederacy: The Story of the Alabama and her Captain, Raphael Semmes. New York: Funk & Wagnalls, 1957. 404p.

307. -----. Sea Devil of the Confederacy: the Story of the Florida and Her Captain, John Newland Maffitt. New York: Funk & Wagnalls, 1959. 306p.

308. Boynton, C. B. History of the Navy During the Rebellion. 2 vols. New York: D. Appleton, 1867.
Emphasis on the Federal sea service.

309. Bradford, Gamaliel, Jr. "Raphael Semmes; a Last Confederate Portrait." Atlantic Monthly, CXII (October 1913), 469-480.

310. Bradford, Gershom. "Cushing in Skokokon." American Neptune, XVIII (April 1958), 142-148.
The converted New York ferryboat commanded by the young lieutenant off North Carolina in 1863.

311. -----. "The Granite's Great Day." Rudder, LXXIV (June 1958), 12-14.
A Federal sloop in action off North Carolina, 1862.

312. Bradlee, Francis B. C. Blockade Running During the Civil War, and The Effect of Land and Water Transportation on the Confederacy. Salem, Mass.:

Essex Institute, 1925. 340p.

313. -----. A Forgotten Chapter in Our Naval History. Salem, Mass.: Essex Institute, 1923. 25p.
A brief biography of Commodore Duncan Ingraham, C. S. N.

314. -----. The Kearsarge-Alabama, the Story as Told to the Writer by James Magee of Marblehead, Seaman on the Kearsarge. Salem, Mass.: Essex Institute, 1921. 25p.

315. Bradley, Chester D. "President Lincoln's Campaign Against the Merrimac." Illinois State Historical Society Journal, LI (Spring 1958), 59-85.

316. Bradley, Erwin S. Simon Cameron, Lincoln's Secretary of War; a Political Biography. Philadelphia: University of Pennsylvania Press, 1966. 451p.
Who exchanged notes with Welles on cannon for the Western gunboats in 1861.

317. Bradlow, Edna and Frank. Here Comes the Alabama. Cape Town, South Africa: A. A. Balkema, 1958. 128p.

318. Bradlow, Frank, Joint Author. See Bradlow, Edna, no. 317.

319. Bragg, Braxton. "The Defence and Fall of Fort Fisher." Southern Historical Society Papers, X (1882), 346-349.

320. Bragg, Jefferson D. Louisiana in the Confederacy. Baton Rouge: Louisiana State University Press, 1941. 341p.

321. Braisted, F. A. "The U. S. Navy's First Iron Man-of-War." United States Naval Institute Proceedings, LXXIX (March 1953), 319-320.
The Michigan, prison guardship on Lake Erie during the War.

322. Brand, Robert. "Reminiscences of the Blockade off Wilmington." In War Papers, Read Before the Wisconsin Commandery, Military Order of the Loyal Legion of the United States. 3 vols.

Milwaukee: Burdick, Armitage & Allen, 1891-1903. Vol. III, pp. 14-32.

323. Brand, W. F. "The Capture of the Indianola." Maryland Historical Magazine, IV (December 1909), 353-361.
On the Mississippi in early 1863.

324. Brandt, John D. Gunnery Catechism, as Applied to the Service of Naval Ordnance. New York: D. Van Nostrand, 1864. 197p.

325. Breckenridge, John C., Author of Report. See C.S.A. War Department, no. 584.

326. Breihan, Carl W. "The Battle of Sabine Pass." Gun Reporter, IV (November 1958), 19-21.

327. Brent, Joseph L. "Artillery of the Army of Western Louisiana." Southern Historical Society Papers, IX (1881), 257-264.

328. -----. "The Capture of the Indianola." Southern Historical Society Papers, I (1876), 91-99.

329. Brewer, George E. "The Defenders of Vicksburg." Confederate Veteran, XXII (January-December 1914), 232.

330. A Brief Review of the Navy Yard Question, Showing that New London has the Advantage of Defensibility, Fresh Water, Iron, Coal, Freedom from Ice, etc., etc. New London: Starr & Farnham, 1863. 32p.

331. Briggs, Herbert W. The Doctrine of Continuous Voyage. Baltimore: n.p., 1926. 226p.
The policy by which Union blockaders intercepted neutral, mainly British, ships enroute to the West Indies.

332. Bright, S. R. "Confederate Coast Defense." Unpublished PhD Dissertation, Duke University, 1961.

333. Brinton, John H. Personal Memoirs of John H. Brinton, Major and Surgeon, U.S.V., 1861-1865.

New York: Neale, 1914. 361p.
Glimpses of hospitals for soldiers and sailors of the Union in the Western theatre.

334. "British Neutrality--the Shenandoah." Nautical Magazine (December 1865), 649-655.

335. Brockett, Linus P. "David Glascoe [sic] Farragut." In Charles F. Horne, ed. Great Men and Famous Women. 3 vols. New York: Selmar Hess, 1894. Vol. I, pp. 379-387.

336. -----. Our Great Captains. New York: C. B. Richardson, 1865. 251p.
Includes Farragut, Grant, and Sherman.

337. Brodie, Bernard. A Guide to Naval Strategy. Princeton: Princeton University Press, 1944. 274p.

338. ----- -----. 5th ed. New York: Praeger, 1965. 274p.

339. -----. Sea Power in the Machine Age. Princeton: Princeton University Press, 1941. 462p.

340. Bromwell, William J., Joint Editor. See Lester, William W., no. 1433.

341. Brooke, George M., Jr. "John Mercer Brooke." Rockbridge Historical Society Papers, IV (1954), 32-34.

342. -----. "John Mercer Brooke, Naval Scientist." Unpublished PhD Dissertation, University of North Carolina, 1956.

343. Brooke, John Mercer. "Ordnance." In Lewis R. Hamersly, ed. A Naval Encyclopedia. p. 617-627.

344. -----. "The Plan and Construction of the Merrimac." By John Mercer Brooke and John L. Porter. In Robert U. Johnson and Clarence C. Buell, eds. B & L. Vol. I, pp. 715-717.

345. -----. "The Real Projector of the Virginia." Southern Historical Society Papers, XIX (1891), 3-34.

346. [Brother, Charles]. "The Journal of Private Charles Brother." In U.S. Navy Department, Naval History Division. Civil War Naval Chronology. 6 vols. Washington: U.S. Government Printing Office, 1961-1966. Vol. VI, pp. 47-89.
Of a marine aboard the Hartford in 1864.

347. -----. Two Naval Journals, 1864, at the Battle of Mobile Bay. By [Charles Brother] and [John C. O'Connell]. Edited by C. Carter Smith. Chicago: Wyvern Press, 1964. 51p.
The Hartford's marine again plus the journal of a man aboard the Confederate ship Tennessee.

348. Broughton, John W. "The Capture of Plymouth, North Carolina." Confederate Veteran, XXIV (January-December 1916), 200-201.
By Rebel troops in co-operation with the ironclad Albemarle in 1864.

349. Brown, Alexander C. "Monitor-Class Warships of the United States Navy." In The Society of Naval Architects and Marine Engineers. Historical Transactions, 1893-1943. New York: The Society, 1945. p. 330-340.

350. Brown, Allan D. "Naval Architecture Past and Present, Part II." Harper's New Monthly Magazine, XLIV (April 1872), 676-684.
Details on several Civil War vessels.

351. -----. "Torpedoes and Torpedo Boats." Harper's New Monthly Magazine, LXV (June 1882), 36-47.
With stress on those of the Civil War.

352. Brown, Campbell H. "Forrest's Johnsonville Raid." Civil War Times Illustrated, IV (June 1965), 48-57.
In which three Federal gunboats were captured, November 1864.

353. Brown, Claude. The Ram Switzerland. n.p., 1958. lv.
Data on her run by Vicksburg in 1863 gathered from newspapers and tradition.

354. Brown, D. Alexander. "The Battle of Chickasaw Bluffs." Civil War Times Illustrated, IX (July 1970), 4-9, 44-48.
In which the river gunboats supported the attempt by Sherman's troops to turn Vicksburg's northern flank, December 1862.

355. Brown, George, ed. The Navy. Vol. VII of The Union Army; a History of Military Affairs in the Loyal States, 1861-1865. 8 vols. Madison, Wisc.: Federal Publishing, 1908.
By the commander of the Indianola.

356. Brown, H. D. "The First Successful Torpedo." Confederate Veteran, XVIII (January-December 1910), 169-170.

357. Brown, Harry B., Jr. "Port Hudson: A Study in Historical Geography." Unpublished M. A. Thesis, Louisiana State University, 1934.

358. Brown, Isaac N. "The Confederate Gun-Boat Arkansas." In Robert U. Johnson and Clarence C. Buell, eds. B & L. Vol. III, pp. 572-579.
By her captain.

359. -----. "Confederate Torpedoes in the Yazoo." In Robert U. Johnson and Clarence C. Buell, eds. B & L. Vol. III, pp. 579-580.

360. Brown, James W. The Mississippi River Ram Fleet and Marine Brigade. Remarks of Hon. James W. Brown, of Pennsylvania, in the House of Representatives, Friday, March 3, 1905. Washington: n.p., 1905.

361. [Brown, Laurence and Isaac Colby]. "The Sonora and the Alabama." Civil War Times Illustrated, X (October 1971), 32-39.
Contemporary description of the capture of a New England merchantman by the Rebel raider.

362. Brown, S. H. "A Minor Naval Engagement." Confederate Veteran, XXIII (January-December 1915), 165-166.
Between the Federals and elements of Rebel Commodore William F. Lynch's flotilla at

Roanoke Island, February 21, 1862.

363. Brown, Walter E. "The Daddy of 'em All." United States Naval Institute Proceedings, L (October 1924), 1687-1694.
The iron U.S.S. Michigan.

364. Browne, A. K. The Story of the Kearsarge-Alabama. San Francisco: H. Payot, 1868. 27p.

365. [Browne, Henry]. "The Dark and the Light Side of the River War." Civil War Times Illustrated, IX (December 1970), 12-18.

366. -----. From the Fresh-Water Navy: 1861-64, The Letters of Acting Master's Mate Henry R. Browne and Acting Ensign Symmes E. Browne. Edited by John D. Milligan. Naval Letter Series, v. 3. Annapolis: U.S. Naval Institute, 1970. 327p.

367. Browne, John M. "The Duel Between the Alabama and the Kearsarge." In Robert U. Johnson and Clarence C. Buell, eds. B & L. Vol. IV, pp. 615-624.

368. Browne, Junius H. Four Years in Secessia: Adventures Within and Beyond the Union Lines: Embracing a Great Variety of Facts, Incidents, and Romance of the War. Hartford: O. D. Case, 1865. 450p.
By a newsman who viewed much of the Western war from the decks of various Federal gunboats.

369. Browne, Samuel T. "The First Cruise of the Montauk." Personal Narratives of Events in the War of the Rebellion, Being Papers Read Before the Rhode Island Soldiers and Sailors Historical Society. 2nd Series, no. 1. Providence: N. B. Williams, 1880.

370. Browne, Symmes E. See Browne, Henry, no. 366.

371. Browne, W. B. "Capture of the Steamer Maple Leaf." Southern Historical Society Papers, XXXIX (1914), 181-185.
Rebel prisoners enroute to Fort Delaware overpowered the guard and took the ship, June 1863.

372. Brownlee, Richard S., III. Gray Ghosts of the Confederacy: Guerrilla Warfare in the West, 1861-1865. Baton Rouge: Louisiana State University Press, 1958. 274p.

373. Bruce, George A. "The Strategy of the Civil War." In Publications of the Military History Society of Massachusetts. 14 vols. Boston: The Society, 1895-1918. Vol. XIII, pp. 393-412.

374. Bruce, Robert. Lincoln and the Tools of War. Indianapolis: Bobbs-Merrill, 1956. 369p.
Demonstrates the President's interest in the military and naval build up of the Union.

375. Bruzek, Joseph C. The "IX" Dahlgren Broadside Gun. n.p., 1964.

376. -----. "The U.S. Schooner Yacht America." United States Naval Institute Proceedings, XCIII (September 1967), 1159-1187.

377. Bryan, Anna S. "The Virginia and the Monitor." Confederate Veteran, XXXII (January-December 1924), 346-347.

378. Buchanan, Franklin. "Official Report of the Battle of Hampton Roads." Southern Historical Society Papers, VII (1879), 305-314.

379. -----. "Official Report of the Fight in Mobile Bay." Southern Historical Society Papers, VI (1878), 220-224.

380. -----. Author of Report. See C.S.A. Navy Department, no. 574.

381. Buckner, William P. Calculated Tables of Ranges for Navy and Army Guns. With a Method of Finding the Distance of an Object at Sea. New York: D. Van Nostrand, 1865. 79p.
Inaccurate.

382. Buell, Clarence C., Joint Editor. See Johnson, Robert U., no. 1294.

383. Buell, Don Carlos. "Shiloh Reviewed." In Robert U.

Johnson and Clarence C. Buell, eds. B & L. Vol. I, pp. 487-536.

384. Bullard, F. Laureston. "Anna Ella Carroll and Her 'Modest Claim.' " Lincoln Hearld, L (January 1948), 2-10.

385. Bullock, James D. "Building Confederate Vessels in France." Southern Historical Society Papers, XIV (1886), 454-465.

386. -----. The Secret Service of the Confederate States in Europe, or How the Confederate Cruisers Were Equipped. 2 vols. New York: Putnam, 1884.

387. "The Bureau of Naval Personnel." United States Naval Institute Proceedings, LXXV (June 1949), 693-704.
Includes the Civil War period.

388. "The Bureau of Ordnance." United States Naval Institute Proceedings, LXXV (February 1949), 213-214.
Includes the Civil War period.

389. "The Bureau of Supplies and Accounts." United States Naval Institute Proceedings, LXXV (March 1949), 343-354.
And its predecessor agencies including the time of the Civil War.

390. Burgess, George W. "The Ram Arkansas and the Battle of Baton Rouge." East and West Baton Rouge Historical Society Proceedings, II (1918), 34-37.

391. Burnett, Alfred. Incidents of the War: Humerous, Pathetic, and Descriptive. Cincinnati: Rickey & Carroll, 1863. 310p.
By a Cincinnati Times reporter covering the Western theatre.

392. "Burning of the Alice Dean." Confederate Veteran, XXI (January-December 1913), 111-112.
By Morgan's men after crossing the Ohio to begin their two state 1863 raid.

393. Burnside, Ambrose E. "The Burnside Expedition." In Robert U. Johnson and Clarence C. Buell, eds. B & L. Vol. I, 660-669.

394. Burpo, Robert S., Jr. "Notes on the First Fleet Engagement in the Civil War." American Neptune, XIX (October 1959), 265-273.
On the Mississippi at Plum Point Bend.

395. Burton, Amos. Journal of the Cruise of the Susquehanna, 1860-63. New York: J. O. Jenkins, 1863. 177p.

396. Burton, E. Milby. The Siege of Charleston, 1861-1865. Columbia: University of South Carolina Press, 1970. 373p.

397. Butler, Benjamin F. Autobiography and Personal Reminiscences of Major-General Benjamin F. Butler; Butler's Book. Boston: A. M. Thayer, 1892. 1,154p.
A Union political general often involved with the Navy, particularly at New Orleans.

398. -----. Private and Official Correspondence of General Benjamin F. Butler, during the Period of the Civil War. 5 vols. Norwood, Mass.: Plimpton, 1917.

399. -----. Statement of Facts in Relation to Admiral D. D. Porter's Claim Not to Have Run Away from Forts St. Philip and Jackson, in April 1862, by which His Cowardice and Falsehood are Fully Shown from Official Documents and Porter's own Self Contradictions. Boston: Priv. Print., 1889. 22p.

400. Butler, Edward. "Personal Experiences in the Navy, 1862-1865." In War Papers, Read Before the Commandery of the State of Maine, Military Order of the Loyal Legion of the United States. 3 vols. Portland: Thurston, 1898-1908. Vol. II, pp. 184-200.

401. Butler, P. R. "Cruise of the Sumter." Blackwood's Magazine, CCLXIII (May 1948), 351-362.
A Confederate cruiser.

402. Butt, Marshall W., Author. <u>See</u> U.S. Norfolk Naval Shipyard, no. 2612.

403. Buttgenbach, Walter J. "Coast Defense in the Civil War." <u>Journal of the U.S. Artillery</u>, XXXIX (March-May 1913), 210-216, 331-338; XL (July-November 1913), 47-58, 205-215, 306-313; XLI (January-June 1914), 19-47, 191-211, 317-336; XLII (July-September 1914), 68-83, 185-213.
Battles and operations along the sea coasts and the banks of inland rivers.

404. -----. Joint Author. <u>See</u> Holcombe, John L., no. 1164.

405. Buttry, Virginia A., Joint Author. <u>See</u> Jones, Allen W., no. 1305.

406. Butts, Francis B. <u>A Cruise Along the Blockade. Personal Narratives of Events in the War of the Rebellion, Being Papers Read Before the Rhode Island Soldiers and Sailors Historical Society</u>. 2nd Series, no. 12. Providence: N. B. Williams, 1881.

407. -----. "The Loss of the <u>Monitor</u>." In Robert U. Johnson and Clarence C. Buell, eds. <u>B & L</u>. Vol. I, pp. 745-747.

408. -----. <u>The Monitor and the Merrimac. Personal Narratives of Events in the War of the Rebellion, Being Papers Read Before the Rhode Island Soldiers and Sailors Historical Society</u>. 4th Series, no. 6. Providence: N. B. Williams, 1890.

409. -----. <u>My First Cruise at Sea and the Loss of the Iron-Clad Monitor. Personal Narratives of Events in the War of the Rebellion, Being Papers Read Before the Rhode Island Soldiers and Sailors Historical Society</u>. 1st Series, no. 4. Providence: N. B. Williams, 1878.

410. -----. <u>Reminiscences of the Gunboat Service on the Nansemond. Personal Narratives of Events in the War of the Rebellion, Being Papers Read Before the Rhode Island Soldiers and Sailors Historical Society</u>. 3rd Series, no. 8, Providence: N. B.

Williams, 1884.

411. Cable, George W. "New Orleans Before the Capture." In Robert U. Johnson and Clarence C. Buell, eds. B & L. Vol. II, pp. 14-21.

412. -----. ed. "A Woman's Diary of the Siege of Vicksburg: Under Fire from the Gunboats." Century Illustrated Magazine, VIII (September 1885), 767-775.

413. Cadwalader, John H. Cadwalader's Cases, 1858-1879.... With Decisions on Cases Arising During the Civil War. 2 vols. Philadelphia: R. Welsh, 1907.
Includes prize cases argued before him as Judge of the U. S. District Court, Eastern District of Pennsylvania.

414. [Cadwallader, Sylvanus]. Three Years with Grant, As Recalled by War Correspondent Sylvanus Cadwallader. Edited by Benjamin P. Thomas. New York: Knopf, 1955. 353p.
Has no use for Admiral David D. Porter.

415. Calhoun, John. Petition of Commander John Calhoun, U. S. Navy, Protesting Against the Action of the Late Advising Board and Praying for Relief. Philadelphia: J. B. Chandler, 1863. 12p.

416. Calkin, Homer L. ed. See Fauntleroy, James H., no. 834.

417. Callender, Eliot. "What a Boy Saw on the Mississippi River." In Military Essays and Recollections; Papers Read Before the Illinois Commandery, Military Order of the Loyal Legion of the United States. 4 vols. Chicago: A. C. McClurg, 1891-1912. Vol. I, pp. 51-68.
Aboard Yankee ironclads.

418. Callwell, Charles E. The Effect of Maritime Command on Land Campaigns Since Waterloo. London: W. Blackwood, 1897. 380p.
Includes the Civil War.

419. -----. Military Operations and Maritime Preponder-

ance, Their Relations and Interdependence. London: W. Blackwood, 1905. 473p.

420. Cameron, W. L. "In Mobile Bay." Confederate Veteran, XXV (January-December 1917), 260.
A C.S.N. cutter attempts to scout below the U.S.S. Metacomet.

421. Cameron, William E. "Historic Waters of Virginia." Southern Historical Society Papers, XXXII (1904), 347-354.

422. [Camm, William]. "Diary of Colonel William Camm, 1861-1865." Edited by Fitz Haskall. Journal of the Illinois State Historical Society, XVIII (January 1926), 793-969.
Tells of the Yankee gunboats at Shiloh, 1862.

423. Campbell, Mrs. A. A. "The First Fight of Ironclads." Confederate Veteran, XXIX (January-December 1921), 290-291.
The Monitor vs. Merrimac.

424. Campbell, James E. "Recent Addresses of James Edwin Campbell." Ohio Archaeological and Historical Quarterly, XXXIV (January 1925), 29-62.
On the crews of Western gunboats.

425. Candler, W. A. "The Merrimac." Confederate Veteran, XVI (January-December 1908), 192.

426. Canfield, Eugene B. Notes on Naval Ordnance of the American Civil War. Washington: American Ordnance Association, 1960. 24p.

427. -----. "Porter's Mortar Schooners." Civil War Times Illustrated, VI (October 1967), 28-36.

428. -----. Author. See U.S. Navy Department. Naval History Division, no. 2565.

429. Canfield, H. S. "Aboard a Semmes Prize." In Magazine of History, Extra Numbers 1-4. New York: William Abbatt, 1908. p. 137-139.

430. Cannon, Le Grand B. Personal Reminiscences of the Rebellion, 1861-1865. New York: Burr, 1895.

228p.
By a staff officer at Hampton Roads, 1862.

431. -----. "Personal Reminiscences of the Rebellion: the Monitor and Merrimac." Magazine of History, XV (June 1912), 190-210; XVII (July 1913), 11-17.

432. -----. Recollections of the Ironclads Monitor and Merrimack, and Incidents of the Fight. Burlington: Free Press, 1875. 10p.

433. Capers, Gerald M. The Biography of a River Town; Memphis: Its Heroic Age. Chapel Hill: University of North Carolina Press, 1939. 292p.

434. -----. "Confederates and Yankees in Occupied New Orleans, 1862-1865." Journal of Southern History, XXX (November 1964), 405-425.

435. -----. Occupied City: New Orleans Under the Federals, 1862-1865. Lexington: University of Kentucky Press, 1965. 248p.

436. "Captain R. N." "The Coming Struggle for Sea Power: The Rise of the United States Navy." United Service Magazine, CLIX (October-December 1908, January, March 1909), 23-32, 140-150, 253-262, 360-372, 575-586.
The Civil War; part of a longer series.

437. "Captain Thomas Jefferson Page." Southern Historical Society Papers, XXVII (1890), 219-231.
Skipper of the C. S. S. Stonewall.

438. "Captain William T. Sampson, U. S. N." United Service, New Series, III (May 1890), 563-564.

439. "The Capture of the Florida." Nautical Magazine, (December 1864), 679-681.

440. "Capture of the Gunboats on the Cumberland River." Confederate Veteran, XIV (January-December 1906), 17-18.

441. "Capture of the Maple Leaf." Confederate Veteran, VI (January-December 1898), 529-530.

442. -----. Confederate Veteran, XXIX (January-December 1921), 375-376.

443. "Capture of the Water Witch." Confederate Veteran, XVII (January-December 1909), 604-605.

444. Caraway, L. B. "The Battle of Arkansas Post." Confederate Veteran, XXXVI (January-December 1928), 171-173.

445. The Career of the Alabama, No. 290. From July 29, 1862 to June 19, 1864. London: Dorrell, 1864. 43p.

446. Carnegie Endowment for International Peace. Division of International Law. Prize Cases Decided in the United States Supreme Court, 1789-1918. Edited by James B. Scott. 3 vols. Oxford: Clarendon Press, 1923.
Civil War cases are in Vol. III.

447. Carpenter, Cyrus C. "James W. Grimes, Governor and Senator." Annals of Iowa, 3rd Series, I (October 1894), 505-525.
A U. S. Senate friend of the Navy.

448. Carraway, L. V. "The Battle of Arkansas Post." Confederate Veteran, XIV (January-December 1906), 127-128.

449. Carrington, Charles S., Author of Report. See C. S. A. Justice Department, no. 570.

450. Carrison, Daniel J. The Navy From Wood to Steel: 1860-1890. New York: Franklin Watts, 1965. 186p.
Good discussion of the effect of "plunging fire" on the Western gunboats.

451. Carroll, Anna E. "Plan of the Tennessee Campaign." North American Review, CXLII (April 1886), 342-347.

452. Carry, Clarence. "Journal of a Confederate Midshipman." All Hands, No. 472 (June 1956), 59-63.

453. Carse, Robert. Blockade. New York: Rinehart,

1958. 279p.

454. Carson, John M. "Capture of the Indianola." Confederate Veteran, XXXII (January-December 1924), 380-381.

455. Carter, Mrs. B. M. "Chain Armor for Warships." Confederate Veteran, VII (January-December 1899), 77.

456. Carter, Hodding. The Lower Mississippi. Rivers of America. New York: Farrar & Rinehart, 1942. 467p.

457. [Cary, Clarence]. "The War Journal of Midshipman Cary." Edited by Brooks Thompson and Frank L. Owsley, Jr. Civil War History, IX (June 1963), 187-202.
Aboard the C. S. S. Chickamauga.

458. The Case of the Trent Examined. London: Ridgway, 1862. 24p.

459. Caskie, J. A. The Life and Letters of Matthew Fontaine Maury. Richmond: Richmond Press, 1928. 191p.

460. Cassidy, John F. "Field Service in the Civil War; Squadron Marines in Combined Operations." Marine Corps Gazette, I (September 1916), 290-297.

461. Cassidy, Vincent H. and Amos E. Simpson. Henry Watkins Allen of Louisiana. Baton Rouge: Louisiana State University Press, 1964. 201p.
Rebel governor during the Red River Campaign, 1864.

462. Castell, Albert G. "The Battle of Helena, Arkansas." Civil War Times Illustrated, VII (August 1968), 12-17.

463. -----. "The Fort Pillow Massacre: A Fresh Examination of the Evidence." Civil War History, IV (March 1958), 37-51.
Which the gunboat New Era, stationed in the river below, was powerless to prevent.

464. Castlen, Harriet (Gift). Hope Bids Me Onward. Savannah: Chatham, 1945. 198p.

A biography, liberally spliced with letters and family documents, of George W. Gift, C.S.N., one-time officer aboard the Arkansas.

465. Catton, Bruce. The Centennial History of the Civil War. E. B. Long, Director of Research. 3 vols. Garden City, New York: Doubleday, 1961-1966.

466. -----. "Glory Road Began in the West." Civil War History, VI (June 1960), 229-237.

467. -----. Grant Moves South. Boston: Little, Brown, 1960. 564.

Second of a three-volume biography; often cites Army-Navy co-operation.

468. -----. "When the Monitor Met the Merrimac." New York Times Magazine, (March 4, 1962), 16, 68, 70-71.

469. -----. Author of Narrative. See American Heritage Picture History of the Civil War, no. 63.

470. Cauthen, Charles C. South Carolina Goes to War, 1860-1865. Chapel Hill: University of North Carolina Press, 1950. 256p.

471. Chadwick, French E. "The Federal Navy and the South." Review of Reviews, XLIII (April 1911), 438-440.

472. Chalmers, James R. "Forrest and His Campaigns." Southern Historical Society Papers, VII (1879), 451-486.

Including his success at Johnsonville, 1864.

473. Chandler, Alfred D., Jr. "DuPont, Dahlgren, and the Civil War Nitre Shortage." Military Affairs, XIII (Fall 1949), 142-149.

474. Chandler, Walter. "The Memphis Navy Yard." West Tennessee Historical Papers, I (1947), 68-72.

475. Chaplain, C. T. and J. M. Keeling. "Operations on the Blackwater River." Confederate Veteran,

XXVII (January-December 1919), 304-305.
The Federal expedition against Franklin, Virginia, September 1862.

476. "Charging a Gunboat with a Bayonet." Confederate Veteran, I (January-December 1893), 308-309.
The vessel is not named.

477. Chase, Lew A. "The Alabama and the Emden." Nation, XCIX (December 3, 1914), 99.
A comparison with illustrations between the Confederate raider and the World War I German cruiser.

478. -----. "The Search for the Alabama and the New Era in Naval Warfare." Sewanee Review, XVIII (July 1910), 344-358.

479. [Chase, Salmon P.]. The Diary and Correspondence of Salmon P. Chase. Part IV of The Annual Report of the American Historical Association for the Year 1902. Washington: Government Printing Office, 1903. 458p.

480. -----. Inside Lincoln's Cabinet; the Civil War Diaries of Salmon P. Chase. Edited by David Donald. New York: Longmans, Green, 1954. 342p.
Sheds some light on the Trent affair.

481. -----. Author of Report. See U.S. Treasury Department, no. 2618.

482. [Cheavens, Henry M.]. "A Missouri Confederate in the Civil War: the Journal of Henry Martyn Cheavens, 1862-1863." Edited by James E. Moss. Missouri Historical Review, LVII (October 1962), 16-53.
Reports the sinking of the ironclad U.S.S. Cincinnati at Vicksburg, May 1863.

483. Chesnut, Mary B. A Diary from Dixie. Edited by Isabella D. Martin and Myrta Lockett Avery. New York: D. Appleton, 1905. 424p.
Sights and sounds of the river war in the West.

484. Chesny, Charles C. Essays in Modern Military

Biography. London: Longmans, Green, 1874. 398p.
Includes Admirals Farragut and Porter.

485. Chester, Colby M. Chasing the Blockaders. District of Columbia Commandery, Military Order of the Loyal Legion of the United States. War Papers, no. 94. Washington: The Commandery, 1913.

486. -----. Showing the Way. District of Columbia Commandery, Military Order of the Loyal Legion of the United States. War Papers, no. 79. Washington: The Commandery, 1910.
Into Mobile Bay.

487. Chisolm, Robert. "The Battle of Port Royal." In George M. Vickers, ed. Under Both Flags. p. 255-257.

488. Chitty, Arthur B. "Leonidas K. Polk--A Profile." Civil War Times Illustrated, II (October 1963), 17-23.
The Bishop-General who opposed Grant and the gunboats at Belmont, 1861.

489. Choate, Joseph H. Farragut. Mr. Choate's Address Made at the Request of the Farragut Monument Association on the Occasion of the Unveiling of the St. Gaudens' Statue, May 25, 1881. New York: Evening Post, 1881. 19p.

490. Church, Henry F. "The Harbor Defense of Charleston." Military Engineer, XXIII (January-February 1931), 11-14.

491. Church, William C. The Life of John Fricsson. 2 vols. New York: Scribner, 1890.

492. -----. "The Naval Victory at Port Royal, S. C., November 7, 1861." In Personal Recollections of the War of the Rebellion; Papers Read before the New York Commandery, Military Order of the Loyal Legion of the United States. 4 vols. New York: The Commandery, 1891-1912. Vol. II, pp. 255-266.

493. "Civil War Blockade Runners." In U.S. Navy Depart-

ment. Naval History Division. Civil War Naval Chronology. 6 vols. Washington: U. S. Government Printing Office, 1961-1966. Vol. VI, pp. 335-347.

Pictures from the Spurling Collection at the Confederate Museum, St. Georges Historical Society, Bermuda.

494. "Civil War Gunboat." All Hands. No. 534 (July 1961), 18-19.

The ironclad Cairo.

495. "Civil War Hospital Ship." All Hands. No. 541 (February 1962), 59-63.

The Red Rover.

496. "Civil War Ships Salvaged or Memorialized." In U. S. Navy Department. Naval History Division. Civil War Naval Chronology. 6 vols. Washington: U. S. Government Printing Office, 1961-1966. Vol. VI, pp. 347-384.

497. "A Civil War Torpedo." Hobbies, LXXII (August 1967), 127.

498. Clagett, Mrs. W. S. "The Virginia and the Monitor." Confederate Veteran, XXI (January-December 1913), 25-26.

499. Clark, Charles. The Trent and San Jacinto. London: Butterworths, 1862. 46p.

A legal pamphlet.

500. Clark, Charles E. My Fifty Years in the Navy. Boston: Little, Brown, 1917. 346p.

Autobiography of a Rear Admiral who, years earlier, served aboard the U. S. S. Ossipee of the West Gulf Coast Blockading Squadron.

501. -----. Prince and Boatswain; Sea Tales from the Recollections of Rear Admiral Charles E. Clark as Related to James Morris Morgan and John Philip Marquand. Greenfield, Mass.: E. A. Hall, 1915. 105p.

Includes stories of "Savez" Read and Cushing.

502. Clark, George E. Seven Years of a Sailor's Life.

Boston: Adams, 1867. 358p.
How a merchant sailor joined the Union blockade.

503. Clarke, H. C. Diary of the War for Seperation, a Daily Chronicle of the Principal Events and History of the Present Revolution, to Which is Added Notes and Descriptions of all the Great Battles, Including Walker's Narrative of the Battle of Shiloh. Augusta: Chronicle and Sentinal, 1862. 191p.

504. Clarke, Norman E., Sr., ed. See Currie, George E., no. 641.

505. Clayton, William F. First Annual Report of William F. Clayton, Secretary of the Association of Survivors of the Confederate States Navy. Florence, S.C.: Times-Messenger, 1900. 11p.

506. -----. A Narrative of the Confederate States Navy. Weldon, N.C.: Harrell, 1910.

507. Clemens, Samuel L. Life on the Mississippi. Boston: J. R. Osgood, 1883. 624p.

508. Clendenen, Clarence C. "The Expedition that Never Sailed: A Mystery of the Civil War." California Historical Society Quarterly, XXXIV (June 1955), 149-156.
Countermanded plan to ferry Yankee troops from California to Mexico and march them overland to San Antonio.

509. Clift, Brooks. "The Confederate Navy." Confederate Veteran, XXXVIII (January-December 1930), 350-351.

510. Cline, William R. "The Ironclad Ram Virginia." Southern Historical Society Papers, XXXII (1904), 243-249.

511. Clubbs, Occi. "Stephen Russell Mallory." Florida Historical Quarterly, XVI (January-April 1947), 221-245, 295-318.
Confederate Secretary of the Navy.

512. Coates, Joseph H. "The Advent of the Ironclads."

United Service, I (October 1879), 586-600.

513. Cochran, Hamilton. Blockade Runners of the Confederacy. Indianapolis: Bobbs-Merrill, 1958. 350p.

514. Coddington, Edwin B. "Activities and Attitudes of a Confederate Businessman: Gazaway B. Lamar." Journal of Southern History, IX (February 1943), 3-36.
The blockade-running business.

515. -----. "The Civil War Blockade Reconsidered." In Dwight E. Lee and George E. McReynolds, eds. Essays in History and International Relations in Honor of George Hubbard Blakeslee. Worchester, Mass.: Clark University Press, 1949. p. 284-305.

516. Coffin, Charles C. The Boys of '61; or, Four Years of Fighting; Personal Observation with the Army and Navy, From the First Battle of Bull Run to the Fall of Richmond. Boston: Estes and Lauriat, 1896. 572p.

517. -----. Four Years of Fighting: A Volume of Personal Observations with the Army and Navy. Boston: Ticknor and Fields, 1866. 558p.

518. -----. My Days and Nights on the Battlefield. Boston: Estes and Lauriat, 1887. 234p.
Recollections of a newsman who spent a large part of his time aboard Western gunboats.

519. Coggins, Jack. Arms and Equipment of the Civil War. Garden City, New York: Doubleday, 1962. 160p.
Many illustrations; includes the Navies.

520. -----. "Civil War Naval Ordnance--Weapons and Equipment." Civil War Times Illustrated, IV (November 1964), 16-20.

521. -----. "New Guns and Projectiles Ended the Reign of Wooden Ships." Civil War Times Illustrated, IV (October 1964), 22-25.

522. Coghlan, Joseph B. "The [Union] Navy." In Personal Recollections of the War of the Rebellion; Papers Read before the New York Commandery, Military Order of the Loyal Legion of the United States. 4 vols. New York: The Commandery, 1891-1912. Vol. II, pp. 384-392.

523. Cohen, Victor H. "Charles Sumner and the Trent Affair." Journal of Southern History, XXII (May 1956), 205-219.

524. [Colby, Carlos W.]. "Bullets, Hardtack and Mud: A Soldier's View of the Vicksburg Campaign." Edited by John S. Painter. Journal of the West, IV (April 1965), 129-168.
Letters of a soldier assigned to Sherman's Yazoo Expeditionary Force, December 1862-August 1863.

525. Colby, Isaac, Joint Author. See Brown, Laurence, no. 361.

526. Coleman, S. B. A July Morning with the Rebel Ram Arkansas. War Papers Read before the Commandery of the State of Michigan, Military Order of the Loyal Legion of the United States, No. 1. Detroit: Winn & Hammond, 1890. 13p.
By an officer aboard the U. S. S. Tyler.

527. -----. "A July Morning with the Rebel Ram Arkansas [and a sketch of the vessel's history]." By S. B. Coleman and Paul Stevens. United States Naval Institute Proceedings, LXXXVIII (July 1962), 84-97.

528. Coles, Frederick C., Joint Author. See Edwards, V. B., no. 785.

529. Collier, Mrs. B. W. "The Alabama." Confederate Veteran, XXXIX (January-December 1931), 342-343.

530. [Collins, James B. and Joseph T.]. "Two New Yorkers in the Union Navy: Narrative Based on Letters of the Collins Brothers." Edited by James J. Heslin. New York Historical Society Quarterly, XLIII (April 1959), 160-201.

On the North Atlantic Blockade, September 1862-July 1863.

531. Collins, R. M. Chapters from the Unwritten History of the War Between the States; or, the Incidents in the Life of a Confederate Soldier in Camp, on the March, in the Great Battles, and in Prison. St. Louis: Nixon-Jones, 1893. 335p.
Captured at Arkansas Post, 1863.

532. Collum, Richard S. The Services of the [U. S.] Marines During the Civil War. Philadelphia: Hamersly, 1886. 8p.

533. -----. "The United States Navy During the Civil War." American Historical Register, I (October-December 1893), 113-122, 243-253, 325-336.

534. -----. comp. See Aldrich, Almy M., no. 49.

535. Colston, R. E. "Watching the Merrimac." In Robert U. Johnson and Clarence C. Buell, eds. B & L. Vol. I, pp. 712-713.

536. Colvocoresses, George M. "Admiral Porter." United States Naval Institute Proceedings, XXXIV (March 1908), 309-314.

537. Colvocoresses, Harold. "Captain George Musalas Colvocoresses, U. S. N." Washington Historical Quarterly, XXV (July 1934), 163-170.
While in command of the store ship Supply in 1861-1863, he captured the blockade runner Stephen Hart.

538. Commager, Henry Steele, ed. The Blue and the Gray: The Story of the Civil War as Told by Participants. 2 vols. Indianapolis: Bobbs-Merrill, 1950.
Much naval data.

539. "Commanders of the Confederate Navy." Confederate Veteran, XXXVII (January-December 1929), 58-59.

540. "A Comprehensive Sketch of the Merrimac and Monitor Naval Battle, Giving an Accurate Account of

the Most Important Naval Engagement in the Annals of the War.... New York: Merrimac and Monitor Panorama Company, 1886. 16p.

541. "Confederate Forces Afloat." In U.S. Navy Department. Naval History Division. Dictionary of American Naval Fighting Ships. Washington: U.S. Government Printing Office, 1959--. Vol. II, pp. 487-590.
Histories of the individual vessels.

542. "Confederate Naval Officers." Confederate Veteran, XXXIX (January-December 1931), 355-356.

543. "Confederate Naval Veterans." Confederate Veteran, XXII (January-December 1914), 255-256.
A list.

544. "Confederate States Naval Academy." Confederate Veteran, XXIII (January-December 1915), 402-403.

545. "The Confederate States Navy." Southern Historical Society Papers, XXXV (1907), 290-297.

546. Confederate States of America. Army. Department of Mississippi and East Louisiana. Report of General Joseph E. Johnstone of His Operations in the Department of Mississippi and East Louisiana, Together with Lieutenant General [John] Pemberton's Report on the Battles of Port Gibson, Baker's Creek, and the Siege of Vicksburg. Richmond: R. M. Smith, 1864. 213p.

547. ----- -----. Department of South Carolina, Georgia, and Florida. Report of the Affair at Port Royal Ferry on 1st January 1862, J. C. Pemberton, Brigadier General Commanding. n.p. n.d. 21p.

548. ----- ----- -----. Report of General [Pierre] G. T. Beauregard of the Defence of Charleston. Richmond: R. M. Smith, 1864. 91p.

549. ----- -----. Trans-Mississippi Department. Report of Major General Thomas C. Hindman of His Operations in the Trans-Mississippi Department. Richmond: R. M. Smith, 1864. 26p.

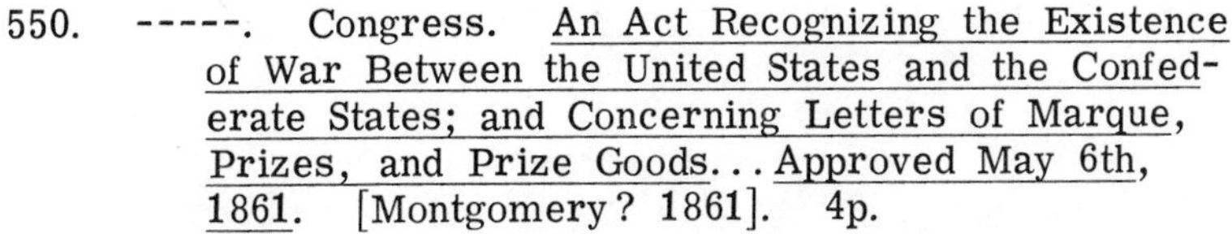

550. -----. Congress. An Act Recognizing the Existence of War Between the United States and the Confederate States; and Concerning Letters of Marque, Prizes, and Prize Goods... Approved May 6th, 1861. [Montgomery? 1861]. 4p.

551. ----- -----. Joint Resolutions on the Subject of the War, and in Regard to the Free Navigation of the Mississippi River. Richmond: 1863. 3p.

552. ----- -----. Laws for the Government of the Navy of the United States. Adopted by Act of Congress, Approved March 16, 1861, for the Government of the Navy of the Confederate States. [Montgomery? 1861]. 14p.

553. ----- -----. Letter of the Secretary of the Navy April 17th, 1862, Transmitting the Report of Lieutenant Commanding Robert B. Pegram, Commanding the Steamer Nashville, and the Correspondence Accompanying the Same. Richmond: 1862. 16p.

554. ----- -----. Minority Report of the Special Committee to Investigate the Affairs of the Navy Department. Richmond: 1863. 4p.

555. ----- -----. Report From the Joint Select Committee to Investigate the Management of the Navy Department. Richmond: 1864. 7p.

556. ----- -----. Report of Evidence Taken Before a Joint Special Committee of Both Houses of the Confederate Congress to Investigate the Affairs of the Navy Department. Richmond: G. P. Evans, 1863. 472p.

557. ----- -----. House of Representatives. Communication From the Secretary of the Navy Transmitting a Copy of [Flag Officer French] Forrest's Report of the Engagement between the Steamer Harmony and the U.S. Frigate Savannah. Richmond: 1862. 1p.

The small armed tug inflicted much damage upon the large Federal ship, August 1861.

558. ----- ----- -----. Report of the Special Committee

on the Fall of Fort Donelson, etc., February 23, 1863. Richmond: 1863. 2p.

559. ----- ----- -----. Report of the Special Committee on the Recent Military Disasters at Forts Henry and Donelson, and the Evacuation of Nashville. Richmond: Enquirer Book and Job Press, 1862. 178p.

560. ----- ----- -----. Committee on Naval Affairs. Report of the Committee on Naval Affairs on Promotions in the Navy. Richmond: 1862. 4p.

561. ----- ----- -----. Roanoke Island Investigation Committee. Report of the Roanoke Island Investigation Committee. Richmond: Enquirer Book and Job Press, 1862. 14p.

562. ----- -----. Senate. Communications from the Secretary of the Navy and the Postmaster General, Relative to the Number of White Men Between the Ages of 18 and 45, and of Negroes, Whose Services are Necessary to Their Respective Departments. Richmond: 1865. 9p.

563. ----- ----- -----. Report of the Committee on Foreign Relations, in Relation to the Capture of the Florida in the Bay of Bahia, Brazil.... Richmond: 1864. 9p.

564. ----- ----- -----. Committee on Naval Affairs. Report of the Committee on Naval Affairs, on the Memorial of Zedekiah McDaniel and Francis M. Ewing. Richmond: 1864. 2p.

For sinking the Federal ironclad Cairo in the Yazoo with a "torpedo" of their invention.

565. -----. District Court of Alabama. Standing Interrogatories in Prize Causes, by Authority of Hon. William G. Jones, Judge of the District Court of Alabama, Confederate States of America. Mobile: S. H. Goetzel, 1863. 8p.

566. -----. Engineer Department. Estimate for the Steamer Phoenix, Impressed by Military Authority and Sunk as an Obstruction in the Harbor of Mobile, Alabama, August 7, 1864. Richmond:

1864. 2p.

567. ----- -----. Estimate for the Value of the Schooner Isabel, Seized by Military Authority and Sunk as an Obstruction in Dog River Bar Channel, Mobile Bay, May 5, 1862. Richmond: 1865. 2p.

568. ----- -----. Official Report of the Chief Engineer of the District of Georgia of the Attack by the Enemy's Turreted Iron Clads on Genesis Point Battery. March 3, 1863. n.p., 1863. 8p.
The U.S. S. Passaic, Nahant, and Patapsco bombard Fort McAllister, at Savannah, as a dry-run for the later attack on Charleston.

569. ----- -----. Official Reports of the Military Engineers of the Engagement of the Enemy's Iron-Clad Fleet with the Forts and Batteries Commanding the Outer Harbor of Charleston, on the Seventh of April 1863. Charleston: 1863. 10p.
A great Confederate victory and the largest defeat handed Yankee monitors during the war.

570. -----. Justice Department. Report on Vessels Sunk and Burnt in the Pamunkey River, by Captain Chas. S. Carrington, A.Q.M., Under the Orders of General Joseph E. Johnston and Others. Richmond: 1863. 5p.
In eastern Virginia.

571. -----. Navy Department. Finding and Opinion of a Naval Court of Inquiry Convened in the City of Richmond, Va., January 5, 1863, to Investigate the Official Conduct of Comdr. John K. Mitchell, C.S. Navy. Richmond: 1863. 4p.
Exonerating him of charges of misconduct at New Orleans in 1862.

572. ----- -----. Message of the President... January 5, 1865 [Transmitting a Communication from the Secretary of the Navy, which Conveys the Information that "no coals Were Taken from the Steamer Advance, in October Last, or at any Other Time, for the Naval Service."] Richmond: 1865. 1p.

573. ----- -----. Official Report of the Battle Between the C.S.S. Virginia (Formerly U.S.S. Merrimack)

and the U. S. S. Monitor, on March 9, 1862. By Flag Officer Franklin Buchanan. Washington: Naval Historical Foundation [1962?]. 8p.
Reprint of the original.

574. ----- -----. Ordnance Instructions for the Confederate States Navy Relating to the Preparation of Vessels of War for Battle, to the Duties of Officers and Others When at Quarters, to Ordnance and Ordnance Stores, and to Gunnery. 3rd ed. London: Otley, 1864. 171p.

575. ----- -----. Proceedings of a Naval General Court-Martial, in the Case of Captain Josiah Tattnall. Richmond: Macfarlane & Fergusson, 1862. 90p.
Exonerating him of charges of misconduct for burning the Merrimac in the face of Federal advances on her anchorage, 1862.

576. ----- -----. Register of the Commissioned and Warrant Officers of the Navy of the Confederate States. To January 1, 1863. Richmond: Macfarlane & Fergusson, 1863. 15p.

577. ----- ----- -----. To January 1, 1864. Richmond: 1864. 96p.

578. ----- -----. Regulations for the Interior Police of the Confederate States School-ship Patrick Henry. [Richmond?, 1863]. 16p.

579. Confederate States of America. Navy Department. Report of the Secretary of the Navy, March 29, 1862. Richmond: 1862.

580. ----- -----. Report of the Secretary of the Navy, November 5, 1864. Richmond: G. P. Evans, 1864. 52p.

581. -----. Ordnance Bureau. Reports: October 13 and December 31, 1864; February 2 and 9, 1865. Southern Historical Society Papers, II (1876), 58-63.

582. -----. President. A Compilation of the Messages and Papers of the Confederacy, Including the Diplomatic Correspondence, 1861-1865.... 2 vols. Nashville: United States Publishing, 1905.

583. -----. State Department. Instructions Upon Neutral and Belligerent Rights, Prepared by the Hon. J. P. Benjamin, Secretary of State, Under the Orders of the President, and Issued by the Secretary of the Navy for the Government of the Cruizing [sic] Ships of the C. S. Navy. Richmond: Macfarlane & Fergusson, 1864. 12p.

584. -----. War Department. Official Reports of Battles, Embracing the Defence of Vicksburg, by Major General Earl Van Dorn, and the Attack on Baton Rouge, by Major-General [sic] Breckenridge.... Richmond: Smith, Barley, 1863. 170p.

585. ----- -----. Report of Lieutenant General [Theophilus] Holmes of the Battle of Helena.... Richmond: R. M. Smith, 1864. 63p.

586. ----- -----. Uniform and Dress of the Army and Navy of the Confederate States of America. With an Introduction by Richard Harwell. Rev. ed. Philadelphia: R. Riling, 1960. 12p.

587. Conger, Arthur L., comp. See U.S. Army General Service Schools, no. 2429.

588. Conger, Charlotte M. "Rear Admiral Thomas H. Stevens, U.S.N." United Service, New Series XV (June 1896), 566-570.

589. Congressional Globe. Washington: 1833-1873.
Within these 46 volumes is much data on the Navy and the Civil War. The appendices contain Messages of the President and the Reports of Heads of Departments.

590. Connecticut Historical Society. "U.S.S. Hartford, 1858-1956." Connecticut Historical Society Bulletin, XXII (April 1957), 53-58.

591. Connelly, Thomas L. "The [Albert Sidney] Johnston Mystique--A Profile." Civil War Times Illustrated, V (February 1967), 14-23.
Originator of the Confederate defense line broken by Grant and Foote at Forts Henry and Donelson.

592. -----. The Army of the Heartland; the Army of Tennessee, 1861-1862. Baton Rouge: Louisiana State University Press, 1967. 305p.

593. Conrad, Daniel B. "Boarding, Capturing, and Burning the Gunboat Underwriter." United Service, New Series VII (June 1892), 598-604.
By a Confederate force led by Commander John Taylor Wood; Near New Bern, North Carolina, February 1864.

594. -----. "Burning the Gunboat Underwriter." In George M. Vickers, ed. Under Both Flags. p. 120-124.

595. -----. "Capture of the C. S. Ram Tennessee." Southern Historical Society Papers, XIX (1891), 72-82.

596. -----. "Capture of the Federal Gunboat Underwriter." Southern Historical Society Papers, XIX (1891), 93-100.

597. -----. "Capture of the Underwriter, 1864." Magazine of History, VIII (September 1908), 125-129.

598. -----. "What the Fleet-Surgeon Saw of the Fight in Mobile Bay, August, 1864, Whilst on Board the Confederate Ironclad Tennessee." United Service, New Series, VIII (September 1892), 261-270.

599. -----. "With Buchanan on the Tennessee." In George M. Vickers, ed. Under Both Flags. p. 62-68.

600. "Contribution of the Confederacy to Naval Architecture and Naval Warfare." Confederate Veteran, XXXI (January-December 1923), 334-338.

601. Cooling, Benjamin F., III "The Attack on Dover, Tennessee." Civil War Times Illustrated, II (August 1963), 10-14.
Led by Forrest; Routed by gunboats under Fitch, February 1863.

602. -----. "The Battle of Dover." Tennessee Historical Quarterly, XXII (March 1963), 143-151.

603. -----. "Fort Donelson National Military Park." Tennessee Historical Quarterly, XXIII (March 1964), 203-223.

604. Copeland, A. C. "The Alabama Never in a Confederate Port." Confederate Veteran, XVIII (January-December, 1910), 160-161.

605. Coppee, Henry, ed. See Paris, L. P. Comte de., no. 1842.

606. Corbin, Diana F. (Maury). A Life of Matthew Fontaine Maury. London: S. Low, Marston, Searle & Rivington, 1888. 326p.

607. -----. "Monument to Commodore Maury." Southern Historical Society Papers, XVIII (1890), 365-371.

608. Coste, Angelo M. Memoir of the Trent Affair. With an Introduction by Charles Wilkes. Washington: McGill & Witherow, 1865. 23p.

609. Coulter, E. Merton. "Commercial Intercourse with the Confederacy in the Mississippi Valley, 1861-1865." Mississippi Valley Historical Review, V (March 1919), 377-395.

610. -----. "Effects of Secession Upon the Commerce of the Mississippi Valley." Mississippi Valley Historical Review, III (December 1916), 275-300.

611. Courtenay, William A. "The Coast Defence of South Carolina." Southern Historical Society Papers, XXVI (1898), 62-87.

612. Cowen, E. G. "The Battle of Johnsonville." Confederate Veteran, XXII (January-December 1914), 174-175.

613. Cowles, Calvin P., comp. See U.S. War Department, no. 2624.

614. Cowley, Charles. Leaves From a Lawyer's Life Afloat and Ashore. Lowell, Mass.: Penhallow, 1879. 245p.
By Dahlgren's Judge Advocate.

615. Cox, Benjamin B. "Mobile in the War Between the States." Confederate Veteran, XXIV (January-December 1916), 209-210.

616. Cox, Jacob D. Military Reminiscences of the Civil War. 2 vols. New York: Scribner, 1900.
A friend of the Union's inland navy.

617. Cox, Merlin G. "John Pope, Fighting General from Illinois." Unpublished PhD Dissertation, University of Florida, 1955.
In charge of the Federal Army's half of the combined operations at Island No. 10.

618. Coxe, Lewis. "Matthew Fontaine Maury, U.S.N." United States Naval Institute Proceedings, LI (July 1925), 1193-1196.

619. Crabtree, John. "From Helena to Vicksburg in August 1863." In Military Essays and Recollections; Papers Read Before the Illinois Commandery, Military Order of the Loyal Legion of the United States. 4 vols. Chicago: A. C. McClurg, 1891-1912. Vol. IV, pp. 105-147.

620. Crandall, Warren D. and Isaac D. Newell. History of the Ram Fleet and the Mississippi Marine Brigade. 2 vols. in 1. St. Louis: Buschart Brothers, 1907. 464p.
The basic account.

621. Cranwell, John P. Spoilers of the Sea: Wartime Raiders in the Age of Steam. New York: W. W. Norton, 1941. 308p.
Includes the Civil War.

622. Craven, Thomas T., Defendant. Record of Testimony Taken at the Trial of Commodore T. T. Craven, U.S.N., Before a Court-Martial Held in Washington, November 1865. New York: C. S. Westcott, 1866. 170p.
A messy affair. Craven in the U.S.S. Niagra, supported by Captain Henry Walke in the Sacramento, refused to fight the C.S.S. Stonewall off Spain in 1864. The court, chaired by Farragut, accepted his judgment. Secretary Welles did not.

623. Creecy, Richard B. "The Bombardment." Pasquotank Historical Society Yearbook, I (1955), 75-76.
Of Roanoke Island.

624. -----. "The Capture of the Maple Leaf." Pasquotank Historical Society Yearbook, III (1958), 108-109.

625. Creese, James. "John Ericsson, Engineer." American Scandinavian Review, XIV (May 1926), 286-301.

626. Crenshaw, Edmund A. "Germantown's Own Sloop-of-War." Germantowne Crier, V (September 1953), 11-12.
Burned by the Federals at Norfolk, 1861.

627. Crenshaw, R. S., contributor. See Page, Thomas J., no. 1832.

628. [Crippin, Edward W.]. "The Diary of Edward W. Crippin, Private, 27th Illinois Volunteers, War of the Rebellion, August 7, 1861-September 19, 1863." In Transactions of the Illinois Historical Society for the Year 1909. Illinois State Library Publication, no. 14. Springfield: The Society, 1910. p. 220-281.
One of those rescued by the Lexington at Belmont in 1861. A close observer of the role of the gunboats in the Western theatre.

629. Crockett, Albert S., ed. See Stodder, Louis N., no. 2315.

630. Cron, Frederick W. "Colonel Bailey's Red River Dams." Military Engineer, XXIX (November-December 1937), 421-424.
Which saved the gunboats, 1864.

631. Cronin, Cornelius. Recollections of Service in the United States Navy While Serving Aboard the U.S. Ships Sabine, Brooklyn, and Richmond. n.p., n.d.
As a gunner during the Civil War.

632. Crowley, R. O. "The Confederate Torpedo Service." Century Illustrated Magazine, LVI (June 1898), 290-300.

633. Crozier, Emmet. Yankee Reporters, 1861-1865. New York: Oxford University Press, 1956. 441p.

634. "The Cruise of the Clarence-Tacony-Archer, C.S. Navy." Maryland Historical Magazine, X (March 1915), 42-55.

635. "The Cruise of the Nashville." Confederate Veteran, XXVI (January-December 1918), 249-250.

636. Crummer, Wilbur F. With Grant at Fort Donelson, Shiloh, and Vicksburg. Oak Park, Ill.: E. C. Crummer, 1915. 190p.

637. Cumberland, C. C. "The Confederate Loss and Recapture of Galveston, 1862-1863." Southwest Historical Quarterly, LI (October 1947), 109-130.

638. Cunningham, Edward C. The Battle of Baton Rouge, 1862. Baton Rouge: Kennedy Print Shop, 1962.

639. -----. The Port Hudson Campaign, 1862-1863. Baton Rouge: Louisiana State University Press, 1963. 174p.

A modern study with ample space devoted to the Union Navy.

640. Currie, George E. "A Naval Battle off Memphis." In Sketches of War History; Papers Read before the Ohio Commandery, Military Order of the Loyal Legion of the United States. 6 vols. Cincinnati: Robert Clarke, 1888-1908. Vol. V, pp. 167-175.

641. -----. Warfare Along the Mississippi: The Letters of Lieutenant Colonel George E. Currie. Edited by Norman E. Clarke, Sr. Mount Pleasant, Mich.: Central Michigan University, 1961. 153p.

Member of the Mississippi Marine Brigade.

642. Curtis, F. H., ed. See Alger, F. S., no. 54.

643. Curtis, John A. The Squib vs. the Minnesota." United States Naval Institute Proceedings, LXXXVI (May 1960), 154-155.

In the James River, 1864.

644. Curtis, N. Martin. "The Capture of Fort Fisher."

In Civil War Papers, Read Before the Commandery of the State of Massachusetts, Military Order of the Loyal Legion of the United States. 2 vols. Boston: The Commandery, 1890. Vol. I, pp. 299-330.

645. Curtis, Walter G. Reminiscences of Dr. Walter G. Curtis; for Thirty Years State Quarantine Surgeon for the Port of Wilmington. Southport, N. C.: Herald Job Office, 1905. 64p.
Scenes of the port during the Rebellion.

646. Cushing, William B. "The Destruction of the Albemarle." In Robert U. Johnson and Clarence C. Buell, eds. B & L. Vol. IV, pp. 634-640.

647. -----. "War Experiences of William B. Cushing as Told by Himself." United States Naval Institute Proceedings, XXXVIII (September 1912), 940-991.

648. Cushman, Joseph D., Jr. "The Blockade and Fall of Apalachicola, 1861-1862." Florida Historical Quarterly, XLI (July 1962), 38-46.

649. Dahlgren, C. B. The Dahlgren Shell-Gun and Its Services During the Late Civil War. Trenton: Priv. Print., 1887. 23p.

650. Dahlgren, John A. B. List of Vessels of the South Atlantic Blockading Squadron, Commanded by Rear Admiral John A. Dahlgren, With Their Armament, Rate, Stations, etc., Also Regular Line Officers of the Squadron, August 1864. n.p., n.d. 16p.

651. -----. Author of Report. See U.S. Navy Department, nos. 2577 and 2586.

652. Dahlgren, Madeleine. Memoirs of John A. Dahlgren, Rear Admiral, United States Navy, by His Widow. Boston: J. R. Osgood, 1882. 660p.

653. -----. The Petition to the National Government of Madeleine V. Dahlgren, Widow of the Late Rear Admiral Dahlgren, Submitting Her Claim for Compensation for the Adoption and Use by the United States Navy of Certain Inventions of the Late Rear Admiral Dahlgren Relating to Ordnance. Washing-

ton: Gideon Brothers, 1872. 32p.

654. Dale, Ira D. "Thomas Jefferson Griffin." Staten Island Historian, XI (July-December 1950), 17-20, 22, 25-28.

655. Daly, Charles P. Are the Southern Privateersmen Pirates? Letter to the Hon. Ira Harris. New York: J. B. Kirker, 1862. 13p.

656. Daly, Robert W. "Burnside's Amphibious Division." Marine Corps Gazette, XXXV (December 1951), 30-38.

657. -----. How the Merrimac Won: the Strategic Story of the C. S. S. Virginia. New York: Crowell, 1957. 211p.

658. -----. "Joe Fyffe--Officer and Gentleman." United States Naval Institute Proceedings, LXXXII (April 1956), 416-425.

Lieutenant Joseph P. Fyffe, commander of the U. S. S. Hunchback.

659. -----. "Pay and Prize Money in the Old Navy, 1776-1899." United States Naval Institute Proceedings, LXXIV (August 1948), 967-971.

660. -----. ed. See Keeler, William F., nos. 1342 and 1343.

661. Dalzell, George W. The Flight From the Flag; the Continuing Effect of the Civil War Upon the American Carrying Trade. Chapel Hill: University of North Carolina Press, 1940. 292p.

662. Damaree, Albert L. "Our Navy's Worst Headache: The Merrimack." United States Naval Institute Proceedings, LXXXVIII (March 1962), 66-84.

663. "'Damn the Torpedoes!' Courage and a Quick Decision Lay Back of Admiral Farragut's Historic Phrase." Fortune, XXVI (December 1942), 130-132.

664. Dana, Charles A. Recollections of the Civil War: With the Leaders at Washington and In the Field in the Sixties. New York: D. Appleton, 1899.

296p.
Including the Western theatre.

665. Dana, Richard H., Jr. Enemy's Territory and Alien Enemies; what the Supreme Court Decided in the Prize Cases. Boston: Little, 1864. 11p.

666. -----. The Trent Affair, an Aftermath. Cambridge: Priv. Print., 1912. 20p.

667. Daniels, Josephus. "John Newland Maffitt." Confederate Veteran, XXX (January-December 1922), 218-221.

668. Davenport, Charles B. Naval Officers, Their Heredity and Development. Publication no. 259. Washington: The Carnegie Institution of Washington, 1919. 286p.
Including some from the Civil War period.

669. "David Glasgow Farragut." In George C. Eggleston. American Immortals. New York: Putnam, 1901. p. 270-286.

670. Davidson, Donald. The Tennessee. Rivers of America. 2 vols. New York: Rinehart, 1946-1948.

671. Davidson, Hunter. "Electrical Torpedoes as a System of Defence." Southern Historical Society Papers, V (1878), 1-6.
During the Civil War.

672. -----. "Mines and Torpedoes During the Rebellion." Magazine of History, VIII (November 1908), 255-261.

673. -----. "Torpedoes in Our War." United States Naval Institute Proceedings, XXIV (June 1898), 349-354.

674. Davis, Burke. To Appomattox: Nine April Days, 1865. New York: Rinehart, 1959. 433p.
Includes the activities of Admiral Semmes.

675. Davis, Charles H. "History of the U.S. Steamer Merrimack." New England Historical and Genealogical Register, XXVII (July 1874), 245-248.

676. Davis, Charles H. The Life of Charles H. Davis,

Rear Admiral, 1807-1877. Boston: Houghton, Mifflin, 1899. 349p.
A biography by his son; many letter excerpts.

677. Davis, Charles S. "Stephen R. Mallory: Leader of Confederate Sea Power." Florida State University Studies, X (1953), 49-61.

678. Davis, Charles W. "New Madrid and Island No. 10." In Military Essays and Recollections; Papers Read Before the Illinois Commandery, Military Order of the Loyal Legion of the United States. 4 vols. Chicago: A. C. McClurg, 1891-1912. Vol. I, pp. 75-92.

679. Davis, Clyde B. The Arkansas. Rivers of America. New York: Farrar and Rinehart, 1940. 340p.

680. Davis, Ellsworth I. "Vicksburg, the Mississippi, and the U.S. Army." Military Engineer, LV (July-August 1963) 259-261.
And indirectly, the U.S. Navy.

681. Davis, Jackson B. "The Life of Richard Taylor." Louisiana Historical Quarterly, XXIV (January 1941), 54-55.

682. Davis, Jefferson. "Confederate Privateersmen." Southern Historical Society Papers, XI (1883), 181-184.

683. -----. "Davis and [Hunter] Davidson." Southern Historical Society Papers, XXIV (1896), 284-291.

684. -----. The Rise and Fall of the Confederate Government. 2 vols. New York: D. Appleton, 1881.
By its President; includes some naval data.

685. ----- -----. With a Foreword by Bell I. Wiley. 2 vols. New York: Yoseloff, 1958.

686. -----. "Sabine Pass." Southern Historical Society Papers, XII (1884), 133-137.

687. Davis, Manton. "The Alabama." Confederate Veteran, XV (January-December 1907), 414-415.

688. Davis, Nora M. Military and Naval Operations in South Carolina, 1860-1865: A Chronological List, with References to Sources of Further Information. Columbia: South Carolina Civil War Centinnial Commission, 1959. 24p.

689. Davis, Robert S. History of the Rebel Steam Ram Atlanta, Now on Exhibition at Foot of Washington Street, for the Benefit of the Union Volunteer Refreshment Saloon, Philadelphia, with an Interesting Account of the Engagement which Resulted in Her Capture. Philadelphia: G. H. Ives, 1863. 10p.
When she visited that city in November 1863.

690. Davis, T. Frederick. "Engagements at St. John's Bluff, St. John's River, Florida. September-October 1862." Florida Historical Quarterly, XV (October 1936), 77-84.
Involving the Union navy.

691. Davis, William J., ed. See Johnson, Adam R., no. 1280.

692. Davis, William W. The Civil War and Reconstruction in Florida. A Facsim. Reproduction of the 1913 Edition. With an Introduction by Fletcher M. Green. Gainesville: University of Florida Press, 1964. 747p.

693. Davison, Louis. United States Monitors and Confederate Rams. Waterline Shipmodelers' Planbook Series. Pensacola, Fla.: The Author, 1970.

694. Dawson, Francis W. Reminiscences of Confederate Service, 1861-1865. Charleston, S.C.: The News and Courier Book Presses, 1882. 180p.
By an Englishman who served aboard the Nashville and Beaufort.

695. Dawson, Sarah (Morgan). A Confederate Girl's Diary. Edited by Warrington Dawson. Boston: Houghton, Mifflin, 1913. 473p.
Includes an account of the Battle of New Orleans, 1862.

696. Dawson, Warrenton, ed. See Dawson, Sarah (Morgan), no. 695.

697. Day, Harry E. "Ellet's Horse Marines." Marine Corps Gazette, XXIII (March 1939), 30-33, 57.
The Mississippi Marine Brigade.

698. "The Defense of New Orleans." United States Service Magazine, V (May 1866), 385-396.
Against the Federal fleet, April 1862.

699. DeForest, J. W. "Port Hudson." Harper's New Monthly Magazine, XXXV (August 1867), 334-344.

700. DeLeon, Perry M. Navies in War and the Confederate Navy in the War Between the States. Washington: Show Brothers, 1910. 46p.

701. Dennett, Tyler, ed. See Hay, John, no. 1085.

702. Denson, A. Clark. Westmoreland; or, Secession Ferocity at the Breaking Out of the Rebellion. St. Louis: P. M. Pinchard, 1865. 48p.
Account of Confederate fire into an unarmed steamer on the Western rivers in 1861.

703. DePeyster, J. Watts. "George H. Preble, Rear Admiral, U. S. N." United Service, XII (April 1885), 455-462.

704. -----. Nashville: the Decisive Battle of the Rebellion. n. p.: 1876. 14p.

705. "Destruction of the British Ship Martaban by the Alabama." Nautical Magazine (March 1864), 141-144.

706. "Destruction of the Confederate Ship Alabama by the United States Ship Kearsage [sic] Nautical Magazine (July 1864), 375-382.

707. Devens, Edward F., Author of Letter. See U. S. Congress. House of Representatives, no. 2444.

708. Devol, George H. Forty Years a Gambler on the Mississippi. Cincinnati: Devol and Haines, 1887. 300p.

709. Dew, Charles B. Ironmaker to the Confederacy: Joseph R. Anderson and the Tredegar Iron Works.

New Haven: Yale University Press, 1966. 345p.
Maker of armor plate for Rebel ironclads.

710. Dewey, George. Autobiography of George Dewey, Admiral of the Navy. New York: Scribner, 1913. 337p.
Aboard the Mississippi at Port Hudson, 1863.

711. Dickerson, Edward N. The Navy of the United States; an Exposure of Its Conditions, and the Causes of Its Failure. New York: Gray and Green, 1864. 80p.
Mostly Secretary Welles.

712. -----. The Steam Navy of the United States: Its Past, Present, and Future. A Letter to the Hon. Gideon Welles. New York: J. A. Gray, 1863. 20p.

713. Dickinson, A. G. "Blockade Running from Wilmington." Confederate Veteran, III (January-December 1895), 361-362.

714. Dickinson, T. "Running the Blockade." Era, XIII (April 1904), 249-254.

715. Didier, Eugene L. "The Active Rear-Admirals of the United States Navy." Chautauguan, XXIV (February 1897), 569-576.
Includes George Brown, John G. Walker, Francis M. Ramsay, Thomas O. Selfridge, Jr.; All held commands during the Civil War.

716. Dillahunty, Albert. Shiloh National Military Park, Tennessee. National Park Service Historical Handbook Series, no. 10. Washington: U.S. Government Printing Office, 1951. 47p.

717. Dillon, Richard H., ed. "First Word from Kearsarge." American Neptune, XIX (April 1959), 126-128.
Of her victory over the Alabama.

718. Dimitry, John. Louisiana. Vol. X of Clement A. Evans, ed. Confederate Military History; a Library of Confederate States History. 12 vols. Atlanta: Confederate Publishing, 1899.

719. Dinkins, James. "The Capture of Fort Pillow." Confederate Veteran, XXXIII (January-December 1925), 460-462.

720. -----. "The Confederate Ram Albermarle." Southern Historical Society Papers, XXX (1902), 205-214.

720a. Dismukes, Camillus J., jt. editor. See Morrissett, Algernon S., no. 1703a.

721. Ditzel, Paul. "The Fantastic Struggle of the Monitor and Merrimac." American Legion Magazine, XLIX (March 1969), 30-34, 51-57.

722. Dixon, Frank H., Author. See U.S. National Waterway Commission, no. 2563.

723. Dohrman, Horatio G. "Diplomacy and Inland Naval Warfare." Military Engineer, XXVI (May-June 1934), 212-215.
The Red River Expedition, 1864.

724. -----. "Old Man River, 1863." United States Naval Institute Proceedings, LX (June 1934), 809-816.
The campaign on the Western rivers.

725. Donald, David. et al. Divided We Fought: A Pictorial History of the War, 1861-1865. New York: Macmillan, 1961. 454p.

726. -----. ed. See Chase, Salmon P., no. 480.

727. -----. Joint Author. See Randall, James G., no. 1992.

728. Donnelly, Ralph W. "Battle Honors and Services of Confederate Marines." Military Affairs, XXIII (Spring 1959), 37-40.

729. -----. "The Charlotte, North Carolina, Navy Yard." Civil War History, V (March 1959), 72-79.

730. -----. "The Confederate Marines at Drewry's Bluff." Virginia Calvalcade, XVI (Autumn 1966), 42-47.

731. -----. "A Confederate Navy Forlorn Hope." Military Affairs, XXVIII (Summer 1964), 73-78.

To send torpedo boats overland from Petersburg, Virginia, to the James River in February 1865.

732. -----. "Uniforms and Equipment of Confederate Marines." Military Collector and Historian, IX (Spring 1957), 1-7.

733. Donovan, Frank R. Ironclads of the Civil War. American Heritage Junior Library. New York: American Heritage, 1964. 153p.
While listed as "junior," the illustrations at least should interest adults.

734. Doran, Charles. "Franklin Buchanan." Confederate Veteran, VIII (January-December 1900), 68.

735. Dorr, Eben P. A Brief Sketch of the First Monitor and Its Inventor. A Paper Read before the Buffalo Historical Society. Buffalo: Matthews and Warren, 1894. 52p.

736. Dorsey, Florence L. Road to the Sea: The Story of James B. Eads and the Mississippi River. New York: Rinehart, 1947. 340p.

737. Dorsey, Sarah A. (Ellis). Recollections of Henry Watkins Allen, Brigadier-General, C. S. A., Ex-Governor of Louisiana. New Orleans: J. A. Gresham, 1866. 420p.
Includes a strong defense of General Pemberton's activities at Vicksburg.

738. Doubleday, Abner. "From Moultrie to Sumter." In Robert U. Johnson and Clarence C. Buell, eds. B & L. Vol. I, pp. 40-49.

739. -----. Reminiscences of Forts Sumter and Moultrie in 1860-'61. New York: Harper, 1876. 184p.

740. "Dowling at Sabine Pass." Confederate Veteran, IV (January-December 1896), 366-367.

741. Drayton, Percival. Naval Letters of Captain Percival Drayton, 1861-1865; Printed from the Original Manuscripts Presented to the New York Public Library by Miss Gertrude L. Hoyt. New York: The Library, 1906. 81p.

742. ----- -----. New York Public Library Bulletin, X (November 1906), 587-625.
Frank letters to the officer's friends.

743. -----. "What Its Captain Thought of the Monitor Passaic: 'I Rue the Day I got into the Ironclad Business.'" Edited by Ashley Halsey, Jr. Civil War Times Illustrated, IV (April 1965), 28-34.
He also had little use for Ericsson and thought monitors only good for defense.

744. Drewry, Augustus H. "Drewry's Bluff Fight." Southern Historical Society Papers, XXIX (1901), 284-285.

745. Driggs, George W. Opening of the Mississippi; or, Two Years Campaigning in the South-west. Madison: W. J. Park, 1864. 149p.

746. Drury, Clifford M., Author. See U.S. Navy Department, no. 2579.

747. Dudley, Dean. Officers of Our Union Army and Navy. Their Lives, Their Portraits. Boston: Washington, L. Pring, 1862. 148p.
An early effort; brief biographies.

748. Dufour, Charles L. The Night the War Was Lost. Garden City, New York: Doubleday, 1960. 427p.

749. -----. "The Night the War Was Lost: the Fall of New Orleans; Causes, Consequences, Culpability." Louisiana History, II (Spring 1961), 157-174.

750. -----. Nine Men in Gray. Garden City, New York: Doubleday, 1963. 364p.
Includes biographies of Richard Taylor and Charles "Savez" Read.

751. Cuke, Basil W. et al. The Great Indiana-Ohio Raid by Brig.-General John Hunt Morgan and His Men, July, 1863. Louisville: Book Nook Press, 1956. 32p.
Testimony as to the effectiveness of Fitch's gunboats in halting the proceedings.

752. -----. A History of Morgan's Calvalry. Edited with

an Introduction by Cecil Fletcher Holland. Civil War Centennial Series. Bloomington: Indiana University Press, 1960. 595p.

753. -----. "Morgan's Indiana and Ohio Raid." In Annals of the War. p. 241-256.

754. -----. Reminiscences of General Basil W. Duke. Garden City, New York: Doubleday, Page, 1911. 512p.

755. Dukeshire, T. S. "The Confederate Marine Corps." Weekly Philatelic Gossip, LXII (April 14, 1956), 222-225.
A general account.

756. Dundas, William O. "Blockade Running in the Civil War." Bellman, XXVI (March 31, 1919), 606-608.

757. ----- -----. United Daughters of the Confederacy Magazine, XV (November 1952), 5, 8-9, 12.

758. Dunlap, Lloyd A., Joint Editor. See Lincoln, Abraham, no. 1454.

759. DuPont, H. A. Rear Admiral Samuel Francis duPont, United States Navy; a Biography. New York: National Americana Society, 1926. 320p.

760. DuPont, Samuel F. Abstract of the Cruise of the U. S. Frigate Wabash, Bearing the Flag of Rear Admiral Samuel F. DuPont, 1861-62 & '63. New York: Edward O. Jenkins, 1863. 31p.

761. -----. Official Dispatches and Letters of Rear Admiral DuPont, U. S. Navy, 1846-48, 1861-63. Wilmington, Del.: Ferris Brothers, 1883. 531p.

762. -----. Samuel Francis DuPont: A Selection from His Civil War Letters. Edited by John D. Hayes. 3 vols. Ithica: Cornell University Press, 1969.

763. Durkin, Joseph T. Stephen R. Mallory: Confederate Navy Chief. Chapel Hill: University of North Carolina Press, 1954. 446p.

764. DuVal, Miles P. Matthew Fontaine Maury: Benefactor of Mankind. An Address before the United Daughters of the Confederacy. In the Old House of Delegates Hall, State Capitol, Richmond, Va.... January 19, 1964. Washington: Priv. Print., 1964. 41p.

765. Duvall, Ruby R. "U.S. Navy Honors James Iredell Waddell." Shipmate, XXV (December 1962), 2-3.

766. Dyer, Brainerd. "Confederate Naval and Privateering Activities in the Pacific." Pacific Historical Review, III (December 1934), 433-443.

767. -----. "Thomas H. Dudley." Civil War History, I (December 1955), 401-413.
U.S. Counsel, Liverpool, England; Active in Union efforts to stop British building of Confederate commerce raiders.

768. Dyer, Brainerd, ed. See Simmons, William B., no. 2178.

769. Dyer, Frederick H. A Compendium of the War of the Rebellion. Edited with an Introduction by Bell Irvin Wiley. 3 vols. New York: Yoseloff, 1959.
Lists many minor battles in which the navies aided or attacked the armies.

770. Dyer, John P. "Fighting Joe" Wheeler. Baton Rouge: Louisiana State University Press, 1941. 417p.
Aided Forrest in the February 1863 drive on Dover, Tennessee.

771. -----. The Gallant Hood. Indianapolis: Bobbs-Merrill, 1950. 383p.
Chief of the December 1864 Rebel drive on Nashville--the last important battle in which the Union's inland navy took part.

772. Dyson, George W. "Benjamin Franklin Isherwood." United States Naval Institute Proceedings, LXVII (August 1941), 1139-1146.
The Federal Navy's Chief Engineer.

773. "E. S." "Fort Fisher, December 1864 and January 1865." United Service, New Series II (July 1889), 11-24.

774. Eads, James B. Addresses and Papers of James B. Eads. Together with a Biographical Sketch. Edited by Estill McHenry. St. Louis: Slaivson, 1884. 654p.

775. -----. "Recollections of Foote and the Gun-Boats." In Robert U. Johnson and Clarence C. Buell, eds. B & L. Vol. I, pp. 338-346.

776. Eagle, Henry. Biographical Sketch of Commodore Henry Eagle, U. S. N. New York: Atlantic Publishing, 1883. 7p.

777. Earle, Ralph. "John Adolphus Dahlgren." United States Naval Institute Proceedings, LI (March 1925), 424-436.

778. East, Sherrod E. "Montgomery C. Meigs and the Quartermaster Department." Military Affairs, XXV (Winter 1961-1962), 183-196.
Project overseer for the building of the Cairo-class river gunboats by Eads, 1861-1862.

779. Ebaugh, David C. "David C. Ebaugh on the Building of the David." South Carolina Historical Magazine, LIV (January 1953), 32-36.

780. Edge, Frederick M. The Alabama and the Kearsarge. London: W. Ridgway, 1864. 48p.

781. -----. Destruction of the American Carrying Trade: A Letter to Earl Russell. London: W. Ridgway, 1863. 27p.

782. -----. An Englishman's View of the Battle between the Alabama and the Kearsarge. New York: A. D. F. Randolph, 1864. 48p.

783. Edwards, E. M. H. Commander William Barker Cushing of the United States Navy. Genealogy, Reminiscences of Childhood, Boyhood, and Manhood; Incidents of His Naval Career. New York: F. T. Neeley, 1898. 202p.

784. Edwards, Frank T. "The United States Consular Service in the Bahamas During the American Civil War: A Study of its Function Within a Naval and Diplomatic Context." Unpublished PhD Dissertation, Catholic University of America, 1968.

785. Edwards, V. B. and Fred C. Coles. "Water Transportation on the Inland Rivers." In The Society of Naval Architects and Marine Engineers. Historical Transactions, 1893-1943. New York: The Society, 1945. p. 400-425.
Includes a brief account of the Union's Western navy.

786. Eggleston, E. T. "Captain [John] Ericsson's Narrative of the Battle of the Merrimac." Southern Historical Society Papers, XLIV (1916), 166-178.
With the Monitor.

787. Eggleston, J. R. "The Confederate States Navy." Confederate Veteran, XV (January-December 1907), 449-450.

788. Eisenschiml, Otto and Ralph Newman. The American Illiad; The Epic Story of the Civil War as Narrated by Eyewitnesses and Contemporaries. Indianapolis: Bobbs-Merrill, 1946. 720p.

789. "Electrical Submarine Mine." Confederate Veteran, XVI (January-December 1908), 456.

790. Eliot, George F. Daring Sea Warrior; Franklin Buchanan. New York: Messner, 1962. 191p.

791. Eller, Ernest M. and Dudley W. Knox. The Civil War at Sea. Washington: Naval Historical Foundation, 1961. 22p.

792. -----. "Seapower--Decisive Influence of the Civil War." Navy, IV (January-February 1961), 17-30, 25-30.

793. Ellerbe, Mrs. J. E. "Raphael Semmes." Confederate Veteran, XXX (January-December 1922), 178-180.

794. Ellet, Alfred W. "[Charles] Ellet and His Steam-Rams at Memphis." In Robert U. Johnson and

Clarence C. Buell, eds. B & L. Vol. I, pp. 453-459.
An account of his late brother's 1862 victory by the commander of the Mississippi Marine Brigade.

795. Ellet, Charles, Jr. Coast and Harbour Defences; or, the Substitution of Steam Battering Rams for Ships of War. Philadelphia: J. C. Clark, 1855. 17p.
An idea he was able to test during the Civil War on Western rivers.

796. -----. Military Incapacity and What it Costs the Country. New York: Ross and Tousey, 1862. 15p.
A criticism of General McClellan.

797. Ellicott, John M. The Life of John Ancrum Winslow, Rear Admiral, United States Navy. New York: Putnam, 1902. 281p.

798. Elliott, James W. Transport to Disaster. New York: Holt, Rinehart and Winston, 1962. 247p.
The Sultana.

799. Elliott, Charles W. Winfield Scott, the Soldier and the Man. New York: Macmillan, 1937. 817p.
Author of the "Anaconda Plan" of blockade and assault.

800. Elliott, Gilbert. "The First Battle of the Confederate Ram Albermarle." In Robert U. Johnson and Clarence C. Buell, eds. B & L. Vol. IV, pp. 625-627.

801. Ellis, Leonard B. The History of New Bedford and Its Vicinity, 1602-1892. Syracuse: D. Mason, 1892. 731p.
Includes the town's contribution to the Union's "Stone Fleets."

802. Ellsworth, Harry A., Author. See U. S. Marine Corps, no. 2550.

803. Ely, Robert B. "This Filthy Ironpot; Ironclads in the Battle of Mobile Bay." American Heritage, XIX (February 1968), 46-51, 108-111.

By an Acting Volunteer Lieutenant aboard the U. S. S. Manhattan.

804. Emilio, Louis F. Roanoke Island: Its Occupation, Defense and Fall. A Paper Read before the Roanoke Association. New York: The Association, 1891. 18p.

805. "Earstus Corning, Silent Partner." New York State and the Civil War, I (January 1962), 18-20.
In building the Monitor.

806. Erben, Henry. "Surrender of the Navy Yard at Pensacola, Florida, January 12, 1861." In Personal Recollections of the War of the Rebellion; Papers Read Before the New York Commandery, Military Order of the Loyal Legion of the United States. 4 vols. New York: The Commandery, 1891-1912. Vol. II, pp. 213-222.
By a lieutenant (later Rear Admiral) from Henry Walke's ship U. S. S. Supply, who attempted to persuade Commodore Armstrong not to give up.

807. Erickson, Edgar L., ed. See Wilcox, Charles E., no. 2781.

808. Ericsson, John. "The Building of the Monitor." In Robert U. Johnson and Clarence C. Buell, eds. B & L. Vol. I, pp. 730-744.

809. -----. "The Monitors." Century Illustrated Magazine, XXXI (December 1885), 280-299.

810. Ernst, Dorothy J., ed. See Pratt, Albert H., no. 1917.

811. Esposito, Vincent J., ed. The West Point Atlas of American Wars. 2 vols. New York: Frederick A. Praeger, 1959.
Includes the river battles.

812. Evans, Clement A., ed. Confederate Military History; a Library of Confederate States History. 10 vols. Atlanta; Confederate Publishing Company, 1899.
Appropriate titles also listed under their authors.

813. Evans, Robley D. A Sailor's Log. New York: D. Appleton, 1901. 467p.
A midshipman during the Rebellion; wounded at Fort Fisher.

814. Evans, S. H. The United States Coast Guard, 1790-1915. Annapolis: U.S. Naval Institute, 1949. 228p.

815. Everett, Edward. An Address Delivered at the Annual Examination of the United States Naval Academy, 28th May, 1863. Boston: Ticknor and Fields, 1863.

816. Everhart, William C. Vicksburg National Military Park, Mississippi. National Park Service Historical Handbook Series, no. 21. Washington: U.S. Government Printing Office, 1954. 60p.

817. "F. J. B." "Fire-Ships, Powder-Vessels, and Obstructions During the Civil War." United Service, New Series II (August 1889), 142-149.

818. Fairbanks, Henry. "The Red River Expedition of 1864." In War Papers, Read Before the Commandery of the State of Maine, Military Order of the Loyal Legion of the United States. 3 vols. Portland: Thurston, 1898-1908. Vol. I, pp. 181-190.

819. Fairfax, D. M. "Captain Wilke's Seizure of Mason and Slidell." In Robert U. Johnson and Clarence C. Buell, eds. B & L. Vol. II, pp. 135-142.

820. Falero, Frank. "Naval Engagements in Tampa Bay." Florida Historical Quarterly, XLVI (October 1967), 134-140.

821. "The Fall of Fort Fisher." All Hands, No. 467. (January 1956), 59-63.

822. The Fanny: First Aircraft Carrier (1861). Tales of Old Fort Monroe, no. 11. Fort Monroe, Va.: The Casemate Museum, n.d. 4p.
The balloon boat of John La Mountain.

823. Farenholt, Oscar W. From Ordinary Seaman to Rear

Admiral. Military Order of the Loyal Legion of the United States, California Commandery. War Papers, no. 22. San Francisco: Shannon-Conmy, 1910.

824. -----. The Monitor Catskill; a Year's Reminiscences. Military Order of the Loyal Legion of the United States, California Commandery. War Papers, no. 23. San Francisco: Shannon-Conmy, 1913.

825. -----. "Punishment in the Old Navy." Military Surgeon, LXXVI (1935), 210-213.
In the 1850's and 1860's.

826. -----. "Some Autobiographical Notes Concerning the Service of the late Oscar W. Farenholt, Rear Admiral, U. S. N., Rt." United States Naval Institute Proceedings, LIV (June 1928), 1047-1050; LV (July 1928), 139-140.

827. -----. "The U. S. S. Oneida." United States Naval Institute Proceedings, XL (July-August 1914), 1109-1118.

828. -----. "The Volunteer Navy in the Civil War." United States Naval Institute Proceedings, XLV (October 1919), 1691-1694.

829. Farragut, David G., Author of Report. See Naval Historical Foundation, no. 1737.

830. Farragut, Loyall. "Admiral David Glasgow Farragut, U. S. N." In Lewis R. Hamersly, ed. A Naval Encyclopedia. p. 272-273.
By the Admiral's son.

831. -----. "Farragut at Port Hudson." Putnam's Magazine, V (October 1908), 44-53.

832. -----. The Life and Letters of Admiral Farragut, First Admiral of the United States Navy. New York: D. Appleton, 1879. 586p.
Still one of the "best books" on the Admiral.

833. -----. "Passing the Port Hudson Batteries." In Personal Recollections of the War of the Rebellion; Papers Read Before the New York Commandery, Military Order of the Loyal Legion of the United

States. 4 vols. New York: The Commandery, 1891-1912. Vol. I, pp. 314-321.

834. [Fauntleroy, James H.]. "Elk Horn to Vicksburg." Edited by Homer L. Calkin. Civil War History, II (March 1956), 7-44.
Journal of a soldier able to hear the bombardment of Grand Gulf, April 1863, and occasionally view Yankee gunboats in the river.

835. Faust, Harold P. "They Who Go Down to the Sea in Ships: U.S. Army Hospital Ships." American Philatelist, LXI (January 1948), 274-279.

836. "Federal Raid in Tampa Bay." Florida Historical Quarterly, IV (January 1926), 130-139.

837. Federal Writers Project. Florida. Florida; A Guide to the Southernmost State. American Guide Series. New York: Oxford University Press, 1944. 600p.
Including Civil War naval spots.

838. -----. Illinois. Illinois; a Descriptive and Historical Guide. American Guide Series. Chicago: A. C. McClurg, 1947. 707p.

839. ----- -----. Cairo. Cairo Guide. Sponsored by the Cairo Public Library. American Guide Series. Nappanee, Ind.: E. B. Publishing, 1938. 62p.
Base of the Union's inland navy.

840. -----. Louisiana. New Orleans. New Orleans City Guide. American Guide Series. Boston: Houghton, Mifflin, 1938. 430p.

841. -----. Mississippi. Mississippi; a Guide to the Magnolia State. American Guide Series. New York: Viking, 1938. 545p.

842. -----. North Carolina. North Carolina; a Guide to the Old North State. American Guide Series. Chapel Hill: University of North Carolina Press, 1939. 601p.

843. -----. Ohio. Cincinnati. Cincinnati; Glimpses of its Youth. American Guide Series. Cincinnati: The Public Schools, 1938. 42p.

844. -----. South Carolina. Beaufort and the Sea Islands. American Guide Series. Savannah: Review Printing, 1938. 47p.

845. -----. Tennessee. Tennessee; a Guide to the State. American Guide Series. New York: Viking, 1939. 558p.

846. Fee, Robert Grand-Crawford. C. S. S. Alabama, Confederate States Navy. n. p., n. d. 18pp.
A paper with illustrations describing a model built by the author.

847. Fentress, Walter E. H. Centennial History of the United States Navy Yard at Portsmouth, New Hampshire. Portsmouth: O. M. Knight, 1876. 84p.
By the Acting Master of the river gunboat U. S. S. Rattler, who went ashore to church one Sunday and was promptly taken by the Rebels, 1863.

848. Fessenden, B. L. "The Yankee Clipper and the Cape Cod Bay." American Neptune, XXIII (October 1964), 264-269.
On the Jacob Bell; captured by the Florida.

849. "Firms that Created the Monitor." New York State and the Civil War, I (January 1962), 21.

850. "First Capture of the Federals at Sea." Confederate Veteran, I (January-December 1893), 300-301.
July 3, 1861.

851. "First Federal Defeat at Sabine Pass." Confederate Veteran, XX (January-December 1912), 108-109.

852. "First Fight of Gunboats with Cavalry." Confederate Veteran, XIX (January-December 1911), 84-85.
An attack by North Carolina mounted units on Yankee vessels in the Roanoke River, July 1862."

853. "The First Ironclad." Southern Historical Society Papers, XXX (1902), 196-204.
The Manassas.

854. "The First Steam Torpedo Boat." Confederate

Veteran, XII (January-December 1904), 106.
The David.

855. Fishbaugh, Charles P. From Paddle Wheels to Propellors. Indianapolis: Indiana Historical Society, 1970. 240p.
The Howard family of Jeffersonville, steamboat builders; includes the Civil War years.

856. Fisk, A. C. "Running the Batteries at Vicksburg." Ohio Soldier, V (1889), 491-492.
By Union Army transports, April 1863.

857. Fiske, John. The Mississippi Valley in the Civil War. Boston: Houghton, Mifflin, 1900. 368p.
Gives credit for the fall of Island No. 10 to Henry Walke and the Carondelet.

858. -----. Joint Editor. See Wilson, James G., no. 2809.

859. Fitts, James F. "A June Day at Port Hudson." Galaxy, II (September 1866), 121-131.

860. Fitzgerald, O. P. "Matthew Fontaine Maury." Confederate Veteran, IV (January-December 1896), 175.

861. Fitzgerald, W. Norman. President Lincoln's Blockade and the Defense of Mobile. Lincoln Fellowship of Wisconsin Bulletin, no. 2. Madison: The Fellowship, 1954. 15p.

862. Fitzhugh, Lester N. "Texas Forces in the Red River Campaign, March-May, 1864." Texas Military History, III (February 1963), 15-22.

863. Fiveash, Joseph G. The Virginia-(Merrimac)-Monitor Engagement, and a Complete History of the Operations of These Two Historic Vessels in Hampton Roads and Adjacent Waters. Norfolk, Va.: Fiveash Publishing, 1907. 29p.

864. -----. "The Virginia's Great Fight on Water." Southern Historical Society Papers, XXXIV (1906), 316-326.

865. Flatau, L. S. "A Great Naval Battle." Confederate Veteran, XXV (January-December 1917), 458-459.
The Arkansas vs. the Federal Fleet, July 1862.

866. Fleming, Francis P., ed. See Rerick, Rowland H., no. 2023.

867. [Fleming, Robert H.]. "The Confederate Naval Cadets and the Confederate Treasure: the Diary of Midshipman Robert H. Fleming." Edited by G. Melvin Heindon. Georgia Historical Quarterly, L (June 1960), 207-216.
Taken from Richmond before its fall.

868. [Fletcher, Elliot, Jr.]. "A Civil War Letter of Captain Elliot Fletcher, Jr." Edited by J. H. Alkinson. Arkansas Historical Quarterly, XXII (Spring 1963), 49-54.
How a company of Southern troops was transported from Fort Pillow to the Black River in 1861.

869. Flinn, Frank M. Campaigning with Banks in Louisiana, '63 and '64, and with Sheridan in the Shenandoah Valley in '64 and '65. Lynn, Mass.: T. P. Nichols, 1887. 239p.
Useful for the Red River Expedition.

870. Florance, John E., Jr. "Morris Island: Victory or Blunder?" South Carolina Historical Magazine, LV (July 1954), 143-152.

871. Floyd, William B. "The Burning of the Sultana." Wisconsin Magazine of History, XI (September 1927), 70-76.

872. Foard, Charles H. "The Confederate States Steamer Tallahassee." Nautical Research Journal, XXI (Summer 1969), 72-81.
Includes the ship's plans.

873. Folk, Winston. "The Confederate States Naval Academy." United States Naval Institute Proceedings, LX (September 1934), 1235-1240.

874. -----. "A Treasure Hunt in Reverse." United

States Naval Institute Proceedings, LXVII (March 1937), 380-386.

To locate the Confederate gold hidden in 1865.

875. [Foltz, Jonathan M.] Surgeon of the Seas: the Adventurous Life of Surgeon General Jonathan M. Foltz in the Days of Wooden Ships.... Edited by Charles S. Foltz. Indianapolis: Bobbs-Merrill, 1931. 351p.

876. Foote, Andrew H., Author. See U.S. Congress, no. 2469.

877. Foote, John A. "Notes on the Life of Admiral Foote." In Robert U. Johnson and Clarence C. Buell, eds. B & L. Vol. I, p. 347.

878. Foote, Shelby. "DuPont Storms Charleston." American Heritage, XIV (June 1963), 28-34, 89-92.

879. Forbes, Hildegarde B., ed. See Wheelwright, C. H., no. 2760.

880. [Forbes, John M.]. Letters and Recollections of John Murray Forbes. Edited by His Daughter, Sarah Forbes Hughes. 2 vols. Boston: Houghton, Mifflin, 1899.

Correspondence of a Union merchant sent to England in 1863 to purchase vessels.

881. Force, Manning F. From Ft. Henry to Cornith. Vol. II of Campaigns of the Civil War. New York: Scribners, 1881. 204p.

882. Ford, Arthur P. Life in the Confederate Army; Being Personal Experiences of a Private Soldier in the Confederate Army. New York: Neale, 1905. 136p.

Discusses the achievements of the Hunley.

883. Forman, Jacob G. The Western Sanitary Commission.... St. Louis: R. P. Studley, 1864. 144p.

Aid to the Navy, as well as the Army.

884. Fornell, Earl W. "Confederate Seaport Strategy." Civil War History, II (December 1956), 61-68.

885. -----. "Mobile During the Blockade." Alabama Historical Quarterly, XXIII (Spring 1961), 29-43.

886. Forrest, French, Author of Report. See C. S. A. Congress. House of Representatives, no. 543.

887. Fort, W. B. "First Submarine in the Confederate Navy." Confederate Veteran, XXVI (January-December 1918), 459-460.
Known as the "Fish Boat."

888. Fort Monroe in the Civil War. Tales of Old Fort Monroe, no. 6. Fort Monroe, Va.: The Casemate Museum, n. d. 12p.
Includes naval activities.

889. Fortney, John F. M. "The Wreck of the James Watson: A Civil War Disaster." Journal of the Illinois State Historical Society, XXXVII (September 1944), 213-228.
On the Western rivers.

890. Foster, Amos P. "Reminiscences of Service in the U. S. Navy, Potomac River." In War Papers, Read Before the Wisconsin Commandery, Military Order of the Loyal Legion of the United States. 3 vols. Milwaukee: Burdick, Armitage & Allen, 1891-1903. Vol. III, pp. 463-469.
With the Potomac Flotilla.

891. Foster, G. A. "The Woman Who Saved the Union Navy." Ebony, XIX (July 1964), 48-50, 52-55.
A slave who supplied data on the Virginia to the Navy Department, 1862.

892. Foster, Wilber F. "The Building of Forts Henry and Donelson." In Bromfield L. Ridley, ed. Battles and Sketches of the Army of the Tennessee. Mexico, Mo.: Missouri Printing, 1906. p. 63-66.

893. Foute, Robert C. "Echoes from Hampton Roads." Southern Historical Society Papers, XIX (1891), 246-248.
Monitor vs. Merrimac.

894. Fowler, G. L. "Ericsson's Monitor and Later Turret Ships." Engineering Magazine, VI (October 1897) 111-119.

895. Fowler, Robert H. "The Capture of New Orleans." Civil War Times, II (May 1960), 4-7.

896. [Fox, Gustavus V.]. Advantages of League Island for a Naval Station, Dockyard, and Fresh-Water Basin for Iron Ships and Other Vessels of War, as Recommended by Public Authorities, with all the Objections Heretofore Officially Advanced, Substantially and Textually Reproduced, and Severally Answered by a New England Man. Philadelphia: Board of Trade, 1866. 74p.
Another installment in a war-time fued between the Navy Department and authorities in New London, Connecticut.

897. -----. The Confidential Correspondence of Gustavus V. Fox. Edited by Robert Means Thompson and Richard Wainwright. 2 vols. New York: Naval History Society, 1919.
Letters to and from the Assistant Secretary of the Navy, mostly from Squadron Chiefs.

898. Franklin, Robert M. The Battle of Galveston, January 1, 1863. Galveston: Galveston News, 1911. 11p.
By an ex-Rebel "horse marine."

899. Franklin, Samuel R. Memoirs of a Rear Admiral Who Has Served for More than Half a Century in the Navy of the United States. New York: Harper, 1898. 397p.
Farragut's Fleet Captain.

900. Fredd, John P. "Civil War Blockade." Recruiter's Bulletin, II (March 1916), 12.
Brief memoir of a former marine private who served aboard the San Jacinto when she took the Trent.

901. Fremont, Jessie B. The Story of the Guard: A Chronicle of the War. Boston: Ticknor and Fields, 1863. 227p.
Highly biased; tells of General John's plan to have Foote push to "New Orleans straight."

902. [French, James C.]. The Trip of the Steamer Oceanus to Fort Sumter and Charleston, S. C. Brooklyn: Union Steam Printing, 1865. 172p.

A committee of the ship's passengers, chaired by French, wrote up their memoirs of the raising of the Federal flag over Sumter in April 1865.

903. Freret, James, Joint Author. See Smith, Marshall, no. 2226.

904. Frohman, Charles E. "Piracy on Lake Erie." Inland Seas, XIV (Fall 1958), 172-180.
By Confederates attempting to capture the Michigan and free the POWs on lake islands.

905. Frost, H. H. "Let's Pull Together." United States Naval Institute Proceedings, LVIII (August 1932), 1175-1185.
The Yankee Army and Navy on inland rivers.

906. Fullam, George T. The Cruise of the Alabama from Her Departure from Liverpool Until Her Arrival at the Cape of Good Hope. Liverpool: Lee and Nightingale, W. H. Peat, 1863. 48p.
An officer's journal.

907. Fuller, John F. C. Grant and Lee: A Study in Personality and Generalship. New York: Scribner, 1933. 323p.
The capture of Vicksburg by the Yankee Army and Navy "was the decisive factor in the war."

908. "Gallant Destruction of the Confederate Ram Albemarle." Nautical Magazine (December 1864), 681-682.

909. Gambrell, Herbert. "After the Merrimac." Readers Digest, XXXI (October 1937), 39-42.

910. -----. "Rams and Gunboats." Southwest Review, XXIII (October 1937), 46-78.

911. [Gardner, Henry R.]. "A Yankee in Louisiana: Selections From the Diary and Letters of Henry R. Gardner." Edited by Kenneth E. Shewmaker and Andrew K. Prinz. Louisiana History, V (Summer 1964), 271-295.
Includes the Teche Campaign and Port Hudson.

912. Garland, Robert R. "The Fall of Arkansas Post." Southern Historical Society Papers, XXII (1894), 10-13.

913. Garnett, Theodore S. "The Cruise of the Nashville." Southern Historical Society Papers, XII (1884), 329-334.

914. Gasser, James C. "Confederate Marines in the Civil War." Unpublished M. A. Thesis, Alabama Polytechnic Institute, 1956.

915. [Gayle, Richard H.]. "The Capture of a Confederate Blockade Runner; Extracts from the Journal of a Confederate Naval Officer." Edited by Frank E. Vandiver. North Carolina Historical Review, XXI (April 1944), 136-138.

916. -----. "Extracts from the Diary of Richard H. Gayle, Confederate States Navy." Edited by Frank E. Vandiver. Tyler's Quarterly Historical and Genealogical Magazine, XXX (October 1948), 86-92.

Mostly a prison journal kept in Boston from January 20-April 3, 1865.

917. Geoghegan, William E. "The Auxilary Steam Packet Massachusetts." Nautical Research Journal, XVI (Spring 1969), 27-35.

A naval store-ship; named changed to Farralones, later to Alaska. Sold in 1867.

918. ----- -----. Steamboat Bill of Facts, XXVII (Spring 1970), 26-33.

919. -----. "The South's Scottish Seamonster." American Neptune, XXIX (January 1969), 5-29.

Frigate No. 61, later purchased by Denmark and called the Danmark.

920. -----. "Study for a Scale Model of the U. S. S. Carondelet." Nautical Research Journal, XVII (Fall and Winter 1970-1971), 147-163, 231-236.

Includes the most complete set of plans yet published for the "City-Series" ironclads.

921. -----., Joint Editor. See Basoco, Richard W., no. 157.

922. Gerdes, F. H. "Reconnaissance Near Fort Morgan and the Expedition in Lake Pontchartrain and the Pearl River by the Mortar Flotilla of Captain D. D. Porter, U. S. N." Continental Monthly, IV (September 1863), 269-273.

923. -----. "The Surrender of Forts Jackson and St. Philip on the Lower Mississippi." Continental Monthly, III (May 1863), 557-561.

924. Gerson, Noel B. Yankee Admiral; a Biography of David Dixon Porter. By Paul Lewis [pseud.] New York: McKay, 1968.

925. Gibson, William. "Life on Board a Man-of-War." Harper's New Monthly Magazine, XLVI (March 1873), 481-494.
Excellent detail; much of the routine identical to that practiced a decade before.

926. "Gideon Welles and Lincoln." Magazine of History, XX (January 1915), 34-40.

927. Gift, George W. "The Story of the Arkansas." Southern Historical Society Papers, XII (1884), 48-54, 115-119, 163-170, 205-212.

928. Gilbert, Benjamin F. "California and the Civil War: A Bibliographic Essay." California Historical Society Quarterly, XL (December 1961), 289-307.
Includes naval activities.

929. -----. "The Confederate Raider Shenandoah." In Morgan B. Sherwood, ed. Alaska and Its History. Seattle: University of Washington Press, 1967. p. 189-207.

930. -----. "The Confederate Raider Shenandoah: the Elusive Destroyer in the Pacific and Arctic." Journal of the West, XIV (April 1965), 169-182.

931. -----. "Confederate Warships off Brazil." American Neptune, XV (October 1955), 287-302.

932. -----. "French Warships on the Mexican West Coast, 1861-1866." Pacific Historical Review, XXIV (February 1955), 25-37.

Civil War naval diplomacy.

933. -----. "Kentucky Privateers in California." Register of the Kentucky Historical Society, XXXVIII (July 1940), 256-266.

934. -----. "Lincoln's Far Eastern Navy." Journal of the West, VIII (July 1969), 355-368.

935. -----. "Naval Operations in the Pacific, 1861-1866." Unpublished PhD Dissertation, University of California at Berkeley, 1951.

936. Gilbert, Benjamin F. "Rumours of Confederate Privateers Operating in Virginia, Vancouver Island." British Columbia Historical Quarterly, XVIII (July-October 1954), 239-255.
In 1863-1864.

937. -----. "The Salvado Pirates." Civil War History, V (September 1959), 294-307.
Confederate Thomas H. Hogg's efforts to take Salvado for operations against Yankee gold shipments on the California coast.

938. -----. "San Francisco Harbor Defense During the Civil War." California Historical Society Quarterly, XXXIII (September 1954), 229-240.

939. -----. "The Shenandoah Down Under: Her Sojourn at Melbourne." Journal of the West, V (July 1966), 321-335.

940. -----. "Welcome to the Czar's Fleet--An Incident of Civil War Days in San Francisco." California Historical Society Quarterly, XXVI (March 1947), 13-19.

941. Gillmore, Q. A. Engineer and Artillery Operations Against the Defenses of Charleston Harbor, 1863. New York: D. Van Nostrand, 1865. 314p.

942. ----- -----. Supplementary Report. Professional Papers, Corps of Engineers, U.S.A., no. 16. New York: D. Van Nostrand, 1868. 172p.

943. -----. "Siege and Capture of Fort Pulaski." In

Robert U. Johnson and Clarence C. Buell, eds. B & L. Vol. II, pp. 1-12.

944. Gilman, J. H. "With Slemmer in Pensacola Harbor." In Robert U. Johnson and Clarence C. Buell, eds. B & L. Vol. I, pp. 26-32.
The Army lieutenant who co-operated with Henry Walke in attempting to prevent Commodore Armstrong from surrendering the post in early 1861.

945. [Ginder, Henry.] "A Louisiana Engineer at the Siege of Vicksburg: Letters of Henry Ginder." Edited by L. Moody Simms, Jr. Louisiana History, VIII (Fall 1967), 371-378.
Assistant to chief engineer of the fortress.

946. Giuliana, John J. Field Encounters and Naval Engagements of the Civil War. N.p., 1962. 45p.
A list.

947. Glassell, W. T. "Torpedo Service in Charleston Harbor." Confederate Veteran, XXV (January-December 1917), 113-114.

948. [Glazier, James E.] "The Roanoke Island Expedition: Observations of a Massachusetts Soldier." Edited by James I. Robertonson, Jr. Civil War History, XII (December 1966), 321-346.

949. Gleaves, Albert. "The Affair of the Blanche, an Incident of the Civil War." United States Naval Institute Proceedings, XLVIII (October 1922), 1661-1675.
Story of her October 7, 1861 destruction by U.S.S. Montgomery and the diplomatic controversey with Spain which resulted from the violation of her neutrality.

950. -----. Life and Letters of Rear Admiral Stephen B. Luce, U.S. Navy, Founder of the Naval War College. New York: Putnam's, 1925. 381p.
During the war, he commanded the ironclad Nantucket off Charleston.

951. -----. "An Officer of the Old Navy: Rear Admiral Charles Steedman, U.S.N." United States Naval

Institute Proceedings, XXXIX (March 1913), 197-210.
Active in Yankee naval operations in Florida.

952. Glenney, Daniel W. "Attempted Sale of the Federal Fleet." Southern Historical Society Papers, XXXII (1904), 58-67.

953. Goggin, Daniel T., Comp. See U.S. National Archives, no. 2556.

954. Golder, F. A. "The Russian Fleet and the Civil War." American Historical Review, XX (July 1915), 801-812.

955. Goldsborough, Louis M. "Narrative of Rear Admiral Goldsborough, U.S. Navy." United States Naval Institute Proceedings, LIX (July 1933), 1023-1031.
Includes his version of the Peninsular Campaign of 1862.

956. Goodrich, Albert M. Cruise and Captures of the Alabama. Minneapolis: Wilson, 1906. 216p.

957. Goodrich, Casper F. "Farragut." United States Naval Institute Proceedings, XLIX (December 1923), 1961-1986.

958. -----. Rope Yarns From the Old Navy. Navy Historical Society Publications, no. 11. New York: The Society, 1931.
Served aboard the Colorado after graduation from the Naval Academy in 1864.

959. Goodspeed's Book Shop. "The Merrimac Before she Became the Virginia and Fought the Monitor." Month at Goodspeed's, XXVIII (March-April 1957), 119-122.

960. -----. "Prize of the Confederate Raider Florida: Manuscript Log of the Anglo-Saxon." Month at Goodspeed's, XXIX (October 1957), 13-14.

961. Goodwin, Martha. "The Ram Arkansas." Confederate Veteran, XXVIII (January-December 1920), 263-264.

962. Gorden, Arthur. "The Great Stone Fleet: Calculated Catastrophe." United States Naval Institute Proceedings, XLIV (December 1968), 72-82.

963. -----. "Union Stone Fleets of the Civil War." In U.S. Navy Department, Naval History Division. Dictionary of American Naval Fighting Ships. Washington: U.S. Government Printing Office, 1959--. Vol. V, pp. 424-441.

964. [Gorgas, Josiah.]. The Civil War Diary of General Josiah Gorgas. Edited by Frank E. Vandiver. University, Ala.: University of Alabama Press, 1947. 208p.
Includes some dealing with blockade runners.

965. -----. "The Confederate Ordnance Department." Southern Historical Society Papers, XII (1884), 66-94.

966. Gosnell, Harper Allen. Guns on the Western Waters: The Story of the River Gunboats in the Civil War. Baton Rouge: Louisiana State University Press, 1949. 273p.

967. -----., ed. See Semmes, Raphael, no. 2150.

968. Gould, Emerson W. Fifty Years; or, Gould's History of River Navigation. St. Louis: Nixon-Jones, 1889, 749p.

969. Gould, James W. "The Civil War in the Far East." United States Naval Institute Proceedings, LXXXVIII (September 1962), 160-164.
Operations of the Alabama.

970. Gould, John M. History of the First-Tenth-Twenty-Ninth Maine Regiment. Portland: S. Berry, 1871. 709p.
This oft-renamed band was up the Red River in 1864 and worked on the dams which saved Porter's gunboats.

971. Grabeau, Warren E., Joint Author. See Bearss, Edwin C., nos. 199 and 210.

972. Graf, L. P. "The Economic History of the Lower

Rio Grande Valley, 1820-1875." Unpublished PhD Dissertation, Harvard University, 1942.
Description of the effect of the Yankee blockade.

973. Grant, Frederick D. "With Grant at Vicksburg." _Outlook_, LIX (July 2, 1898), 532-543.
By the General's son.

974. Grant, Richard S. "Captain William Sharp of Norfolk, Virginia, U. S. N. -C. S. N." _Virginia Magazine of History and Biography_, XLVII (January 1949), 44-54.

975. Grant, Ulysses S. "The Battle of Shiloh." _In_ Robert U. Johnson and Clarence C. Buell, eds. _B & L_. Vol. I, pp. 465-486.

976. -----. _The Papers of Ulysses S. Grant_. Edited by John Y. Simon. Carbondale, Illinois: Southern Illinois University Press, 1967--.

977. -----. _Personal Memoirs. A Modern Abridgement_. With an Introduction by Philip Van Dorn Stern. "Premier Civil War Classics, no. 48." Greenwich, Conn.: Fawcett Publications, 1962. 464p.

978. -----. _Personal Memoirs of U. S. Grant_. 2 vols. New York: Charles L. Webster, 1885.

979. -----. "The Vicksburg Campaign." _In_ Robert U. Johnson and Clarence C. Buell, eds. _B & L_. Vol. III, pp. 493-538.

980. [Graves, Charles I.]. "A Confederate Sailor's Lament." Edited by William B. Hesseltine. _Civil War History_, V (March 1959), 99-102.
Problems of married life as seen from the C. S. S. _Morgan_ in Mobile Bay.

981. [Graves, Henry L.]. _A Confederate Marine; a Sketch of Henry Lea Graves with Excerpts from the Graves Family Correspondence, 1861-1865_. Edited by Richard Harwell. Confederate Centennial Studies, no. 24. Tuscalosa, Ala.: Confederate Publishing Company, 1963. 140p.

982. Great Britain. Foreign Office. _The Case of Great_

Britain as Laid Before the Tribunal of Arbitration. 3 vols. Washington: Government Printing Office, 1872.

Much data on Confederate cruisers.

983. ----- -----. Correspondence Arising out of the Conflict between the Kearsarge and Alabama. North America, no. 3. London: Harrison, 1865. 15p.

984. ----- -----. Correspondence Relating to the Steamers Nashville and Tuscarora at Southampton. North America, no. 6. London: Harrison, 1862. 30p.

985. ----- -----. Correspondence Respecting Instructions Given to Naval Officers of the United States in Regard to Neutral Vessels and Mails. London: Harrison, 1863. 7p.

986. ----- -----. Correspondence Respecting the Seizure of Messrs. Mason, Slidell, McFarland, and Eustis, from on board the Royal Mail-Packet Trent, by the Commander of the United States Ship-of-War San Jacinto. North America, no. 5. London: Harrison, 1862. 37p.

987. ----- -----. Correspondence Respecting the Seizure of the British Vessels Springbok and Peterhoff, by United States' Cruisers in 1863. London: R. M. Stationery Office, 1900. 69p.

988. ----- -----. Correspondence with the United States Government Respecting the Blockade. London: Harrison, 1861. 16p.

989. ----- -----. Dispatch from Lord Lyons Referring to the Alledged Report of the Secretary of the So-Styled Confederate States. North America, no. 10. London: Harrison, 1864. 1p.

990. Great Britain. Foreign Office. Papers Relating to the Blockade of the Ports of the Confederate States. North America, no. 8. London: Harrison, 1862. 126p.

991. -----. Parliament. Return of Claims of British Subjects Against the United States Government from the Commencement of the Civil War. London:

Harrison, 1864.
Names of British ships captured.

992. Green, J. V. "Capture of the Federal Steamer Maple Leaf." Southern Historical Society Papers, XXIV (1896), 165-171.

993. Green, Thomas. "Battle of Atchafalya River." Southern Historical Society Papers, III (1877), 62-63.

994. Green, Thomas W., Joint Author. See Merli, Frank J., no. 1617.

995. Greenbie, Marjorie B. My Dear Lady; the Story of Anna Ella Carroll, the "Great Unrecognized Member of Lincoln's Cabinet." New York: McGraw-Hill, 1940. 316p.

996. -----. Joint Author. See Greenbie, Sydney, no. 997.

997. Greenbie, Sydney and Marjorie B. Anna Ella Carroll and Abraham Lincoln: A Biography, Manchester, Me.: Falmouth Publishing, 1952. 539p.

998. Greene, Albert S. Organization of the Engineer Corps of the Navy and Education of its Officers. N.p., 1864.

999. Greene, Francis V. The Mississippi. Vol. VIII of Campaigns of the Civil War. New York: Scribner's, 1885. 276p.

1000. Greene, S. Dana. An Eye-Witness Account of the Battle Between the U.S.S. Monitor and the C.S.S. Virginia (Formerly U.S.S. Merrimac) on March 9, 1862. Washington: Naval Historical Foundation, n.d. 6p.
Letter of the Union craft's executive officer written to his parents on March 14, 1862.

1001. -----. "The Fight Between the Monitor and Merrimac." United Service, XII (April 1885), 448-454.

1002. -----. "I Fired the First Gun and thus Commenced the Great Battle." American Heritage, VIII

(June 1957), 10-13, 102-105.

1003. -----. "In the Monitor's Turret." In Robert U. Johnson and Clarence C. Buell, eds. B & L. Vol. I, pp. 719-729.

1004. -----. "The Monitor at Sea and in Battle." United States Naval Institute Proceedings, XLIX (November 1923), 1839-1849.

1005. -----. "The Monitor Repels the Merrimac." In Lydia M. Post, ed. Soldiers Letters from Camp, Battle-Field, and Prison. New York: Bunce and Huntington, 1865. p. 109-113.

1006. -----., Joint Author. See Worden, John L., no. 2828.

1007. Greer, Mrs. Hal W. "Sabine Pass Battle." Southern Historical Society Papers, XXIX (1901), 314-319.

1008. Gregory, Edward S. "Vicksburg During the Siege." In Annals of the War. p. 111-133.

1009. Gregory, Thomas B. "The Battle of Sabine Pass." Confederate Veteran, XIX (January-December 1911), 531-532.

1010. Griffis, William E. Charles Carleton Coffin, War Correspondent, Traveller, Author, and Statesman. Boston: Estes and Lauriat, 1898. 357p.
Reporter saw much of early Western theatre from deck of Yankee ironclads.

1011. Grimball, John. "Career of the Shenandoah." Southern Historical Society Papers, XXV (1897), 116-130.

1012. [Grimes, Absalom]. Absalom Grimes, Confederate Mail Runner. Edited from Captain Grimes' Own Story by M. M. Quaife. New Haven: Yale University Press, 1926. 216p.
Operations often in the face of Yankee ships.

1013. Grimes, James M. Achievements of the Western Naval Flotilla. Washington: L. Towers, 1862. 8p.
A Senate speech of March 13, 1862 in praise

of Andrew H. Foote.

1014. -----. The Navy in Congress; Being Speeches of the Hon. Messrs. Grimes, [James R.] Doolittle, and [James W.] Nye; of the Senate, and the Hon. Messrs. [Alexander H.] Rice, [Frederick A.] Pike, [John A.] Griswold, and [Henry T.] Blow; of the House of Representatives. Washington: F. Taylor, 1865. 53p.
Pro-Navy; comments on appropriations and expenditures.

1015. -----. Speeches of the Hon. James W. Grimes and the Hon. John P. Hale, in the United States Senate, May 23, 1864. Boston: Office of the Boston Courier, 1864. 26p.

1016. Groh, George W. "The Curious Cruise of the Shenandoah." Ships and the Sea, VI (Fall 1956), 42-45.

1017. -----. "Last of the Rebel Raiders." American Heritage, X (December 1958), 48-51.
The Shenandoah.

1018. Grotenrath, Mary Jo, Comp. See U.S. National Archives, no. 2560.

1019. Guernsey, A. H. "Iron-Clad Vessels." Harper's New Monthly Magazine, XXV (September 1862), 443-446.
Based upon "an elaborate paper on the manufacture of iron-clad vessels" furnished by Egbert P. Watson, "an iron-worker at the Novelty Works."

1020. Gutheim, Frederick. The Potomac. Rivers of America. New York: Rinehart, 1949. 436p.

1021. Haberlein, Charles R. "Former Blockade Runners in the United States Navy." Unpublished B.A. Paper, Kalamazoo College, 1965.

1022. Hackett, Frank W. Deck and Field; Addresses before the United States Naval War College and on Commemorative Occasions. Washington: W. H. Loudermilk, 1909. 222p.

Includes a piece on Farragut.

1023. Hagood, Johnson. "The Battle of Drewry's Bluff, 1864." Southern Historical Society Papers, XII (1884), 229-232.
Primarily an army operation; however, some small gunboats did participate.

1024. Hague, Parthenia A. A Blockaded Family; Life in Southern Alabama during the Civil War. Boston: Houghton Mifflin, 1888. 176p.

1025. Haines, Peter C. "The Vicksburg Campaign." Military Engineer, XIII (May-June 1921), 189-196, 270-272.

1026. Halbert, Henry S. "Daring Capture of a Federal Transport." Confederate Veteran, XIV (January-December 1906), 309.
Taking of the transport Miller on the Arkansas River, August 1864.

1027. Hale, John P. Speech on Frauds in Naval Contracts. Washington: Palkinhorn, 1864. 16p.

1028. -----. Joint Author. See Grimes, James W., no. 1015.

1029. Hale, John R. Famous Sea Fights from Salamis to Tsushima. London: Methuen, 1911. 349p.
Includes a chapter on the Monitor and Merrimack.

1030. Hall, A. D. Uncle Sam's Ships; Being a History of the American Navy. Historical Series, no. 6. New York: Street and Smith, 1899. 198p.
Including those of the Civil War period.

1031. Hall, Anne M., Joint Author. See Benham, Edith W., no. 241.

1032. Hall, Asaph. John Rogers, 1812-1882. Washington: Judd and Detweiller, 1906. 12p.

1033. Hall, Frederic B. M., ed. See Hollyday, Henry, no. 1176.

1034. Hall, Henry, Author. <u>See</u> U.S. Department of Interior, no. 2547.

1035. Hall, Thomas, Contributor. "Naval Battles in Mexico Gulf." <u>Confederate Veteran</u>, IV (January-December), 280-281.
Abreast of Biloxi, April 4, 1862.

1036. Hall, Winchester. <u>The Story of the 26th Louisiana Infantry in the Service of the Confederate States.</u> N.p., 1890. 228p.
Includes the defenses of New Orleans and Vicksburg.

1037. Hallock, C. "Bermuda in Blockade Times." <u>New England Magazine</u>, VI (May 1892), 337-343.

1038. Halsey, Ashley, Jr. "The Plan to Capture the <u>Monitor</u>: 'Seal the Turtle in its Shell.'" <u>Civil War Times Illustrated</u>, V (June 1966), 28-31.

1039. -----., ed. <u>See</u> Drayton, Percival, no. 743.

1040. Hamersly, Lewis R. <u>A Naval Encyclopedia, Comprising a Dictionary of Nautical Words and Phrases; Biographical Notices, and Records of Naval Officers; Special Articles on Naval Art and Science, Written Expressly for this Work by Officers and Others of Recognized Authority in the Branches Treated by Them, Together with Descriptions of the Principal Naval Stations and Seaports of the World.</u> Complete in One Volume. Philadelphia: Hamersly, 1884. 872p.

1041. -----. <u>The Records of Living Officers of the U.S. Navy and Marine Corps; with a History of Naval Operations During the Rebellion of 1861-5, and a List of the Ships and Officers Participating in the Great Battles. Compiled from Official Sources.</u> Philadelphia: Lippincott, 1870. 350p.

1042. Hamersly, Thomas H. S. <u>General Register of the United States Navy and Marine Corps, Arranged in Alphabetical Order, for One Hundred Years (1782 to 1882)</u>... <u>Including Volunteer Officers</u>...

With a Sketch of the Navy from 1775-1778. Baltimore: W. K. Boyle, 1882. 940p.

1043. Hamilton, Doris H., ed. See Morgan, James M., no. 1699.

1044. -----., ed. See Ranson, Thomas, no. 2000.

1045. Hamilton, F. E. "Chicora, A Blockade Runner Came to the Lakes." Steamboat Bill of Facts, XII (September 1955), 49-52, 57.

The Birkenhead-built steamer which ran the blockade between Bermuda and Charleston in 1864-1865 and how she came to see service as a Great Lakes freighter until 1938.

1046. Hamilton, James A. An Address Delivered Before the Students of the United States Naval Academy at Newport, June 1864. Boston: Tichnor and Fields, 1864. 28p.

1047. Hamilton, James J. The Battle of Fort Donelson. New York: Thomas Yoseloff, 1968. 378p.

1048. Hamilton, Richard V. "Facts Connected with the Naval Operations During the Civil War in the United States." Journal of the Royal United Service Institute, XXII (December 1878), 612-640.

From the British viewpoint.

1049. Hamilton, Schuyler. "Comment on Colonel Bissell's Paper." In Robert U. Johnson and Clarence C. Buell, eds. B & L. Vol. I, p. 462.

On the canal to bypass Island No. 10.

1050. Hammar, Hugo. "The Monitor and the Merrimac." Mariner's Mirror, XXVI (April 1940), 163-184.

1051. Hammond, W. E. "The Stonewall of the Confederate Navy." Confederate Veteran, XII (January-December 1904), 230-231.

1052. Hanaford, Phoebe A. Field, Gunboat, Hospital, and Prison; or, Thrilling Records of the Heroism, Endurance, and Patriotism Displayed by the Union Army and Navy During the Great Rebellion.

Boston: C. M. Dinsmoor, 1866. 379p.

1053. Hand-book for the War; Describing the Military Terms in Use in the United States Service, and Giving a List of the Forts and Ships Belonging to the United States. Boston: 1861. 23p.

1054. [Hander, Christian W.] "Excerpts from the Hander Diary." Edited by Leonard B. Plummer. Journal of Mississippi History, XXVI (April 1964), 141-149.

A Danish Volunteer inside Vicksburg, May-July 1863.

1055. Handford, Stanley W. "Again the Alabama." United States Naval Institute Proceedings, XC (June 1964), 172-174.

1056. Hanford, Franklin. "How I Entered the Navy; Including a Personal Interview with Abraham Lincoln." Edited by S. W. Jackson. United States Naval Institute Proceedings, XCI (June 1965), 75-87.

Life at the Newport-based U. S. Naval Academy.

1057. Hanks, Carlos C. "Blockaders off the American Coast." United States Naval Institute Proceedings, LXVII (February 1941), 172-175.

1058. -----. "The Last Confederate Raider." United States Naval Institute Proceedings, LXVII (January 1941), 21-32.

The Shenandoah.

1059. Hanna, Kathryn A. "Incidents of the Confederate Blockade." Journal of Southern History, V (May 1945), 214-229.

1060. Harbeck, Charles T. A Contribution to the Bibliography of the History of the United States Navy. Cambridge, Mass.: Riverside Press, 1906. 240p.

1061. Harden, William. "The Capture of the U. S. Steamer Water Witch in Ossabaw Sound, Georgia, June 2-3, 1864." Georgia Historical Quarterly, III (March 1919), 11-27.

1062. Harding, James F., Joint Author. See Harding, Ursula, no. 1063.

1063. Harding, Ursula and James F. "The Guns of the Keokuk." Civil War Times Illustrated, I (November 1962), 22-25.
Confederate salvage of the armament of a Yankee ironclad sunk at Charleston, 1863.

1064. Harkness, Edwon J. "The Expeditions Against Fort Fisher and Wilmington." In Military Essays and Recollections; Papers Read Before the Illinois Commandery, Military Order of the Loyal Legion of the United States. 4 vols. Chicago: A. C. McClurg, 1891-1912. Vol. II, pp. 145-188.

1065. Harleston, John. "Battery Wagner on Morris Island." South Carolina Historical Magazine, LVII (January 1956), 1-13.

1066. Harms, F. S. "Bones of the Star of the West." Confederate Veteran, VII (January-December 1899), 457-460.

1067. Harper's Weekly; A Journal of Civilization. 62 vols. New York: Harper, 1857-1916.

1068. Harrell, J. M. Arkansas. In Vol. X of Clement A. Evans, ed. Confederate Military History; a Library of Confederate States History. 12 vols. Atlanta: Confederate Publishing Company, 1899.

1069. Harrington, Frederick H. Fighting Politician: Major General Nathaniel P. Banks. Philadelphia: University of Pennsylvania Press, 1948. 301p.

1070. Harris, Charles. "Newport News." Southern Historical Society Papers, X (1882), 489-503.
Exploits of the U.S.S. Virginia.

1071. Harris, John W. "The Gold of the Confederate Treasury." Southern Historical Society Papers, XXXII (1904), 157-163.
Spirited out of Richmond by midshipmen, 1865.

1072. Harris, Thomas L. The Trent Affair; Including a

Review of English and American Relations at the Beginning of the Civil War. Indianapolis: Bowen-Merrill, 1896. 288p.

1073. Harrison, Robert W. "Levee Building in Mississippi Before the Civil War." Journal of Mississippi History, XII (April 1950), 63-97.
Title misleading; covers period 1819-1865.

1074. Hart, Albert B. The Romance of the Civil War. New York: Macmillan, 1903. 418p.
A "source book"; includes naval aspects.

1075. Harwell, Richard, ed. See Graves, Henry L., no. 981.

1076. ----- , ed. See Taylor, Richard, no. 2349.

1077. Harwood, Andrew A. The Law and Practice of United States Naval Courts-Martial. New York: D. Van Nostrand, 1867. 325p.
Based largely on Civil War justice.

1078. Haskall, Fitz, ed. See Camm, William, no. 422.

1079. Hass, Paul H., ed. See Warmouth, Henry C., no. 2697.

1080. Hassler, Charles W. "Reminiscences of 1861-1863." In Personal Recollections of the War of the Rebellion; Papers Read before the New York Commandery, Military Order of the Loyal Legion of the United States. 4 vols. New York: The Commandery, 1891-1912. Vol. I, pp. 58-70.

1081. Hassler, Warren W., Jr. George B. McClellan: Shield of the Union. Baton Rouge: Louisiana State University Press, 1957. 350p.
The "best" monographic coverage of his relations with the Yankee navy.

1082. -----. "How the Confederacy Controlled Blockade Running." Civil War Times Illustrated, II (October 1963), 43-49.

1083. Hawkins, Rush C. "Early Coast Operations in North Carolina." In Robert U. Johnson and Clarence

C. Buell, eds. B & L. Vol. I, pp. 632-659.

1084. Hawthorne, Harry L. Military Careers of Officers of the Army and Navy in Honor of whom Coast Artillery Posts and Batteries in the Dept. of the Columbia Have been Named. N.p.: 1908. 26p.

1085. [Hay, John]. Lincoln and the Civil War in the Diaries and Letters of John Hay. Edited by Tyler Dennett. New York: Dodd, Mead, 1939. 348p.

1086. ----- , Joint Author. See Nicolay, John G., no. 1792.

1087. Hay, Thomas R. "Confederate Leadership at Vicksburg." Mississippi Valley Historical Review, XI (March 1925), 543-560.

1088. -----. Hood's Tennessee Campaign. New York: W. Neale, 1929. 272p.
Useful for background to the Union Navy's role in the 1864 Battle of Nashville.

1089. Haydon, F. Stansbury. Aeronautics in the Union and Confederate Armies. Baltimore: Johns Hopkins University Press, 1941. 421p.
Data on the Fanny and George Washington Parke Curtis, Yankee balloon barges.

1090. Hayes, D. J. Civil War Military and Naval Engagements in the State of Texas. Houston: 1961. 8p.
Cursory accounts.

1091. Hayes, John D. "Admiral Luce's Pontiac." United States Naval Institute Proceedings, LXXXIII (February 1957), 158-163.
The 1864-1865 command of the Naval War College's founder.

1092. -----. "April 1861--Civil War Comes to the Naval Academy." Shipmate, XXIV (April 1961), 8-10.

1093. -----. "Bitter April." Shipmate, XXII (April 1959), 6-10.

1094. -----. "Captain Fox--He is the Navy Department." United States Naval Institute Proceedings, XCL (November 1965), 64-71.
Gustavus V. Fox, Assistant Secretary.

1095. -----. "Fox Versus DuPont; the Crisis in Civil-Military Relations, 7 April 1863." Shipmate, XXVI (April 1963), 10-11.

1096. -----. "Lee Against the Sea; Port Royal, S. C., 7 November 1861." Shipmate, XXII (November 1959), 4-7.

1097. -----. "Lee Against the Sea; Seapower at Hampton Roads." Shipmate, XX (June 1957), 20-22.

1098. -----. "Loss of the Norfolk Yard." Ordnance, XLVI (September-October 1961), 220-223.

1099. -----. "The Marine Corps in the American Civil War." Shipmate, XXIII (November 1960), 2-4.

1100. -----. "Samuel William Preston, Flag Lieutenant to Three Admirals and Tragic Example of the Staff Officer in War." Shipmate, XXVI (January 1963), 18-19.

1101. -----. "Sea Power in the Civil War." United States Naval Institute Proceedings, LXXXVIII (November 1961), 60-69.
Strategic value of the Navy to the eventual Federal victory.

1102. -----. "Ships Versus Forts." Civil War Times, III (May 1961), 4-6, 24.
Drewry's Bluff, 1862.

1103. -----. "Studies in Naval Failure." Shipmate, XXV (September-October 1962), 32-33.
During the Civil War.

1104. -----. "Up Through the Ranks--Civil War Style." All Hands, No. 536 (September 1961), 12-13.

1105. -----., ed. See Barnes, John S., no. 135.

1106. -----., ed. See DuPont, Samuel F., no. 762.

1107. Haywood, Philip D. The Cruise of the Alabama, by One of the Crew. Boston: Houghton, Mifflin, 1886. 150p.
Authenticity disputed.

1108. Headley, Joel T. Farragut and Our Naval Commanders. New York: E. B. Treat, 1867. 609p.
Biographies of Federal officers.

1109. -----. Our Navy in the Great Rebellion; Heroes and Battles of the War. New York: E. B. Treat, 1891. 616p.

1110. Headley, John W. Confederate Operations in Canada and New York. New York: Neale, 1906. 480p.
Includes the activities of J. Beall.

1111. Headley, Phineas C. The Life and Naval Career of Vice-Admiral David Glascoe [sic] Farragut. New York: William H. Appleton, 1865. 342p.
The first of many biographies.

1112. -----. The Miner Boy and His Monitor; the Career and Achievements of John Ericsson, Engineer. Boston: Lee and Shepard, 1883. 297p.

1113. [Heartsill, William W.]. "A Texas Ranger Company at the Battle of Arkansas Post." Edited by Arthur M. Shaw. Arkansas Historical Quarterly, IX (Winter 1950), 270-297.

1114. Heath, Winifred. "Matthew Fontaine Maury." Catholic World, CLXVIII (February 1949), 349-353.

1115. Hefferman, John B. "The Blockade of the Southern Confederacy; 1861-1865." Smithsonian Journal of History, II (Winter 1967-1968), 23-44.

1116. Heindon, G. Melvin, ed. See Fleming, Robert H., no. 867.

1117. Heinl, Robert D., Jr. "The Cat With More Than Nine Lives." United States Naval Institute Proceedings, LXXX (June 1954), 658-671.
Discussion of the various Civil War attempts to abolish the Federal Marine Corps; strongly

opposed by many naval officers, including Admiral David D. Porter.

1118. -----. Soldiers of the Sea; The United States Marine Corps, 1775-1962. Annapolis: U.S. Naval Institute, 1962. 692p.

1119. Heitman, Francis B., ed. See U.S. Army, no. 2426.

1120. Hellweg, J. F. "The Pathfinder of the Seas." United States Naval Institute Proceedings, LIX (June 1933), 93-96.
Matthew F. Maury.

1121. Helm, Charles J. Letter from Charles J. Helm, Esqr., on the Blockade and Rights of Neutrals to His Excellency, the Captain General, Don Francisco Serrano, Superior Governor of Cuba. N.p.: [1862]. 19p.

1122. Henderson, Daniel M. The Hidden Coasts; a Biography of Admiral Charles Wilkes. New York: Sloane, 1953. 306p.

1123. Henderson, W. J. The Last Cruise of the Mohawk: a Boy's Adventures in the Navy in the War of the Rebellion. New York: Scribner's, 1897. 278p.

1124. Hendren, Paul. "The Confederate Blockade Runners." United States Naval Institute Proceedings, LIX (April 1933), 506-512.

1125. Hendrick, Burton J. "Historic Crises in American Diplomacy." World's Work, XXXII (June 1916), 182-183.
The Trent Affair.

1126. Hendricks, George L. "Union Army Occupation of the Southern Seaboard." Unpublished PhD. Dissertation, Columbia University, 1952.
Includes naval aspects.

1127. Henry, Robert S. "First with the Most" Forrest. Indianapolis: Bobbs, Merrill, 1944. 558p.

1128. Henry-Ruffin, Mrs. M. E. "Running the Blockade." In George M. Vickers, ed. Under Both Flags. p. 556-567.

1129. Henwood, James N., ed. See Ringgold, C., no. 2033.

1130. Herbert, A. Otis, Jr., Joint Author. See Williams, T. Harry, no. 2800.

1131. "Heroes of the Confederate Navy." Confederate Veteran, IV (January-December 1896), 313-314.
C. C. Gore of the 4th Louisiana Volunteers and the C.S.A. steamers Webb, Doctor Beatty, and the ex-Federal ram Queen of the West in the capture of the Indianola.

1132. Heslin, James J., ed. See Collins, James B., no. 530.

1133. Hesmer, James K. "The Battle of the Monitor and the Merrimac." In Ripley Hitchcock, et al. Decisive Battles of America. New York: Harper, 1909. p. 232-273.

1134. -----. "The Capture of Vicksburg." In Ripley Hitchcock, et al. Decisive Battles of America. New York: Harper, 1909. p. 295-305.

1135. -----. "Farragut's Capture of New Orleans, 1862." In Ripley Hitchcock, et al. Decisive Battles of America. New York: Harper, 1909. p. 232-273.

1136. Hesseltine, William B., ed. See Graves, Charles I., no. 980.

1137. Heyl, Erik. "The Blockade Runner Scotia." Steamboat Bill of Facts, XII (December 1955), 79-81.

1138. -----. "The Civil War and Great Lakes Steamers." Inland Seas, XV (Winter 1959), 256-270.

1139. -----. "The Lady was a Tramp." Steamboat Bill of Facts, XX (Fall 1963), 73-77.
Blockade runner Lady Stirling. Captured in 1864 and added to the Yankee navy under that

name with a later name-change to Hornet. Sold out in 1869. Active in Cuban trade to 1894.

1140. -----. "Mystery Picture." Steamboat Bill of Facts, XX (Spring 1963), 15.
An unidentified steamer with U.S. colors snaped off Louisiana in 1862 or 1863.

1141. Hibben, Henry B., Author. See U.S. Congress. Senate. no. 2518.

1142. Hicken, Victor. Illinois in the Civil War. Urbanna: University of Illinois Press, 1966. 391p.

1143. Higginson, Thomas W. Massachusetts in the Army and Navy During the War of 1861-1865. 2 vols. Boston: Wright and Potter, 1895-1896.

1144. Hill, Frederic S. Twenty Years at Sea; or, Leaves from My Old Log Books. Boston: Houghton, Mifflin, 1893. 273p.
By an ex-Master's Mate aboard the U.S.S. Richmond at New Orleans in 1862.

1145. -----. Twenty-Six Historic Ships: The Story of Certain Famous Vessels of War and of Their Successors in the Navies of the United States and of the Confederate States of America from 1775-1902. New York: G. P. Putnam, 1903. 515p.
Civil War ships include the U.S.S. Hartford, Kearsarge, Monitor, and New Ironsides; C.S.S. Alabama, Arkansas, Sumter, and Tennessee.

1146. Hill, Jim Dan. "Charles W. Read, Confederate Von Luckner." South Atlantic Quarterly, XXVIII (October 1929), 390-406.
A comparison with the World War I German captain, Count Felix von Luckner.

1147. -----. "Charles Wilkes--Turbulent Scholar of the Old Navy." United States Naval Institute Proceedings, LVII (July 1931), 867-887.

1148. -----. Sea Dogs of the Sixties; Farragut and Seven

Contemporaries. Minneapolis: University of Minnesota Press, 1935. 265p.
Includes Farragut, Bulloch, Wilkes, Wilkinson, Rogers, Read, Winslow, and Waddell.

1149. Hindman, Thomas C., Author. See C. S. Army. Trans-Mississippi Department, no. 549.

1150. Hippen, James C. "The Influence of Geographical Conditions Upon Civil War Strategy in the Mississippi Delta." Oklahoma Academy of Science Proceedings, XXXVIII (1958), 128-131.

1151. Hirsch, Charles B. "Gunboat Personnel on the Western Waters." Mid-America, XXXIV (April 1952), 75-86.

1152. Hislam, Percival A. "Jubilee of the Turret-Ship." Scientific American, CVI (February 17, 1912), 153-154.
Includes data and diagrams of the Monitor.

1153. Historical Abstracts: a Quarterly, Covering the World's Periodical Literature, 1775-1945. Edited by E. H. Boehm. New York: 1955--
Volumes for 1960-1963 useful to pick up materials where the last (1959) volume of Writings on American History stops and the first volume (1964) of America: History and Life commences.

1154. Hitchcock, Benjamin W. Hitchcock's Chronological Record of the American Civil War, 1860-'65. Also a Complete List of the Vessels Captured by the Confederate Navy. New York: Office of the Soldiers' Friend, 1868. 106p.
List incomplete.

1155. Hobart-Hampton, Augustus C. Hobart Pasha. Edited by Horace Kephart. New York: Outing, 1915. 285p.

1156. -----. Never Caught: Personal Adventures Connected with Twelve Successful Trips in Blockade Running During the American Civil War, 1863-64. By Captain Roberts, pseud. London: John Camden Holten, 1867. 123p.

A man of many names, younger son of the Duke of Buckingham and a favorite of Queen Victoria, this Royal Navy officer captained the famous blockade runner Condor, the same ship from which the spy, "Rebel Rose" Greenhow, was lost in 1864.

1157. -----. Sketches from My Life. New York: D. Appleton, 1887. 282p.
Includes another account of his blockade running, p. 87-185.

1158. Hobson, Henry S. The Famous Cruise of the Kearsarge. Bonds Village, Mass.: The Author, 1894. 167p.

1159. Hoehling, Adolf A. and the Editors of the Army Times Publishing Company. Vicksburg: 47 Days of Siege. Englewood Cliffs, N.J.: Prentice-Hall, 1969. 386p.

1160. Hoffman, Daniel G. "Historic Truth and Ballad Truth: Two Versions of the Capture of New Orleans." Journal of American Folklore, LXV (July-September 1952), 295-303.
On a song composed by Seaman William Densmore.

1161. Hoffman, Wickhan. Camp, Court, and Siege: A Narrative of Personal Adventure and Observation During Two Wars: 1861-1865; 1870-1871. New York: Harper, 1877. 285p.
At New Orleans, Port Hudson, and the Red River Expedition of 1864.

1162. Hogane, James T. "Reminiscences of the Siege of Vicksburg." Southern Historical Society Papers, XI (1883), 4854-4886.
By the Rebel engineer in charge of the defenses at Snyder's and Hayne's Bluffs above the city.

1163. Holberg, Ralph G. "Confederate Defenses of Mobile." Port of Mobile, XLIII (June 1970), 16-22.

1164. Holcombe, John L. and Walter J. Buttgenbach. "Coast Defense in the Civil War." Journal of

U.S. Artillery, XXXVII (March 1912), 169-187; XXXVIII (July-November 1912), 35-41, 198-212, 312-317; XXXIX (January 1913), 83-90.
Includes battles on the Western rivers.

1165. Holden, Edgar. "The Albermarle and the Sassacus." In Robert U. Johnson and Clarence C. Buell, eds. B & L. Vol. IV, pp. 628-633.
After ramming the ironclad on May 5, 1864, the wooden Union ship was forced out of action by a Rebel shot into her starboard boiler.

1166. -----. "A Cruise on the Sassacus." Harper's New Monthly Magazine, XXIX (November 1864), 712-724.

1167. -----. "The First Cruise of the Monitor Passaic." Harper's New Monthly Magazine, XXVII (October 1863), 577-595.

1168. -----. "The Sassacus and the Albemarle." In Personal Recollections of the War of the Rebellion; Papers Read before the New York Commandery, Military Order of the Loyal Legion of the United States. 4 vols. New York: The Commandery, 1891-1912. Vol. I, pp. 96-107.

1169. ----- -----. Magazine of History, V (May 1907), 267-273.

1170. Holladay, Florence E. "The Powers of the Commander of the Confederate Trans-Mississippi Department, 1863-1865." Southwest Historical Quarterly, XXI (January-April 1918), 279-298, 333-359.

1171. Holland, Cecil F. Morgan and His Raiders, a Biography of the Confederate General. New York: Macmillan, 1942. 373p.

1172. Holley, Alexander L. A Treatise on Ordnance and Armor. New York: D. Van Nostrand, 1865. 900p.
Comparison of U.S. and British cannon, ammunition, etc.

1173. Hollins, George N. "Autobiography of Commodore

George Nicholas Hollins, C. S. A." Maryland Historical Magazine, XXXIV (September 1939), 228-243.
Active in the defense of New Orleans.

1174. -----. "Capture of the Steamer St. Nicholas." Southern Historical Society Papers, XXIV (1896), 88-91.
Captured by Confederates in the Potomac River in June 1861 and renamed Rappahannock (not to be confused with the inactive British-built cruiser of the same name). Operated in the Potomac to April 1862 when burned by the Rebels at Fredericksburg.

1175. Hollyday, Henry. "Running the Blockade." Confederate Veteran, XXIX (January-December 1921), 93-96.

1176. -----. "Running the Blockade: Henry Hollyday Joins the Confederacy." Edited by Frederic B. M. Hall. Maryland Historical Magazine, XLI (March 1946), 1-10.

1177. Hollyday, Lamar. "The Virginia and the Monitor." Confederate Veteran, XXX (January-December 1922), 380-382.
Attempts to "clear up" Yankee versions.

1178. Holmes, Jack D. L. "The End of the Star of the West." Civil War Times, III (August 1961), 24.
Under the name St. Philip, sunk in the Tallahatchie River to block the Yazoo Pass Expedition of 1863. Noted for her attempt, when yet in Yankee hands, to reinforce Fort Sumter in 1861.

1179. -----. "The Naval Career of Captain Laurence Rousseau." By Jack D. L. Homes and Raymond J. Martinez. Louisiana History, IX (Fall 1968), 341-354.
Skipper of the C. S. S. Selma.

1180. Holmes, Sarah K. (Stone). Brokenburn: the Journal of Kate Stone, 1861-1868. Edited by John Q. Anderson. Baton Rouge: Louisiana State University Press, 1955. 400p.

The Brokenburn Plantation was 30 miles northwest of Vicksburg. Here the young girl kept her journal and wrote of her loathing for the Federal gunboats which appeared on the Mississippi a few miles away.

1181. Holmes, Theophilus H., Author of Report. See C.S.A. War Department., no. 585.

1182. Holton, William C. Cruise of the U.S. Flag-ship Hartford, 1862-'63; Being a Narrative of all Her Operations Since Going into Commission in 1862, Until Her Return to New York in 1863. From the Private Journal of William C. Holton. Edited by B. S. Osbon. New York: L. W. Paine, 1863. 84p.

1183. Holzman, Robert S. "Ben Butler in the Civil War." New England Quarterly, XXX (September 1957), 330-345.

1184. -----. Stormy Ben Butler. New York: Macmillan, 1954. 297p.

1185. Homans, James E. Our Three Admirals: Farragut, Porter, Dewey. New York: J. T. White, 1899. 93p.

1186. Homans, John. "The Red River Expedition." In Publications of the Military History Society of Massachusetts. 14 vols. Boston: The Society, 1895-1918. Vol. VIII, pp. 65-98.

1187. Hood, John B. Advance and Retreat: Personal Experiences in the United States and Confederate States Army. New Orleans: Hood Orphan Memorial Fund, 1880. 358p.

Useful for background to Nashville Campaign.

1188. Hoogenboom, Ari. "Gustavus Fox and the Relief of Fort Sumter." Civil War History, IX (December 1963), 383-398.

1189. Hooker, C. E. "Mississippi." In Vol. VII of Clement A. Evans, ed. Confederate Military History; a Library of Confederate States History. 12 vols. Atlanta: Confederate Publishing

Company, 1899.

1190. Hoole, William S. "The C.S.S. Alabama at Cape Town: Centennial Celebration, 1863-1963." Alabama Review, XVII (July 1964), 228-233.

1191. -----. Four Years in the Confederate Navy: The Career of Captain John Low of the C.S.S. Fingal, Alabama, Florida, Tuscaloosa, and Ajax. Athens: University of Georgia Press, 1964. 147p.

1192. Hooper, W. R. "Blockade-Running." Harper's New Monthly Magazine, XLII (December 1870), 105-108.

1193. Hopkins, Garland E. The First Battle of Modern Naval History. Richmond: Dietz, 1943. 34p.
Monitor and Merrimack.

1194. [Hopkins, Owen J.]. Under the Flag of the Nation: Diaries and Letters of a Yankee Volunteer in the Civil War. Edited by Otto F. Bond. Columbus: Ohio State University Press, 1961. 308p.
"Johnny" Hopkins was a private in Co. K, 42nd Ohio Volunteers, and saw action at Arkansas Post and Vicksburg. His description of the establishment of the naval siege battery at the latter place is most interesting.

1195. Hoppin, James M. The Life of Andrew Hull Foote, Rear Admiral U.S. Navy. New York: Harper, 1874. 411p.
Still the only book-length biography.

1196. Horan, James D., ed. See Waddell, James I., no. 2654.

1197. Horn, Stanley F. The Army of Tennessee. Norman: University of Oklahoma Press, 1941. 503p.
Includes the Tennessee River campaign, 1862.

1198. -----. The Decisive Battle of Nashville. Baton Rouge: Louisiana State University Press, 1956. 181p.

1199. Horn, Stanley F. Gallant Rebel: The Fabulous Cruise of the C.S.S. Shenandoah. New Brunswick,

N. J.: Rutgers University Press, 1947. 292p.

1200. -----. "Nashville-The Most Decisive Battle of the War." Civil War Times Illustrated, III (December 1964), 4-11, 31-36.

1201. Horne, Charles F., ed. Great Men and Famous Women. 3 vols. New York: Selmar Hess, 1894.

1202. Horner, Dave. The Blockade-Runners; True Tales of Running the Yankee Blockade of the Confederate Coast. New York: Dodd, Mead, 1968. 241p.

1203. Horsley, A. S. "The Invention of Torpedoes." Confederate Veteran, II (January-December 1894), 234-235.

1204. House, Boyce. "Confederate Navy Hero Puts the Flag Back in Place." Tennessee Historical Quarterly, XIX (June 1960), 172-175.

1205. House, E. H. The Shimonoseki Affair. Tokyo: 1875. 35p.

U. S. S. Wyoming's exchange with Japanese forts.

1206. Hovgaard, William. "Who Invented the Monitor?" Army and Navy Journal, XLVII (November 27, 1909), 357.

Dismisses the claims of Theodore Timby.

1207. How, Louis. James B. Eads. Boston: Houghton, Mifflin, 1900. 120p.

1208. Howard, Brett. "The Story of Vicksburg." Mankind, I (July-August 1967), 4-20.

1209. Howe, M. A. De Wolfe, ed. See Sherman, William T., no. 2163.

1210. Howell, Glenn. "Picnic with Cushing." United States Naval Institute Proceedings, LXII (August 1936), 1098-1104.

Against the C. S. gunboat Raleigh.

1211. Howes, Abby W. "Captain Walke Passing Island

Number Ten." Chautauguan, XXXI (August 1900), 527-528.
With the Carondelet, 1862.

1212. Hoyt, Edwin P. From the Turtle to the Nautilus: The Story of Submarines. Boston: Little, Brown, 1963. 134p.
Includes those of the Civil War.

1213. Hubbard, Lucius F. Minnesota in the Red River Expedition, 1864, and the Campaign of Mobile, 1865. Papers Read Before the Minnesota Historical Society by General Lucius F. Hubbard, November 11, 1907 and February 10, 1908. [Minneapolis: The Society, 1908.] 48p.

1214. -----. "The Red River Expedition." In Glimpses of the Nation's Struggle: A Series of Papers Read Before the Minnesota Commandery, Military Order of the Loyal Legion of the United States. 6 vols. St. Paul: St. Paul Book and Stationary, 1887-1909. Vol. II, pp. 267-279.

1215. Huff, Leo E. "The Union Expedition Against Little Rock, August-September 1863." Arkansas Historical Quarterly, XXII (Summer 1963), 224-237.
Including Yankee naval activity in the White River.

1216. Huffmaster, Joseph. "Naval Officers in the '60's." Confederate Veteran, XX (January-December 1912), 19-20.

1217. Huffstot, Robert S. "The Carondelet and Other 'Pook Turtles.'" Civil War Times Illustrated, VI (August 1967), 4-11.
Naval Constructor Samuel Pook drew the plans for the "City Series" gunboats.

1218. -----. "The Post of Arkansas." Civil War Times Illustrated, VII (January 1969), 11-36.

1219. -----. "The Story of the C.S.S. Arkansas." Civil War Times Illustrated, VII (July 1968), 20-27.

1220. Hughes, Nathaniel C., Jr. General William J. Hardee: Old Reliable. Southern Biography

Series. Baton Rouge: Louisiana State University Press, 1965. 329p.
A Confederate general involved in the siege of Savannah and who oversaw the destruction of the Rebel squadron at that place.

1221. Hughes, Robert M. "The Monitor Defeated the Merrimac--Myth." Tyler's Quarterly Historical and Genealogical Magazine, VIII (July 1926), 30-36.
Presents the Southern viewpoint.

1222. Hughes, Sarah F., ed. See Forbes, John M., no. 880.

1223. [Hults, Ellsworth H.]. "Aboard the Galena at Mobile." Civil War Times Illustrated, X (April-May 1971), 12-21, 28-42.
Based on the journal of an officer.

1224. Humphrey, Willis C. The Great Contest: a History of Military and Naval Operations During the Civil War. Detroit: C. H. Smith, 1886. 691p.

1225. Humphreys, Andrew A. and Henry C. Abbot. Report Upon the Physics and Hydraulics of the Mississippi River. Professional Papers of the Corps of Topographical Engineers, United States Army, no. 4. Philadelphia: J. B. Lippincott, 1861. 214p.

1226. Humphreys, H. K. See Pryor, J. P., no. 1979.

1227. Hunt, Aurora. "The Civil War on the Western Seaboard." Civil War History, IX (June 1963), 178-186.
Activities of the Federal Pacific Squadron.

1228. Hunt, Cornelius E. The Shenandoah; or, the Last Confederate Cruiser. New York: G. W. Carleton, 1867. 273p.
By one of the ship's officers.

1229. Hunt, George. "The Fort Donelson Campaign." In Military Essays and Recollections; Papers Read Before the Illinois Commandery, Military Order of the Loyal Legion of the United States. 4 vols.

Chicago: A. C. McClurg, 1891-1912. Vol. IV, pp. 61-82.

1230. Hunt, William H. Address on the Occasion of the Unveiling of the Statue of Admiral Farragut in Madison Square, New York, May 25, 1881. Boston: Franklin Press, 1881. 4p.

1231. Hunter, Louis C. Steamboats on the Western Rivers; an Economic and Technological History. Studies in Economic History. Cambridge, Mass.: Harvard University Press, 1949. 684p.
Useful for understanding the river gunboats, many of which were converted steamers. Some data on steamers used as transports in the war.

1232. Huse, Caleb. The Supplies for the Confederate Army, How They were Obtained in Europe and How Paid for. Personal Reminiscences and Unpublished History. Boston: T. R. Marvin, 1904. 36p.
An interesting account of Confederate purchasing operations and, indirectly, blockade running, by a former Confederate agent.

1233. Hutchins, John G. B. The American Maritime Industries and Public Policy, 1789-1914. Harvard Economic Studies, no. 71. Cambridge, Mass.: Harvard University Press, 1941. 627p.
Includes Civil War.

1234. Hutchinson, William F. The Bay Fight: A Sketch of the Battle of Mobile Bay, August 5, 1864. Personal Narratives of Events in the War of the Rebellion, Being Papers Read Before the Rhode Island Soldiers and Sailors Historical Society. 1st Series, no. 8. Providence: N. B. Williams, 1879.

1235. -----. Life on the Texan Blockade. Personal Narratives of Events in the War of the Rebellion, Being Papers Read Before the Rhode Island Soldiers and Sailors Historical Society. 3rd Series, no. 1. Providence: N. B. Williams, 1883.

1236. Hyde, James N. "Two Stonewalls, from a Seaside View." In Military Essays and Recollections; Papers Read Before the Illinois Commandery, Military Order of the Loyal Legion of the United States. 4 vols. Chicago: A. C. McClurg, 1891-1912. Vol. I, pp. 453-476.
Part I: "A Rebel Ram in European Waters"; Part II: The Stonewall in American and Japanese Waters."

1237. -----. "The Two Stonewalls--The Last Chapter of the Rebellion." Magazine of History, III (January 1906), 11-17.

1238. Hyde, William. "Gay and Festive Times in Old Carondelet." Missouri Historical Society Bulletin, VI (April 1950), 323-332.
Site of Ead's shipyard where gunboats were built; now part of the city of St. Louis.

1239. Hyman, Harold M., Joint Author. See Thomas, Benjamin P., no. 2357.

1240. I. N. The Monitor Ironclads. Boston: Eastburn, 1864. 17p.

1241. "In Memoriam: Commodore Foxhall A. Parker." United States Naval Institute Proceedings, V (1879), 569-571.
One-time commander of the Potomac Flotilla.

1242. "In Memoriam: John Mercer Brooke." Lexington: Virginia Military Institute, 1906. 16p.

1243. "In Memoriam: Rear Admiral John Rogers." United States Naval Institute Proceedings, VIII (1881), 177-180.

1244. "An Incident on the Coast of Maine in 1861." Magazine of History, XV (January 1912), 38-41.
Capture of Confederate vessels by the U.S. Coast Survey schooner Arago.

1245. Inhster, Tom H. "Waddell's War on the Whalers." History Today, XVI (September 1966), 627-632.
Activities of the Shenandoah.

1246. "Ironclad Echo." Newsweek, SIV (August 21, 1939), 14-15.
Proposed memorial for Hampton Roads.

1247. Irwin, Richard B. "The Capture of Port Hudson." In Robert U. Johnson and Clarence C. Buell, eds. B & L. Vol. III, pp. 586-597.

1248. -----. History of the Nineteenth Army Corps. New York: Putnam, 1892. 528p.
Useful discussions of co-operation between General N. Banks and the U. S. Navy by the Assistant Adjutant General of the Federal Department of the Gulf.

1249. -----. "The Red River Campaign." In Robert U. Johnson and Clarence C. Buell, eds. B & L. Vol. IV, pp. 345-361.
The author did not accompany the advance.

1250. Isherwood, Benjamin F. Facts in Relation to the Official Career of Benjamin F. Isherwood, Chief of the Bureau of Steam Engineering of the Navy Department. Philadelphia: The Author, 1866. 57p.

1251. Jackman, S. W. "Admiral Wilkes Visits Bermuda During the Civil War." American Neptune, XXIV (July 1964), 208-211.
In September 1862.

1252. Jackson, Crawford M. "An Account of the Occupation of Port Hudson, La." Alabama Historical Quarterly, SVIII (Winter 1956), 474-485.

1253. Jackson, S. W., ed. See Hanford, Franklin, no. 1056.

1254. Jackson, Walter A. The Story of Selma. [Birmingham, Ala. ?]: 1954. 574p.
The Civil War chapter contains useful data on the naval foundry there.

1255. Jacobi, C. The Rifled Batteries of the Americans at the Siege of Charleston, from 1863-65, Their Use, Effect, and Durability, With a Criticism

of the Attack and Defense. Berlin: 1868. 84p.
By an observing Captain of the Royal Prussian Artillery.

1256. Jahns, Patricia. Matthew Fontaine Maury and Joseph Henry: Scientists of the Civil War. New York: Hastings, 1961. 308p.
The latter, a Smithsonian "professor" of physics, was the first Secretary of the Institution.

1257. James, Alfred P. "The Strategy of Concentration, as Used by the Confederate Forces in the Mississippi Valley in the Spring of 1862." Mississippi Valley Historical Review, VII (November 1921), 363-372.

1258. James, Urian P. James' River Guide: Containing Descriptions of all the Cities, Towns, and Principal Objects of Interest, on the Navigable Waters of the Mississippi Valley. Cincinnati: The Author, 1860. 128p.
Of particular value to students of the Western theatre; the 1858 and 1869 editions also helpful.

1259. "James Buchanan Eads." Scientific American, LVI (April 1887), 263-264.

1260. Jeffers, W. N., Joint Author. See Murphy, John M., no. 1718.

1261. "Jefferson Davis, Privateer." Southern Historical Society Papers, XXXI (1903), 53-55.
The Confederacy's most noted private man-o'-war of the first year of the war. Commonly known as the Jeff Davis.

1262. Jeffries, Clarence. "Running the Blockade on the Mississippi." Confederate Veteran, XXII (January-December 1914), 22-23.

1263. Jeffries, William W. "The Civil War Career of Charles Wilkes." Unpublished PhD. Dissertation, Vanderbilt University, 1941.

1264. ----- -----. Journal of Southern History. XI

(August 1945), 324-348.

1265. Jenkins, Thornton A. Rear Admiral Goldsborough and the Retiring Laws of the Navy. A Paper Read Before the Naval Committee of the House of Representatives, January 21, 1868, in Reply to Rear Admiral Goldsborough's Claim to be Continued on the Active List of the Navy. Washington: McGill and Witherow, [1868]. 38p.

1266. ----- -----. Number Two. Washington: Mohun and Bester, 1868. 19p.

1267. -----. Author. See U.S. Navy Department, no. 2547.

1268. Jennings, William. "On the North Atlantic Blockade." Magazine of History, IV (July 1906), 26-29.
A useful account of dull routine.

1269. Jenrich, Charles H. "An Error in Flags." United States Naval Institute Proceedings, XCIV (January 1968), 138-141.
Capture of the Eric by the U.S.S. Mohican.

1270. -----. "Pathfinder of the Seas." Rudder, LXXV (May 1959), 29-30, 68.
Maury.

1271. Jervey, Theodore D. "Charleston During the Civil War." In Annual Report of the American Historical Association for the Year 1913. 2 vols. Washington: Government Printing Office, 1915. Vol. I, pp. 167-177.

1272. Jocobus, Melancthon. "Six Fighting Ships." Conneticut Historical Society Bulletin, XXI (October 1956), 112-116.
Six warships named Connecticut, including the Union blockader.

1273. John, Evan, pseud. See Simpson, E. J., no. 2183.

1274. "John Ericsson's Deadly Cheeze Box." Life, XXXIX (October 17, 1955), 113.
Monitor.

1275. "John McIntosh Kell." Confederate Veteran, XXIV (January-December 1916), 380.

1276. "John Mercer Brooke." Confederate Veteran, XXXV (January-December 1927), 258.

1277. "John Slidell of Louisiana." Confederate Veteran, XXXVIII (January-December 1930), 47.

1278. Johns, John. "Wilmington During the Blockade." Harper's New Monthly Magazine, XXXIII (September 1866), 497-503.

1279. Johns, John E. Florida During the Civil War. Gainesville: University of Florida Press, 1964. 265p.
Includes naval activities.

1280. Johnson, Adam R. The Partisan Rangers of the Confederate States Army. Edited by William J. Davis. Louisville, Ky.: G. G. Fetter, 1904. 476p.
Johnson was with Morgan at Buffington Island.

1281. Johnson, Allen and Dumas Malone, eds. Dictionary of American Biography. 20 vols. New York: Scribner's, 1930.
Good biographies of many of the leading naval officers, North and South.

1282. Johnson, Arthur M. "Genesis of a Navy Yard." United States Naval Institute Proceedings, LXXXI (September 1955), 993-1003.
League Island, Pennsylvania.

1283. Johnson, Charles F. The Long Roll; Being a Journal of the Civil War, as Set Down During the Years 1861-1863. East Aurora, N.Y.: Roycrofters, 1911. 241p.
Roanoke Island Expedition.

1284. Johnson, Frank. "The Vicksburg Campaign." In Publications of the Military History Society of Massachusetts. 14 vols. Boston: The Society, 1895-1918. Vol. X, pp. 63-90.

1285. Johnson, Howard P. "New Orleans Under General

Butler." Louisiana Historical Quarterly, XXIV (April 1941), 434-536.

1286. Johnson, John. "The Confederate Defense of Fort Sumter." In Robert U. Johnson and Clarence C. Buell, eds. B & L. Vol. IV, pp. 23-26.

1287. -----. The Defense of Charleston Harbor, Including Fort Sumter and the Adjacent Islands, 1863-'65. Charleston, S. C.: Walker, Evans and Cogswell, 1890. 276p.

1288. -----. "The Story of the Confederate Armored Ram Arkansas." Southern Historical Society Papers, XXXIII (1905), 1-16.

Taken from the Charleston, S. C., Sunday News of November 12, 1905.

1289. Johnson, Kenneth R. "Confederate Defenses and Union Gunboats on the Tennessee River: A Federal Raid into Northwest Alabama." Alabama Historical Quarterly, LXIV (Summer 1968), 39-60.

In 1862.

1290. Johnson, Ludwell H. "Contraband Trade During the Last Year of the Civil War." Mississippi Valley Historical Review, XLIX (March 1963), 635-652.

Includes the capture of George W. Lane's tug, Philadelphia, by the Union navy.

1291. -----. Red River Campaign: Politics and Cotton in the Civil War. Baltimore: Johns Hopkins Press, 1958. 317p.

Good coverage of naval activities.

1292. Johnson, Marion M., comp. See U. S. National Archives, nos. 2560 and 2561.

1293. Johnson, Robert E. Rear Admiral John Rogers, 1812-1882. Annapolis: U. S. Naval Institute, 1967. 426p.

1294. Johnson, Robert U. and Clarence C. Buell, eds. Battles and Leaders of the Civil War: Being for the Most Part Contributions by Union and Confederate Officers. 4 vols. New York: Century, 1887.

1295. Johnson, Rossiter. The Hero of Manila, Dewey on the Mississippi and in the Pacific. New York: D. Appleton, 1907. 152p.

1296. Johnston, J. S. "Kentucky." In Clement A. Evans, ed. Confederate Military History; a Library of Confederate States History. 12 vols. Atlanta: Confederate Publishing Company, 1899.

1297. Johnston, James D. "Admiral Buchanan and the Confederate States Ram Tennessee." United Service, VII (August 1882), 202-213.

1298. -----. "The Battle of Mobile Bay." United Service, VI (January 1882), 104-108.

1299. -----. "The Fight in Mobile Bay." Southern Historical Society Papers, VI (1878), 224-227; IX (1881), 471-476.

1300. -----. "The Ram Tennessee at Mobile Bay." In Robert U. Johnson and Clarence C. Buell, eds. B & L. Vol. IV, pp. 401-405.

1301. Johnston, Joseph E. Narrative of Military Operations, Directed During the Late War Between the States. New York: D. Appleton, 1874. 602p.
Including the 1861-1862 Tennessee strategy.

1302. -----., Author of Report. See C. S. A. Army Department of Mississippi and East Louisiana, no. 546.

1303. Johnston, Robert C. "Navy Yards and Dry Docks: A Study of the Bureau of Yards and Docks, 1842-1871." Unpublished M. A. Thesis, Stanford University, 1954.

1304. Johnston, William P. The Life of General Albert Sidney Johnston, Embracing His Services in the Armies of the United States, the Republic of Texas, and the Confederate States. New York: D. Appleton, 1878. 755p.

1305. Jones, Allen W. and Virginia Ann Buttry. "Military [and Naval] Events in Arkansas During the Civil War, 1861-1865." Arkansas Historical Quarterly,

XXII (Summer 1963), 124-170.

1306. -----. "Military [and Naval] Events in Louisiana During the Civil War. Louisiana History, II (Summer 1961), 301-321.

1307. -----., Joint Author. See Letford, William, no. 1434.

1308. Jones, Archer. Confederate Strategy from Shiloh to Vicksburg. Baton Rouge: Louisiana State University Press, 1961. 258p.

1309. -----. "Tennessee and Mississippi: Joe Johnston's Strategic Problem." Tennessee Historical Quarterly, XVIII (June 1959), 134-147.

1310. -----. "The Vicksburg Campaign." Journal of Mississippi History, XXIX (February 1967), 12-27.

1311. Jones, Catesby ap Roger. "The First Confederate Iron-Clad, the Virginia, Formerly the United States Steam Frigate Merrimac." Southern Magazine, XV (December 1874), 200-207.
By her Executive Officer.

1312. ----- -----. In Transactions of the Southern History Society, I (1874), 200-207.

1313. -----. "The Iron-Clad Virginia." Virginia Magazine of History and Biography, XLIX (October 1941), 297-303.

1314. -----. "Services of the Virginia (Merrimac)." Southern Historical Society Papers, I (1876), 90-91; XI (1881), 65-75.

1315. ----- -----. United Service, VIII (June 1883), 660-668.

1316. ----- -----. In Robert A. Brock, ed. General Robert E. Lee; Soldier, Citizen, and Christian Patriot. Richmond: B. F. Johnson, 1897. p. 538-549.

1317. Jones, Charles C. The Life and Services of

of Commodore Josiah Tattnall. Savannah: Morning News Steam Printing, 1878. 255p.
The Rebel Flag Officer forced to order the burning of the Merrimack to prevent her capture.

1318. -----. Military Lessons Inculcated on the Coast of Georgia During the Confederate War. An Address Delivered Before the Confederate Survivors Association in Augusta, Georgia, at Its 5th Annual Meeting on Memorial Day, April 26, 1883. Augusta: Chronicle Printing, 1883. 15p.

1319. Jones, Charles E. Georgia in the War, 1861-1865. Atlanta: Foote and Davies, 1909. 167p.
Contains some data on Confederate navy officers.

1320. Jones, Charles L. "The Naval Expedition from Wilmington, North Carolina, and the Cruise of the C.S. Steamer Tallahassee." In Addresses Delivered Before the Confederate Veteran's Association of Savannah, Georgia, 1898-1902. Savannah: The Association, 1902. p. 106-117.

1321. Jones, Edmund. The U.S. Gunboat Itasca, Lieutenant Commanding C. H. B. Caldwell, Lieutenant and Executive Officer George B. Bacon. During the Siege of Forts Jackson and St. Phillippe [sic] by the West Gulf Squadron Under the Command of Commodore David G. Farragut, April 24, 1862. New York: Belford, 1890. 62p.

1322. Jones, J. L., Joint Author. See Porter, William D., no. 1936.

1323. Jones, James P. "John L. Worden and the Fort Pickens Mission: The Confederacy's First Prisoner of War." Alabama Review, XXI (April 1968), 113-132.
Picked up after carrying Welles' orders to the U.S.S. Sabine to reinforce the Florida post.

1324. Jones, John B. A Rebel War Clerk's Diary, at the Confederate States Capital. 2 vols. Philadel-

phia: Lippincott, 1866.
Includes mention of important naval events.

1325. Jones, Samuel. The Siege of Charleston and the Operations on the South Atlantic Coast in the War Among the States. New York: Neale, 1911. 295p.
Data on Federal amphibious campaigns helpful.

1326. Jones, Virgil C. The Civil War at Sea. 3 vols. New York: Holt, Rinehart, Winston, 1960-1962.

1327. -----. "How the South Created a Navy." Civil War Times Illustrated, VIII (July 1969), 4-9, 42-48.

1328. -----. "The Mighty Ram Albemarle." Civil War Times Illustrated, I (June 1962), 6-11, 43-45.

1329. -----. "Mr. Lincoln's Blockade." Civil War Times Illustrated, X (December 1971), 10-24.

1330. -----. "The Naval War--Introduction." Civil War History, IX (June 1963), 117-120.
A short discussion of the sorry state of research into Civil War naval history--"the ignored war."

1331. -----. "Preparation Paid Off for Farragut at Mobile Bay." Civil War Times Illustrated, III (May 1964), 6-13, 28-31.

1332. -----. "Slipping Through the Blockade." Civil War Times, II (October 1960), 4-6, 18-19.

1333. Jones, Wilbur D. The Confederate Rams at Birkenhead; A Chapter in Anglo-American Relations. Confederate Centennial Studies, no. 19. Tuscaloosa, Ala.: Confederate Publishing Company, 1961. 124p.
Built by the Laird brothers; saw no action due to diplomatic pressure.

1334. Jordan, Thomas. "Recollections of General Beauregard's Service in West Tennessee in the Spring of 1862." Southern Historical Society Papers, VIII (1880), 404-417.

1335. -----. "Seacoast Defences of South Carolina and Georgia." Southern Historical Society Papers, I (1876), 403-407.

1336. -----., Joint Author. See Pryor, J. P., no. 1979.

1337. Kaiser, Leo M., ed. See Bodman, Albert H., no. 285.

1338. Kamm, Samuel R. "The Civil War Career of Thomas A. Scott." Unpublished PhD. Dissertation, University of Pennsylvania, 1939.
As an Assistant Secretary of War, he was present to applaud the success of the Carondelet in passing Island No. 10.

1339. Kaplan, Hyman R. "The U.S. Coast Guard and the Civil War." United States Naval Institute Proceedings, LXXXVI (August 1960), 40-50.

1340. Kassel, Charles. "Opening the Mississippi--A Civil War Drama." Open Court, XL (March 1926), 145-154.

1341. Kautz, Albert. "Incidents in the Occupation of New Orleans." In Robert U. Johnson and Clarence C. Buell, eds. B & L. Vol. II, pp. 91-94.

1342. Keeler, William F. Aboard the U.S.S. Florida, 1863-1865. Edited by Robert W. Daly. Naval Letter Series, v. 2. Annapolis: U.S. Naval Institute, 1968. 272p.
Activity on the Atlantic blockade.

1343. -----. Aboard the U.S.S. Monitor, 1862. Edited by Robert W. Daly. Naval Letter Series, v. 1. Annapolis: U.S. Naval Institute, 1964. 278p.
Routine as pictured by the ship's paymaster.

1344. Keeling, J. M., Joint Author. See Chaplain, C. T., no. 475.

1345. Kell, John McIntosh. "Cruise and Combats of the Alabama." In Robert U. Johnson and Clarence C. Buell, eds. B & L. Vol. IV, pp. 600-614.
By the raider's executive officer.

1346. -----. Recollections of a Naval Life; Including the Cruises of the Confederate States Steamers Sumter and Alabama. Washington: Neale, 1900. 307p.
Also includes his service with the Rebel Squadron on the James River, 1865.

1347. Kellar, Allan. Andrew Hull Foote: Gunboat Commodore (1806-1863). [New Haven?] Connecticut Civil War Centennial Commission, n. d. 48p.

1348. -----. "Morgan's Raid Across the Ohio." Civil War Times Illustrated, II (June 1963), 6-10.

1349. Kellar, A. L. "Confederate Submarines and P. T. Boats." All Hands, no. 470 (April 1956), 59-63.

1350. Kelley, J. D. J. "A Lay Sermon--Armored Vessels." United Service, I (April 1879), 263-274.

1351. Kelln, Albert L. "Confederate Submarines." Virginia Magazine of History and Biography, LXI (July 1953), 292-303.

1352. Kellogg, John J. War Experiences and the Story of the Vicksburg Campaign from "Milliken's Bend" to July 4, 1863; Being an Accurate and Graphic Account of Campaign Events Taken from the Diary of Captain John Jackson Kellogg, of Company B, 113th Illinois Volunteer Infantry. Washington, Ia.: Evening Journal, 1913. 64p.
Includes references to some naval events.

1353. Kelly, W. J. "Steamboats from Baltimore." Maryland Historical Magazine, XXXVII (March 1942), 42-52.
During the Civil War.

1354. Kendall, John S. History of New Orleans. 3 vols. Chicago: Lewis, 1922.
Includes Farragut's capture.

1355. Kendricken, Paul H. Memoirs of Paul H. Kendricken. Boston: Priv. Print., 1910. 355p.
Author served as an engineer aboard the U. S. S. Conemaugh at Port Royal, Charleston, and Mobile Bay.

1356. Kennedy, Charles. "The Civil War Letters of Captain Charles Kennedy." Staten Island History, IX (October-December 1948), 30-32.
Alexandria, La., April 3-24, 1864.

1357. Kenneth, Lee. "The Strange Career of the Stonewall." United States Naval Institute Proceedings, XCIV (February 1968), 74-85.

1358. Kenney, Edward C. "From the Log of the Red Rover, 1862-1865; a History of the First U.S. Navy Hospital Ship." Missouri Historical Review, LX (October 1965), 31-49.

1359. Kennon, Beverly. "Fighting Farragut Below New Orleans." In Robert U. Johnson and Clarence C. Buell, eds. B & L. Vol. II, pp. 76-88.

1360. Kephart, Horace, ed. See Hobart-Hampton, Augustus C., no. 1155.

1361. Kerr, W. M. "William Maxwell Wood, the First Surgeon General of the United States Navy." Annals of Medical History, VI (December 1924), 387-425.
Fleet Surgeon, North Atlantic Blockading Squadron during war; witness to contest between Monitor and Merrimack.

1362. Kessler, James W. "Loss of the Mississippi at Port Hudson." United Service, XII (June 1885), 650-656.

1363. Ketchum, Edgar. "Personal Reminiscences of the Capture of Fort Fisher and Wilmington, North Carolina." United Service, New Series XVI (December 1896), 457-470.

1364. Ketchum, Richard M., ed. See American Heritage Picture History of the Civil War., no. 65.

1365. [Killgore, Gabriel M.]. "Vicksburg Diary: the Journal of Gabriel M. Killgore." Edited by Douglas Maynard. Civil War History, X (March 1964), 33-54.
A soldier from the 17th Louisiana Infantry whose writings date February 13-July 20, 1863.

1366. Kimball, Carol W. "The Valentine's Day Ironclad." Yankee, XXXV (February 1970), 80-83, 148-153.
The U.S.S. Galena, her building and career.

1367. King, Ernest J. "The Fort Fisher Campaigns, 1864-1865." United States Naval Institute Proceedings, LXXVII (August 1951), 842-855; LXXVIII (February 1952), 197-198.

1368. King, Horatio. "The Trent Affair." Magazine of American History, XV (March 1886), 278-291.

1369. King, James W., Author of Report. See U.S. Navy Department., no. 2578.

1370. King, W. R. Torpedoes, Their Invention and Use from the First Application of the Art of War to the Present Time. Washington: Government Printing Office, 1866.

1371. Kinney, John C. "The Battle of Mobile Bay." United Service, VI (February 1882), 209-216.

1372. -----. "Farragut at Mobile Bay." In Robert U. Johnson and Clarence C. Buell, eds. B & L. Vol. IV, pp. 379-399.

1373. Kirk, Neville T. "The Father of American Naval Engineering." United States Naval Institute Proceedings, LXXXI (May 1955), 486-489.
Benjamin Isherwood.

1374. -----. "The Last Battle of the Monitors." United States Naval Institute Proceedings, LXXXI (February 1955), 240-241.
On the James River, January 1865.

1375. -----. "T.A.M. Craven at Mobile Bay." United States Naval Institute Proceedings, LXXXI (August 1955), 962-963.
The skipper of the Tecumseh who was lost when his ship struck a torpedo.

1376. Kirkland, Charles P. Liability of the Government of Great Britain for the Depredations of Rebel Privateers on the Commerce of the United States Considered. New York: Randolph, 1863. 37p.

Holds England fully responsible.

1377. "Klaxon." "Stout Hearts." Blackwood's Magazine, CCXXXVII (April 1935), 540-550.

1378. Klein, Benjamin F. The Ohio River Atlas; a Collection of the Best Known Maps of the Ohio River from 1713 to 1854. Cincinnati: Picture Marine, [1954] 32p.
Latter charts helpful to the Civil War buff.

1379. Klein, Frederic S. "The Sinking of the Ruth." Civil War Times Illustrated, I (July 1962), 10-15.
A Federal steamer sunk below Cairo, Illinois, on August 4, 1863 with 200 passengers and $2.5 millions.

1380. Knapp, David, Jr. "The Rodney Church Incident." Journal of Mississippi History, XXXII (July 1970), 245-249.
Acting Master Walter E. H. Fentress and 20 men from the U.S.S. Rattler were captured by Confederate Soldiers while attending services, September 1863.

1381. Knox, Dudley W. A History of the United States Navy. Rev. Ed. New York: Putnam, 1948. 704p.
Good Civil War coverage.

1382. -----. "The U.S.S. Red Rover." Steamboat Bill of Facts, XIII (December 1944), 269-271.

1383. -----., Joint Author. See Eller, Ernest M., nos. 792-992.

1384. Knox, Thomas W. Campfire and Cotton-field: Southern Adventure in Time of War. Life with the Union Armies and Residence on a Louisiana Plantation. New York: Blelock, 1865. 524p.
Until ordered out of the Western theatre by Sherman for his report of the Chickasaw Bayou expedition of December 1862, the author, like other Yankee reporters, saw much of the inland navy.

1385. Koopman, Harry L. The Great Admiral. Ithaca, New York: 1883. 16p.
Farragut.

1386. Kountz, John S., comp. See U.S. Vicksburg, no. 2626.

1387. Krafft, Herman F. "Seapower and American Destiny." United States Naval Institute Proceedings, XLVII (April 1921), 473-486.
Includes comments on the Civil War.

1388. Krout, Mary H. "Rear Admiral Charles Wilkes and His Exploits." United States Naval Institute Proceedings, L (March, July 1924), 405-416, 1131-1133.

1389. Kurtz, Henry I. "The Battle of Belmont." Civil War Times Illustrated, II (June 1963), 18-24.

1390. Lachlison, J. "Daring Deed in Saving the David--C.S. Navy." Confederate Veteran, XVI (February 1908), 78.
How engineer J. H. Tomb got the craft back to Charleston after her attack on the New Ironsides.

1391. LaFaucheur, L. J. "The Fight Between the Merrimac and Monitor. Account by a Confederate Spectator." Belford's Magazine, VI (December 1890), 104-112.

1392. Laird Brothers. Birkenhead Iron-Clads. Correspondence Between Her Majesty's Government and Messers. Laird Brothers; and Appendix, Containing Correspondence between Officers of H. M.'s Customs and Captain Inglefield, R. N., and Messers. Laird Brothers, Respecting Iron-Clad Vessels Building at Birkenhead, 1863-4. London: Vacher, 1864. 69p.
The ships destined for the Confederacy, but never released due to Union diplomatic pressure.

1393. Lamb, Martha J. "John Ericsson." In Charles F. Horne, ed. Great Men and Famous Women.

3 vols. New York: Selmar Hess, 1894. Vol. III, pp. 311-318.

1394. -----. "John Ericsson, the Builder of the Monitor, 1803-1889." Magazine of American History, XXV (January 1891), 1-17.

1395. Lamb, William. Colonel Lamb's story of Fort Fisher: the Battles Fought Here in 1864 and 1865. Carolina Beach, N. C.: Blockade Runner Museum, 1966. 40p.

1396. -----. "The Defense and Fall of Fort Fisher." Southern Historical Society Papers, X (1882), 257-290.

1397. -----. "The Defense of Fort Fisher." In Robert U. Johnson and Clarence C. Buell, eds. B & L. Vol. IV, pp. 642-654.

1398. -----. "The Defense of Fort Fisher, North Carolina." In Publications of the Military History Society of Massachusetts. 14 vols. Boston: The Society, 1895-1914. Vol. IX, pp. 361-368.

1399. Lambert, William H. The American Navy. An Address. Philadelphia: Culbertson and Bache, 1880. 9p.
In the Civil War.

1400. Landers, H. L. "Wet Sand and Cotton--Bank's Red River Expedition." Louisiana Historical Quarterly, XIX (January 1936), 150-195.
That of 1864.

1401. Landon, F. "The Trent Affair of 1861." Canadian Historical Review, III (March 1922), 48-55.

1402. Landry, Ernest A. "The History of Forts Jackson and St. Philip with Special Emphasis on the Civil War Period." Unpublished M.A. Thesis, Louisiana State University, 1938.

1403. Langdon, Loomis L. "The Relief of Fort Pickens, Florida. The First Expedition. Journal of the U.S. Military Service Institute, (September-October 1909), 267-296.

1404. Langdon, Robert M. "Josiah Tattnall--Blood is Thicker Than Water." United States Naval Institute Proceedings, LXXXV (June 1959), 156-158.
On his decision to "go South."

1404a. Langdon, William C. "A Gunboat Episode." United Service, New Series I (February 1889), 191-195.
Involving the U.S.S. Currituck based at Harve de Grace, Maryland.

1405. Lanier, Robert S., Joint Author. See Miller, F. T., no. 1654.

1406. Lansden, John M. A History of the City of Cairo, Illinois. Chicago: R. R. Donnelley, 1910. 303p.
Including the Civil War period.

1407. Larkin, J. L. "The Battle of Santa Rosa Island." Florida Historical Quarterly, XXXVII (January-April 1959), 372-376.
Pensacola Bay, October 1861.

1408. Larson, Cedric A. "Death on the Dark River." American Heritage, VI (October 1955), 48-51, 98.
The explosion of the steamer Suitana.

1409. "The Late Naval Duel and Its Consequences." United Service Magazine [Great Britain], (May 1862), 34-48.
British view of the importance of the Monitor vs. Merrimac affair.

1410. Lathrop, Barnes F. "The La Fourche District in 1862: Invasion." Louisiana History, II (Spring 1961), 175-201.
That southeast section of Louisiana through which the Mississippi flows and through which Farraguts fleet and Butler's troops advanced on New Orleans.

1411. Lathrop, Constance. "Grog--Its Origin and Use in the United States Navy." United States Naval Institute Proceedings, LXI (March 1935), 377-380.
Use discontinued in 1862.

1412. Lattimore, Ralston B. Fort Pulaski National Monument--Georgia. National Park Service Historical Handbook Series, no. 18. Washington: U.S. Government Printing Office, 1954. 56p.

1413. Lauer, Conrad N. John Ericsson, Engineer, 1803-1889. [Glenlock, Pa.] Newcomen, 1939. 10p.

1414. Laughlin, Patrick. "Rebel Marines." Marine Corps Gazette, XXXVII (November 1953), 52-55.

1415. Lawrence, Alexander A. A Present for Mr. Lincoln: The Story of Savannah from Secession to Sherman. Macon: Ardivan Press, 1971. 321p.

Includes such naval activities as the story of the C.S.S. Atlanta.

1416. Lawson, Raymond S. "It Happened in Bahia." United States Naval Institute Proceedings, LVIII (June 1932), 834-836.

The illegal capture of the C.S.S. Florida.

1417. Leahy, Eugene L. "The Mark of the Ram." Nautical Research Journal, IX (August 1957), 108-111.

1418. Leary, William M., Jr. "Alabama Versus Kearsarge: A Diplomatic View." American Neptune, XXIX (July 1969), 167-173.

1419. LeDuc, William G. "The Little Steambost that Opened the 'Cracker Line.'" In Robert U. Johnson and Clarence C. Buell, eds. B & L. Vol. III, pp. 676-678.

U.S.S. Chattanooga, with a few other steamers, carried supplies to Union forces helping them prepare for the battle and victory at Chattanooga, Tennessee.

1420. Lee, Alfred. Substance of Remarks Made by Bishop Lee, at the Funeral Services for Admiral S. F. DuPont, in Christ Church, June 25, 1865. Wilmington, Del.: H. Eckel, 1865. 8 p.

1421. Lee, George R. "After Donelson: Scene Aboard Ship Loaded with Wounded." Civil War Times Illustrated, V (March 1966), 48-49.

1422. Lee, Samuel P. "Letter of Rear Admiral Samuel Phillips Lee to Senator James Rood Doolittle." Contributed by Duane Moury. Publications of the Southern History Association, IX (1905), 111-122.
Concerning the naval officer's advancement.

1423. -----. Author of General Orders. See U.S. Navy Department. Mississippi Squadron., no. 2594.

1424. Lee, Stephen D. "The Campaign of Generals Grant and Sherman Against Vicksburg in December 1862, and January 1st and 2nd, 1863, Known as the 'Chickasaw Rayou Campaign.'" Publications of the Mississippi Historical Society, IV (1901), 15-36.

1425. -----. "The First Step in the War." In Robert U. Johnson and Clarence C. Buell, eds. B & L. Vol. I, pp. 74-81.

1426. -----. "The War in Mississippi After the Fall of Vicksburg." Publications of the Mississippi Historical Society, X (1909), 47-62.

1427. Leech, Margaret. Reveille in Washington, 1860-1865. New York: Harper, 1941. 483p.
Some references to the U.S. Navy.

1428. Lees, John C. Decree of His Honor, John Campbell Lees, Esquire, Judge of the Vice Admiralty Court of the Bahamas, in the Case of the British Steamship Oreto Seized for an Alleged Violation of the Foreign Enlistment Act. Nassau: Nassau Guardian, 1862. 25p.
The C.S.S. Florida; ordered out of port.

1429. Leftwick, Nina. Two Hundred Years at Muscle Shoals, Being an Authentic History of Colbert County [Alabama], 1700-1900. Tuscumbia, Ala.: The Author, 1935. 279p.
Includes the Civil War period.

1430. Leland, Waldo G. "The Kearsarge and Alabama: French Official Report, 1864." American Historical Review, XXIII (October 1917), 119-123.

1431. Leslie's Illustrated Weekly Newspaper. 13 vols.

New York: Frank Leslie, 1860-1866.
Many drawings of naval ships and battles.

1432. Lester, C. E. "The Gun-Boat Essex." Harper's New Monthly Magazine, XXVI (February 1863), 397-406.
Includes her part in the destruction of the Arkansas.

1433. Lester, William W. and William J. Bromwell, eds. A Digest of the Military and Naval Laws of the Confederate States. Columbia, S. C.: Evans and Cogswell, 1864. 329p.

1434. Letford, William and Allen W. Jones. "Military and Naval Activity in Alabama from 1861-65." Alabama Historical Quarterly, XXIII (Spring 1961), 189-206.

1435. Letters from Naval Officers in Reference to the United States Marine Corps. Washington: F. Taylor, 1864. 39p.
None in favor of abolishing the organization or converting it into an army corps.

1436. Leutze, E. H. C. "A Recollection of 1864." Navy, VII (June 1913), 234-235.

1437. Levy, Uriah P. Manuel of Internal Rules and Regulations for Men-of-War. 2nd ed. New York: D. Appleton, 1862. 70p.

1438. Lewis, Berkeley R. Notes on Ammunition of the American Civil War. Washington: American Ordnance Association, 1959. 32p.
Including naval.

1439. Lewis, Charles B. Field, Fort and Fleet.... Detroit: Free Press, 1885. 520p.

1440. Lewis, Charles L. Admiral Franklin Buchanan, Fearless Man of Action. Baltimore: Norman, Remington, 1929. 285p.

1441. -----. "The Confederate Ironclad Virginia." Southern Magazine, II (June 1935), 12-13, 48-49.

1442. -----. David Glasgow Farragut. 2 vols. Annapolis: U.S. Naval Institute, 1941-1943.

1443. -----. Famous American Naval Officers. Famous Leaders Series. Boston: Page, 1924. 374p.
Includes Farragut.

1444. -----. "Matthew Fontaine Maury." Confederate Veteran, XXXIII (January-December 1925), 296-301.

1445. -----. Matthew Fontaine Maury; the Pathfinder of the Sea. Annapolis: U.S. Naval Institute, 1927. 264p.

1446. Lewis, Mrs. Charles L. "The Marines of the Confederate States of America." United Daughters of the Confederacy Magazine, VII (January 1944), 14-15.

1447. Lewis, Gene D. Charles Ellet, Jr.: the Engineer as Individualist, 1810-1862. Urbanna: University of Illinois Press, 1968. 220p.

1448. Lewis, Lloyd. Sherman, Fighting Prophet. New York: Harcourt, Brace, 1932. 690p.
Useful coverage of the Steele's Bayou Expedition, March 1863.

1449. Lewis, Paul., pseud. See Gerson, Noel B., no. 924.

1450. Lewis, S. E. "The Confederate States Naval Academy." Confederate Veteran, XXIII (January-December 1915), 402-403.

1451. -----. "Ironclad Warships." Confederate Veteran, XXIII (January-December 1915), 315-316.

1452. Lewis, Samuel. "Life on the Monitor; a Seaman's Story of the Fight with the Merrimac; Lively Experiences Inside the Famous 'Cheezebox on a Raft.'" By Peter Truskitt, pseud. In William C. King and William P. Derby, comp. Camp-Fire Sketches and Battlefield Echoes of 61-5. Springfield, Mass.: King, Richardson, 1888. p. 257-261.

1453. Liddell Hart, B. H. Sherman: Soldier, Realist, American. New York: Dodd, Mead, 1929. 456p.

1454. [Lincoln, Abraham]. Collected Works. Edited by Roy P. Basler, Marion D. Pratt, and Lloyd A. Dunlap. 9 vols. New Brunswick, N. J.: Rutgers University Press, 1953-1955.

1455. Lincoln, Abraham., Author. See U. S. President, no. 2613.

1456. Lining, Charles. "The Cruise of the Confederate Steamship Shenandoah." Tennessee Historical Quarterly, VIII (July 1924), 102-111.

1457. Littlepage, H. B. "Career of the Merrimac." Confederate Veteran, II (January-December 1894), 86-87.

1458. -----. "The Merrimac and the Monitor." Southern Historical Society Papers, XI (1881), 32-34.

1459. -----. "Merrimac vs. Monitor: A Midshipman's Account of the Battle with the 'Cheeze Box.' " In William C. King and William P. Derby, comp. Camp-Fire Sketches and Battlefield Echoes of 61-5. Springfield, Mass.: King, Richardson, 1888. p. 335-337.

1460. Littleton, William G. The Battle Between the Alabama and the Kearsarge, off Cherbourg France, Sunday, June 19, 1864. Philadelphia: Pennsylvania Commandery, Military Order of the Loyal Legion of the United States, 1930. 19p.

1461. -----. The Cumberland, the Monitor, and the Virginia (Popularly Called the Merrimac). Philadelphia: Pennsylvania Commandery, Military Order of the Loyal Legion of the United States, 1933.

1462. Lockett, S. H. "The Defense of Vicksburg." In Robert U. Johnson and Clarence C. Buell, eds. B & L. Vol. III, pp. 482-492.

1463. Lockwood, H. C. "The Capture of Fort Fisher." Atlantic Monthly, XXVII (May-June 1871),

622-636, 684-690.

1464. Loehr, Charles T. "The Battle of Drewry's Bluff." Southern Historical Society Papers, XIX (1891), 100-111.

1465. Logan, Frenise A. "Activities of the Alabama in Asian Waters." Pacific Historical Review, XXXI (May 1962), 143-150.

1466. Logan, George W. "The Federal Gunboats and Fort Beauregard." Southern Historical Society Papers, XI (1881), 497-501.
Port Royal, S. C.

1467. Logan, John A. The Volunteer Soldier of America, with a Memoir of the Author and Military Reminiscences. Chicago: R. S. Peale, 1887. 706p.
"Military Reminiscences" cover Belmont, Forts Henry and Donelson, and Vicksburg campaigns.

1468. Long, E. B., Director of Research. See Catton, Bruce, no. 465.

1469. -----., Joint Author. See Newman, Ralph G., no. 1783.

1470. Long, John S. "The Civil War Career of Charles Wilkes." Unpublished PhD Dissertation, University of California at Los Angeles, 1952.

1471. -----. "Glory-Hunting off Havana: Wilkes and the Trent Affair." Civil War History, IX (June 1963), 133-144.

1472. -----. "The Gosport Affair." Journal of Southern History, XXIII (May 1957), 155-172.

1473. Long, Richard A. "Send Me Thirty Marines." Leatherneck, XLIV (April-May 1961), 16-21, 72; 47-53.
U. S. Marine Corps operations in the war.

1474. Lonn, Ella. "The Extent and Importance of Federal Naval Raids on Salt-Making in Florida, 1862-1865." Florida Historical Society Quarterly,

X (July 1932), 167-184.

1475. -----. Foreigners in the Confederacy. Chapel Hill: University of North Carolina Press, 1940. 566p.
Including those in the navy.

1476. -----. Foreigners in the Union Army and Navy. Baton Rouge: Louisiana State University Press, 1952. 725p.

1477. Looker, Thomas H., comp. See U.S. Congress. House. no. 2475.

1478. Lord, Daniel. The Crenshaw and Her Cargo. On Treating Property of Residents in the Seceding States as Subject to... Capture. Argument of Daniel Lord. New York: Chatterton and Parker, 1861. 40p.

1479. Lord, Franics A. "Army and Navy Textbooks Used by the North During the Civil War." Military Collector and Historian, IX (Fall-Winter 1957), 61-67, 95-102.
An annotated bibliography.

1480. -----. They Fought for the Union. Harrisburg: Stackpole, 1960. 375p.
Includes the U.S. Navy and Marines.

1481. Loring, B. W. "The Monitor Weehawken in the Rebellion." United States Naval Institute Proceedings, XII (1886), 111-121.
Under John Rogers, she captured the C.S. ram Atlanta.

1482. Lossing, Benson J. "The First Attack on Fort Fisher." In Annals of the War. p. 228-240.

1483. -----. The Story of the United States Navy. New York: Harper, 1881. 418p.
Includes the Civil War.

1484. Lott, Arnold S. A Long Line of Ships, Mare Island's Century of Naval Activity in California. Annapolis: U.S. Naval Institute, 1954. 268p.
Includes the Civil War years.

1485. -----. Most Dangerous Sea; A History of Mine Warfare and an Account of U.S. Navy Mine Warfare Operations in World War II and Korea. Annapolis: U.S. Naval Institute, 1959. 322p.
Includes Civil War "torpedoes."

1486. Loughborough, Mary Ann (Webster). My Cave Life in Vicksburg. New York: D. Appleton, 1864. 196p.
Under gunboat fire during the siege.

1487. Louisiana. General Assembly. House of Representatives. Special Report of the Committee on Naval Affairs to the House of Representatives. Baton Rouge: Bynum, 1862. 4p.
Concerning defenses of New Orleans.

1488. -----. Governor. Official Reports Relative to the Conduct of Federal Troops in Western Louisiana, During the Invasions of 1863 and 1864, Compiled from Sworn Testimony. Under the Direction of Governor Henry W. Allen. Shreveport: News Printing, 1865. 89p.

1489. Lovell, R. I. "Case for the Alabama." Queen's Quarterly, XLII (November 1935), 515-522.

1490. Low, Alfred M. Blockade and Contraband. Washington: Columbian Printing, 1916. 16pp.
Long range impact on international law of the Civil War prize cases.

1491. Lowrey, W. M. "Navigational Problems at the Mouth of the Mississippi River, 1698-1880." Unpublished PhD. Dissertation, Vanderbilt University, 1956.

1492. Loyal, Benjamin P. "Capture of the Underwriter." Southern Historical Society Papers, XXVII (1899), 136-144.

1493. Lucas, Daniel B. Memoir of John Yates Beall: His Life, Trial, Correspondence, Diary, and Private Manuscript Found Among His Papers, Including His Own Account of the Raid on Lake Erie. Montreal: J. Lovell, 1865. 297p.

1494. Luce, Stephen B. Seamanship. 3rd ed. New York: D. Van Nostrand, 1866. 663p.

1495. -----. "The Story of the Monitor." In Publications of the Military History Society of Massachusetts. 14 vols. Boston: The Society, 1895-1918. Vol. XII, pp. 127-154.

1496. Luce, Stephen Bleecher. "Stephen B. Luce, Rear Admiral U. S. Navy; Family Reminiscences by His Grandson, Stephen Bleecher Luce." Newport Historical Society Bulletin, XCII (1934), 13-28.

1496a. Lull, Edward P. Description and History of the United States Naval Academy, from its Origin to the Present Time. Annapolis: The Academy, 1869. 86p.

Including the war years at Newport.

1497. -----. History of the United States Navy-Yard at Gosport, Virginia (near Norfolk). Washington: Government Printing Office, 1874. 64p.

1498. Luvaas, Jay. "The Fall of Fort Fisher." Civil War Times Illustrated, III (August 1964), 5-9, 31-35.

1498a. -----. The Military Legacy of the Civil War: The European Inheritance. Chicago: University of Chicago Press, 1959.

1499. Lytle, Andrew N. Bedford Forrest and His Critter Company. New York: Minton, Balch, 1931. 402p.

1500. Lytle, William M., comp. Merchant Steam Vessels of the United States, 1807-1868: "The Lytle List." Publication, no. 6. Mystic, Conn.: Steamship Historical Society of America, 1952. 294p.

Extremely useful for determining the pre- and post-war employments of many naval vessels.

1501. McAuley, John. "Fort Donelson and Its Surrender." In Military Essays and Recollections; Papers Read Before the Illinois Commandery, Military Order of the Loyal Legion of the United States. 4 vols. Chicago: A. C. McClurg, 1891-1912.

Vol. I, pp. 69-74.

1502. McBlair, C. H. "Historical Sketch of the Confederate Navy." United Service, III (November 1880), 588-613; 3rd Series III (May 1903), 1155-1183.

1503. Macbride, Robert. Civil War Ironclads: the Dawn of Naval Armor. Philadelphia: Chilton, 1962. 185p.

1504. McCabe, W. Gordon. "McCabe's Impressions of the Bombardment of Charleston, 1863." South Carolina Historical Magazine, L (October 1970), 266-269.

1505. McCarten, Franics. In Peace and in War; or, Seven Years in the U.S. Navy. [Printed aboard the U.S. Flagship Tennessee, 1876-78.] 69p.
Includes summaries of the Civil War cruises of the U.S.S. Augusta and Metacomet.

1506. Macartney, Clarence E. N. Mr. Lincoln's Admirals. New York: Funk and Wagnalls, 1956. 335p.
Brief biographies of Collins, Cushing, Dahlgren, DuPont, Farragut, Foote, Fox, Porter, Welles, Winslow, and Worden.

1507. McClellan, Edwin N. "The Capture of Fort Fisher." Marine Corps Gazette, V (March 1920), 59-80.

1508. -----. "The Capture of New Orleans." Marine Corps Gazette, V (December 1920), 360-369.

1509. McClellan, George B. McClellan's Own Story: the War for the Union, the Soldiers who Fought it, the Civilians who Directed it and His Relations to it and Them. New York: Charles L. Webster, 1887. 678p.

1510. McClinton, Oliver W. "The Career of the Confederate States Ram Arkansas." Arkansas Historical Quarterly, VII (Winter 1948), 329-333.

1511. MacCord, Charles W. "Ericsson and His Monitor." North American Review, CXLIX (October 1889), 460-471.

By the inventor's one-time chief draftsman.

1512. McCordock, Robert S. The Yankee Cheezebox. Philadelphia: Dorrance, 1938. 470p.
Monitor.

1513. Maccoun, R. T. "Reminiscences of the U. S. Ship Mississippi." United Service, V (November 1881), 552-558.

1514. McCready, L. S. "The U. S. S. Hartford: Notes on a 1953 Visit to the Famous Old Veteran of the Battles of New Orleans and Mobile Bay, Then 95 Years Old." Steamboat Bill of Facts, XIII (June 1956), 39-40.

1515. McDiarmid, A. M. "American Civil War Precedents: Their Nature, Application, and Extension." American Journal of International Law, XXXIV (April 1940), 220-237.
Referring to the Yankee blockading practices.

1516. McDonald, Edward H. "Escape from a POW Boat." Civil War Times Illustrated, VI (May 1967), 45-49.
Leave-taking from a prisoner steamer sent north shortly before the fall of Vicksburg.

1517. McDonald, Joseph. "How I Saw the Monitor-Merrimac Fight." New England Magazine, New Series XXXVI, (July 1907), 548-553.
By a Yankee sailor aboard the Minnesota.

1517a. McDonough, John. "Lincoln, Welles, and the Public Service." Quarterly Journal of the Library of Congress, XXVI (October 1969), 213-216.
On the leave request of Lt. Cmdr. James W. A. Nicholson, August 1862.

1518. "McDowell." "Passing the Batteries at Port Hudson." Confederate Veteran, VI (January-December 1898), 250-251.
The destruction of the U. S. S. Mississippi.

1519. McFarland, Baxter. "A Forgotten Expedition to Pensacola in January 1861." Publications of the Mississippi Historical Society, IX (1907), 15-23.

1520. M'Gowan, J. E. "Morgan's Indiana and Ohio Raid." In Annals of the War. p. 750-769.
Federal viewpoint.

1521. McHenry, Estill, ed. See Fads, James B., no. 774.

1522. McIlwaine, Shields. Memphis Down in Dixie. New York: E. P. Dutton, 1948. 400p.
Includes the June 6, 1861 naval battle.

1523. McKean, W. V. "What the [Union] Navy has Done During the [Civil] War." United States Service Magazine, I (April 1864), 337-344.

1524. McKibben, F. P. "The Stone Fleet of 1861." New England Magazine, XVIII (June 1898), 121-125.

1525. McKay, Richard C. "A Famous Shipbuilder Acts as Peace-maker at Home and Abroad." United States Naval Institute Proceedings, LXV (October 1939), 1405-1408.
Activities of David McKay, clipper ship designer, during the war.

1526. Mackie, John F. "The Destruction of the Norfolk Navy Yard, April 21, 1861." Home and Country, IV (March-May 1889), 1011-1012, 1041, 1057-1058, 1062-1063.
By a U.S. Marine who was there.

1527. -----. "Running the Blockade--Escape of the Fox." In George M. Vickers, ed. Under Both Flags. p. 329-332.
As seen from the U.S.S. Seminole off Galveston, April 1865.

1528. Maclay, Edgar S. A History of the United States Navy from 1775-1894. 2 vols. New York: D. Appleton, 1894.

1529. -----., ed. See Trenchard, Edward., no. 2396.

1530. MacLean, G. "The Georgian Affair: an Incident in the American Civil War." Canadian Historical Review, XLII (June 1961), 133-144.
A Canadian ship schemed for by Confederates as a means of spreading terror on the Great

Lakes; no success.

1531. Maclean, Malcolm. "The Short Cruise of the C.S.S. Atlanta." Georgia Historical Quarterly, X (June 1956), 130-143.

1532. McClure, Mary L. and J. Edward Howe. History of Shreveport and Shreveport Builders. Shreveport, La.: Journal Printing, 1937. 463p.
Includes the Civil War years.

1533. McMaster, G. Trotten. "A Little Unwritten History of the Original U.S.S. Monitor." United States Naval Institute Proceedings, XXVII (December 1901), 725-732.

1534. McMaster, John B. Our House Divided; a History of the People of the United States During Lincoln's Administration. Edited by Philip Van Dorn Stern. Premier Civil War Classics. Greenwich, Conn.: Fawcett, 1961. 693p.
Reprint of the 1927 Appleton edition; still very solid with come comments on naval affairs.

1535. McMurtry, R. Gerald. "The Life and Career of John L. Worden." Lincoln Herald, LI (October 1949), 12-20, 25.

1536. -----. "Lincoln's Promotion of John L. Worden." Lincoln Lore, No. 1572 (1969), 1-3.

1537. McNaughtan, J. "The Recapture of the Emily St. Pierre." Blue Peter, XV (January 1935), 10-11.
From the prize crew of the U.S.S. James Adger.

1538. MacNeill, Ben D. The Hatterasman. Winston Salem, N.C.: John F. Blair, 1958. 276p.

1539. McNeilly, James H. "The End of the Vicksburg Campaign." Confederate Veteran, XXVIII (January-December 1920), 58-60.

1540. -----. "Under Fire at Port Hudson." Confederate Veteran, XXVII (January-December 1919), 336-339.

1541. Maffitt, Emma (Martin). "The Confederate Navy."

Confederate Veteran, XXV (January-December 1917), 157-158, 217-218, 264-265, 315-316.
By the wife of the noted Rebel sea captain, John Newland Maffitt.

1542. -----. The Life and Services of John Newland Maffitt. New York: Neale, 1906. 436p.
Draws heavily upon his correspondence.

1543. Maffitt, John Newland. "Blockade-Running." United Service, VI (June 1882), 626-633; VII (July 1882), 14-22; New Series VII (February 1892), 147-173.

1544. -----. Nautilus; or, Crusing Under Sail. New York: United States Publishing, 1872. 352p.
By the captain of C. S. S. Florida.

1545. -----. "Reminiscences of the Confederate Navy." United Service, III (October 1880), 495-514.

1546. Maffitt, Rose D. Romantic Career of a Naval Officer, Federal and Confederate: Captain John N. Maffitt of the U. S. S. Crusader and the C. S. S. Florida. Spray, N. C.: The Author, 1935. 68p.

1547. Magruder, John H. "The Wreck of the Governor." Leatherneck, XXXVIII (November 1955), 74-77.
Loss of the vessel carrying U. S. Marines to the Port Royal operation, November 1862.

1548. Magruder, P. H. "Naval Academy Practice Ships; the Era of Sail and the Square-Rigger at the Naval Academy, 1845 to 1909." United States Naval Institute Proceedings, LX (May 1934), 623-632.

1549. Mahan, Alfred T. Admiral Farragut. Great Commanders Series. New York: D. Appleton, 1892. 333p.

1550. -----. From Sail to Steam; Recollections of a Naval Life. New York: Harper, 1907. 325p.
Served with the West Gulf Coast Blockading Squadron during the war.

1551. -----. The Gulf and Inland Waters. Vol. III of The Navy in the Civil War. New York: Scribner,

1883. 267p.
Much of the data and many opinions based on correspondence with participants, e.g., Henry Walke and Isaac Brown in the matter of the Arkansas vs. Carondelet, July 1862.

1552. -----. "Minor Trials of Blockade Duty." Harper's Weekly, LI (October 26, 1907), 1556.

1553. Mahon, John K., ed. See Bacon, George B., no. 110.

1554. Mahoney, Tom. "The Sinking of the Sultana." American Legion Magazine, LXXVI (May 1965), 14-15.

1555. Maihafer, H. J. "The Partnership." United States Naval Institute Proceedings, XCIII (May 1967), 49-57.
Between Andrew Foote and U.S. Grant.

1556. Mallett, John W. "Work of the Ordnance Bureau." Southern Historical Society Papers, XXXVII (1909), 1-20.

1557. Mallory, Stephen R. "The Last Days of the Confederacy." McClure's Magazine, XVI (January 1901), 104-110.
By the Rebel Secretary of the Navy.

1558. Malone, Dumas., Joint Editor. See Johnson, Allen., no. 1281.

1559. Manarin, Louis H., comp. See North Carolina. Confederate Centennial Committee., no. 1801.

1560. Mannix, D. Pratt. The Extent and Value of the Co-operation of the Navy During our Late Civil War. N.p.; 1878. 31p.
A short naval history by a lieutenant, U.S.N.

1561. Manucy, Albert. Artillery Through the Ages. National Park Service Interpretive Series, no. 3. Washington: U.S. Government Printing Office, 1949. 92p.
Includes those of the Civil War fleets.

1562. "Mariner." pseud. *The Great Naval Battle as I Saw It, and Remarks Upon American Genius.* N. p., n. d. 16p.

Monitor and *Merrimack*.

1563. Markens, Isaac. *President Lincoln and the Case of John Y. Beall.* New York: The Author, 1911. 11p.

1564. Markland, A. H. "Names of Western Gun-boats." *Century Illustrated Magazine*, XXIX (March 1885), 779.

On the different spellings of the name for U. S. S. *Tyler*.

1565. Marshall, Edward C. *History of the United States Naval Academy, with Biographical Sketches and the Names of all the Superintendents, Professors, and Graduates.* New York: 1862. 156p.

1566. Marthon, Joseph., Joint Author. *See* Watson, J. C., no. 2702.

1567. Martin, Charles. *Personal Reminiscences of the Monitor and Merrimac Engagement and the Destruction of the Congress and the Cumberland.* New York: [Macgowan and Slipper] 1886. 8p.

1568. -----. "The Sinking of the *Congress* and *Cumberland* by the *Merrimac*." *In Personal Recollections of the War of the Rebellion; Papers Read Before the New York Commandery, Military Order of the Loyal Legion of the United States.* 4 vols. New York: The Commandery, 1891-1912. Vol. II, pp. 1-16.

1569. Martin, Charles L. "The Red River Campaign." *Confederate Veteran*, XXXIII (January-December 1925), 169-170.

1570. Martin, Christopher. *Damn the Torpedoes: the Story of America's First Admiral, David Glasgow Farragut.* New York: Abelard-Schuman, 1970. 280p.

1571. Martin, Harrison P. "When the *Monitor* Went Down."

United States Naval Institute Proceedings, LXVII (July 1941), 927-931.

1572. Martin, Isabella D., Joint Editor. See Chesnut, Mary B., no. 483.

1573. Martin, John L. "Confederate Torpedo Boats." Confederate Veteran, XXXI (January-December 1923), 93-94.

1574. Martin, Laurence W. "The Historiography of the Laird Rams." New England Social Studies Bulletin, IX (December 1951), 9-15.

1575. Martinez, Raymond J., Joint Author. See Holmes, Jack D. L., no. 1179.

1576. Marvin, David P. "The Harriet Lane." Southwest Historical Quarterly, XXXIX (July 1935), 15-20.

1577. Mason, Augustus L., ed. See Steedman, Charles, no. 2279.

1578. Mason, Edwin C. "The Army and the Navy." In Glimpses of the Nation's Struggle; a Series of Papers Read Before the Minnesota Commandery, Military Order of the Loyal Legion of the United States. 6 vols. St. Paul: St. Paul Book and Stationary, 1887-1909. Vol. II, pp. 429-436.
Stresses their co-operation.

1579. Mason, John T. "Arctic Raiders of the Civil War." All Hands, No. 512 (September 1959), 59063.
Largely the Shenandoah.

1580. -----. "The Last of the Confederate Cruisers." Century Illustrated Magazine, LVI (August 1898), 600-610.
Shenandoah.

1581. Mason, Virginia. The Public Life and Diplomatic Career of James M. Mason, with Some Personal History by Virginia Mason (His Daughter). New York: Neale, 1906. 603p.
Much on the Trent affair.

1582. Masterson, James R., comp. See U.S. National

Archives., no. 2555.

1583. "Matthew Fontaine Maury." Confederate Veteran, XXVI (January-December 1918), 54.

1584. -----. Confederate Veteran, XXII (January-December 1919), 163.

1585. "Matthew Fontaine Maury, the Pathfinder of the Seas--a Profile." Civil War Times Illustrated, II (June 1963), 10-16.

1586. Matthews, Franklin. Our Navy in Time of War. Appleton's Home Reading Books. New York: D. Appleton, 1899. 275p.
1861-1898.

1587. Maurois, André. "A Princely Service." American Heritage, SVII (April 1966), 52-54, 80-81.
The Prince de Joinville, while visiting America, remarked: "In the West, the Union armies marched from success to success thanks to the support of the navy."

1588. Maury, Dabney H. "Exploits of the Torpedo Boat St. Patrick." Southern Historical Society Papers, IX (1881), 81.

1589. -----. "How the Confederacy Changed Naval Warfare." Southern Historical Society Papers, XXII (1894), 75-81.

1590. Maury, Matthew Fontaine. Captain Maury's Letter on American Affairs. Baltimore: "The South" Office, 1862. 10p.

1591. Maury, Richard L. A Brief Sketch of the Work of Matthew Fontaine Maury During the War, 1861-1865, by his son. Richmond: Whittet and Shepperson, 1915. 36p.

1592. -----. "The First Marine Torpedoes." Southern Historical Society Papers, XXXI (1903), 326-333.

1593. "Maury, the Great American." Confederate Veteran, XXII (January-December 1919), 340.
Matthew F.

1594. May, John F. "The Positive Identification of the Body of John Wilkes Booth." In U.S. Navy Department, Naval History Division. Civil War Naval Chronology. 6 vols. Washington: U.S. Government Printing Office, 1961-1966. Vol. VI, pp. 25-28.

1595. Maynard, Douglas H. "The Confederate Super-Alabama." Civil War History, V (March 1959), 80-95.
The Texas; saw no active service.

1596. -----. "The Escape of the Florida." Pennsylvania Magazine of History and Biography, LXXVII (April 1953), 181-197.

1597. -----. "Plotting the Escape of the Alabama." Journal of Southern History, XX (May 1954), 197-209.

1598. -----. "Thomas H. Dudley and Union Efforts to Thwart Confederate Activities in Great Britain." Unpublished PhD. Dissertation, U.C.L.A., 1951.

1599. -----. "Union Efforts to Prevent the Escape of the Alabama." Mississippi Valley Historical Review, XLI (June 1954), 41-60.

1600. -----., ed. See Killgore, Gabriel M., no. 1365.

1601. Meade, Rebecca (Paulding). Life of Hiram Paulding, Rear Admiral, U.S.N. New York: Baker and Taylor, 1910. 321p.
Commander New York Navy Yard.

1602. "Medical Director Edward Shippen." United Service, New Series IV (September 1890), 323-324.
Aboard Congress when sunk by Merrimac.

1603. "Medical Officers of the Army and Navy." Confederate Veteran, IX (January-December 1900), 102.

1604. -----. Confederate Veteran, XIX (January-December 1911), 215.

1605. Meier, Walter F., ed. See Terrell, "Spot" F., no. 2355.

1606. Meigs, Montgomery C., Author of Report. See U.S. Congress. House of Representatives., no. 2468.

1607. Melton, Maurice. Confederate Ironclads. New York: Thomas Yoseloff, 1969. 319p.

1608. -----. "The First and Last Cruise of the C.S.S. Atlanta." Civil War Times Illustrated, X (November 1971), 4-10.

1609. Melville, Philip. "Carondelet Runs the Gauntlet." American Heritage, X (October 1959), 65-77.
Of Island No. 10.

1610. Melvin, Philip. "Stephen Russell Mallory, Southern Naval Statesman." Journal of Southern History, X (May 1944), 137-160.

1611. Meneely, A. H. The War Department, 1861: A Study in Mobilization and Administration. Columbia University Studies in History, Economics, and Public Law, no. 300. New York: Columbia University Press, 1928. 400p.
The Western Flotilla was built under this bureau's supervision and manned by Navy personnel.

1612. Meredith, Roy. Storm Over Sumter: the Opening Engagement of the Civil War. New York: Simon and Schuster, 1957. 214p.

1613. Meredith, William T. "Admiral Farragut's Passage of Port Hudson." In Personal Recollections of the War of the Rebellion; Papers Read Before the New York Commandery, Military Order of the Loyal Legion of the United States. 4 vols. New York: The Commandery, 1891-1912. Vol. II, pp. 118-125.

1614. -----. "Farragut's Capture of New Orleans." In Robert U. Johnson and Clarence C. Buell, eds. B & L. Vol. II, pp. 70-72.

1615. Meriwether, Colyer. Raphael Semmes. American Crises Biographies. Philadelphia: Jacobs, 1913. 367p.

1616. Meriwether, Walter S. "The Paul Jones of the Confederacy; the Brilliant but Forgotten Exploits of Captain Charles W. Read of Mississippi." Munsey's Magazine, LVIII (July 1916), 264-277.

1617. Merli, Frank J. "Crown Versus Cruiser: the Curious Case of the Alexandra." Civil War History, IX (June 1963), 167-177.
Prevented by the British government from being turned over to the Confederates.

1618. -----. "Great Britain and the Confederate Navy, 1861-65." Unpublished PhD. Dissertation, Indiana University, 1964.

1619. ----- -----. Bloomington: Indiana University Press, 1970. 342p.

1620. -----., Joint Editor. See Basoco, Richard W., no. 157.

1621. ----- , and Thomas W. Green. "Could the Laird Rams Have Lifted the Blockade?" Civil War Times Illustrated, II (April 1963), 14-17.

1622. -----, -----. "Great Britain and the Confederate Navy 1861-1865." History Today, XIV (October 1964), 687-695.

1623. Merrick, George B. Old Times on the Upper Mississippi; the Recollections of a Steamboat Pilot from 1854 to 1863. Cleveland: A. H. Clark, 1909. 323p.

1624. Merrill, James M. Battle Flags South; the Story of the Civil War Navies on Western Waters. Rutherford, N. J.: Fairleigh Dickinson University Press, 1970. 334p.

1625. -----. "The Battle for Elizabeth City, 1862." United States Naval Institute Proceedings, LXXXIII (March 1957), 321-323.
Following the capture of Roanoke Island.

1626. -----. "Confederate Shipbuilding at New Orleans." Journal of Southern History, XXVIII (February 1962), 87-94.

1627. -----. "The Hatteras Expedition." North Carolina Historical Review, XXIX (April 1952), 204-219.

1628. -----. "Men, Monotony, and Mouldy Beans--Life on Board Civil War Blockaders." American Neptune, XVI (January 1956), 49-59.

1629. -----. "Naval Operations Along the South Atlantic Coast, 1861-1865." Unpublished PhD. Dissertation, University of California at Berkeley, 1954.

1630. -----. The Rebel Shore; the Story of Union Sea Power in the Civil War. Boston: Little, Brown, 1957. 246p.

1631. -----. "Strategy Makers in the Union Navy Department, 1861-65." Mid-America, XLIV (January 1962), 19-32.

1632. -----. "Union Shipbuilding on Western Waters During the Civil War." Smithsonian Journal of History, III (Winter 1968-1969), 17-44.
Concerns naval shipbuilding.

1633. -----. "U. S. S. Weehawken--Gallant Iron Ship." United States Naval Institute Proceedings, LXXXVI (October 1960), 162-163.

1633a. -----. William Tecumseh Sherman. Chicago: Rand McNally, 1971. 445p.
Includes his co-operation with the navy during the Western campaign, 1861-1863.

1634. -----., ed. Quarterdeck and Fo'c's'le: The Exciting Story of the Navy. Chicago: Rand McNally, 1963. 509p.
Contemporary accounts; includes Civil War.

1635. -----., ed. See Porter, David D., no. 1923.

1636. "The Merrimac and the Monitor." Eclectic Magazine of Foreign Literature, Science, and Art, LVI (June 1862), 528-537.

1637. -----. Gentleman's Magazine, CCXII (May 1862), 631-635.

1638. -----. Quarterly Review, CXI (April 1862), 562-576.

1639. Mervine, Charles R. "Life on a Union Frigate: the Diary of Charles R. Mervine, 1862-1864." Pennsylvania Magazine of History and Biography, LXXI (April 1947), 121-151, 242-282.

1640. Metcalf, Clarence S. "First Iron Vessel on the Great Lakes." Inland Seas, XIII (September 1957), 24-28.
U. S. S. Michigan.

1641. Metcalf, Clyde H. A History of the U. S. Marine Corps. New York: Putnams, 1939. 584p.

1642. Meyer, Marie E. "River Towns." Palimpsest, VII (December 1926), 381-386.
Including many which saw Civil War action.

1643. Meyer, Richard and Lee C. Dickson. "Army Forces in Riverine Operations." Military Review, XLVII (August 1967), 64-74.
Includes the Civil War.

1644. -----. "The Ground-Sea Team in River Warfare." Military Review, XLVI (September 1966), 54-61.

1645. Meyer, Roland L., Jr. "Inland Shipyard Saga." Marine Engineering and Shipping Review, LI (February 1946), 127-129.
Ead's Carondelet, Missouri, boatyard.

1646. Meyers, Lewis. "Greyclad Marines." Marine Corps Gazette, XXXI (March 1947), 26-29.

1647. Michael, William H. Co-operation Between General Grant and Commodore Foote, and Between General Grant and Admiral Porter. Address of Ensign William H. Michael Delivered at the Biennial Meeting, Nineteen Hundred and Four, of Crocker's Iowa Brigade. Waterloo, Ia.: 1904. 29p.

1648. ----- -----. N. p., n. d. 40p.

1649. -----. "The Explosion of the Sultana." In Sketches and Incidents; Papers Read by Companions of the Commandery of the State of Nebraska, Military Order of the Loyal Legion of the United States. Omaha: The Commandery, 1902. p. 253-257.

One volume produced by this state.

1650. -----. "How the Mississippi Was Opened." In Sketches and Incidents; Papers Read by Companions of the Commandery of the State of Nebraska, Military Order of the Loyal Legion of the United States. Omaha: The Commandery, 1902. p. 34-58.

1651. -----. "The Mississippi Flotilla in the Civil War." In Sketches and Incidents; Papers Read by Companions of the Commandery of the State of Nebraska, Military Order of the Loyal Legion of the United States. Omaha: The Commandery, 1902. p. 21-33.

1652. Miers, Earl S. The Web of Victory: Grant at Vicksburg. New York: Alfred A. Knopf, 1955. 320p.

1653. -----., ed. See Sherman, William T., no. 2165.

1654. Miller, Francis T. and Robert S. Lanier, eds. The Photographic History of the Civil War. 10 vols. New York: Review of Reviews, 1911.

While Vol. VI concerns the navies, Vols. I and II also present naval vessels, e.g. Carondelet.

1655. Miller, M. M. "Evansville, Indiana, Steamboats During the Civil War." Indiana Historical Magazine, XXXVII (December 1941), 359-381.

1656. Miller, Marshall C. "A History of the United States Marine Corps During the Civil War Period." Unpublished M.A. Thesis, Colorado State College, 1936.

1657. Miller, Robert R. "The Camanche: First Monitor of the Pacific." California Historical Society Quarterly, XLV (June 1966), 113-124.

1658. Milligan, John D. "Charles Ellet and His Naval

Steam Ram." Civil War History, IX (June 1963), 121-133.

1659. -----. "Charles Ellet, Naval Architect: A Study in Nineteenth Century Professionalism." American Neptune, XXXI (January 1971), 52-72.

1660. -----. "The Federal Fresh Water Navy and the Opening of the Mississippi." Unpublished PhD. Dissertation, University of Michigan, 1961.

1661. -----. "The First American Ironclads: The Evolution of a Design." Missouri Historical Society Bulletin, XXII (October 1965), 3-13.
The "City Series" vessels built by Eads.

1662. -----. Gunboats Down the Mississippi. Annapolis: U.S. Naval Institute, 1965. 217p.
Takes the story to the fall of Vicksburg.

1663. -----., ed. See Browne, Henry., no. 366.

1664. -----., ed. See Stimers, Alban C., no. 2314.

1665. Millis, Walter. "The Iron Sea Elephants." American Neptune, X (January 1950), 15-32.
Federal sea-going monitors of the period.

1666. Minick, Rachel. "New York Ferryboats in the Union Navy." New York Historical Society Quarterly, XLVI (October 1962), 422-436; XLVII (April-October 1963), 173-219, 288-327, 437-462; XLVIII (January 1964), 51-80.
Histories of those converted to war-use, mostly on the blockade.

1667. Minor, Robert D. "Some Notes on the Confederate Navy." Southern Historical Society Papers, XXVIII (1900), 305-307.

1668. "The Mississippi Flotilla in the Red River Expedition." In Robert U. Johnson and Clarence C. Buell, eds. B & L. Vol. IV, p. 366.

1669. Mitcham, Howard. "Old Rodney: A Mississippi Ghost Town." Journal of Mississippi History, XV (October 1953), 242-251.

Includes the "Rodney Church Incident."

1670. Mitchell, John K. "Operations of the Confederate States Navy." Southern Historical Society Papers, II (1876), 240-244.
Particularly at New Orleans.

1671. Mitchell, Joseph B., ed. The Badge of Gallantry: Recollections of Civil War Congressional Medal of Honor Winners. New York: Macmillan, 1968. 194p.
Includes such naval enlisted men as John G. Morrison, who served aboard the Carondelet and Lafayette with such gallantry that Captain Walke recommended him.

1672. Mitchell, R. B. "Capture of the Star of the West." Confederate Veteran, XXXII (January-December 1924), 174-175.

1673. Molloy, Robert. Charleston, a Gracious Heritage. New York: D. Appleton, 1947. 311p.

1674. Monaghan, J. Jay. Diplomat in Carpet Slippers: Abraham Lincoln Deals with Foreign Affairs. Indianapolis: Charter Books, 1962. 505p.
Includes such naval crises as the Trent Affair.

1675. -----. Swamp Fox of the Confederacy: the Life and Services of M. Jeff Thompson. Confederate Centennial Studies, no. 2. Tuscaloosa, Ala.: Confederate Publishing Company, 1956. 123p.
Who often attacked Union shipping on the Western waters.

1676. Monitor, U.S.S. Officers and Crew. "Application for Bounty." Southern Historical Society Papers, XIII (1885), 90-119.

1677. "The Monitor and Merrimac." Leisure Hour, XIII (July 2, 1884), 427-429.

1678. "The Monitor and Merrimac--Ericsson." United States Naval Institute Proceedings, LIII (February 1927), 198-203.

1679. The Monitor and the Merrimack. Tales of Old Fort Monroe, no. 12. Fort Monroe, Va.: The Casemate Museum, n. d. 4p.

1680. "The Monitor Boys." Lincoln Herald, L (February 1948), 32-48.
Letters from the crew to Captain Worden.

1681. Montague, William P. "The Alabama-Kearsarge Fight." Confederate Veteran, II (January-December 1894), 140-141.

1682. Montgomery, James. "General John Morgan Would Not Leave His Men." Confederate Veteran, XIX (January-December 1911), 384.
To the mercy of U. S. S. Moose at Buffington Island.

1683. Moore, Frank., ed. Heroes and Martyrs; Notable Men of the Time. New York: Putnam, 1863. 253p.
Includes DuPont, Stringham, Welles, and Wilkes.

1684. -----. The Portrait Gallery of the War, Civil, Military, and Naval: A Biographical Record. New York: Putnam, 1864. 353p.
Many errors.

1685. -----. The Rebellion Record; a Diary of American Events, With Documents, Narratives, Illustrative Incidents, Poetry, etc. 11 vols. New York: Putnam, 1861-1863; D. Van Nostrand, 1864-1868.
A very useful source.

1686. Moore, J. C. "Missouri." In Vol. IX of Blement A. Evans, ed. Confederate Military History; a Library of Confederate States History. 12 vols. Atlanta: Confederate Publishing Company, 1899.

1687. Moore, Ross H. "The Vicksburg Campaign of 1863." Journal of Mississippi History, I (June 1939), 151-168.

1688. "Moose Chase." All Hands, No. 519 (April 1960), 59-63.

After Morgan, July 1863.

1689. Mordell, Albert. "Farragut at the Crossroads." United States Naval Institute Proceedings, LVII (February 1931), 151-161.
On his decision to remain "loyal."

1690. -----., comp. See Welles, Gideon., no. 2732.

1691. Morgan, George W. "The Assault on Chickasaw Bluffs." In Robert U. Johnson and Clarence C. Buell, eds. B & L. Vol. III, pp. 462-470.
December 1862.

1692. Morgan, Charles. "James Shedden Palmer." United States Naval Institute Proceedings, XLVI (January 1940), '31-48.

1693. Morgan, James M. "The Confederacy's Only Foreign War." Century Illustrated Magazine, LVI (August 1898), 594-600.
By a midshipman aboard the vessel involved, C. S. S. Georgia.

1694. -----. "The Confederate Cruiser Florida." United States Naval Institute Proceedings, XLII (September-October 1916), 1581-1588.

1695. -----. "The Lost Cause." Atlantic Monthly, CXIX (April 1917), 500-508.
Naval defense of the James River, 1865.

1696. -----. "A Mystery of the Seas." United States Naval Institute Proceedings, XL (June 1921), 909-915.
The whereabouts of the Shenandoah.

1697. -----. "The Pioneer Ironclad." United States Naval Institute Proceedings, XLIII (October 1917), 2275-2282.
The Manassas.

1698. -----. "A Realistic War College." United States Naval Institute Proceedings, XLII (March 1916), 543-554.
The C. S. Naval Academy aboard the Patrick Henry.

1699. -----. "A Rebel Reefer Rights the Record." Edited by Doris Hamilton. Hobbies, LXII (January 1958), 106-107.
Manassas vs. U.S.S. Richmond, 1861.

1700. -----. Recollections of a Rebel Reefer. Boston: Houghton, Mifflin, 1917. 491p.
Useful data on the C.S. Naval Academy.

1701. -----. "The St. Lawrence and the Petrel." United States Naval Institute Proceedings, XLVI (August 1920), 1219-1221.
The latter, a Rebel privateer, was sunk by the former in July 1861.

1702. Morgan, Murray C. Dixie Raider: the Saga of the C.S.S. Shenandoah. New York: E. P. Dutton, 1948. 336p.

1703. Morgan, William J. "The Virginia No Longer Exists." Iron Worker, XXIV (Summer 1960), 1-7.
Her fate after the famous battle.

1703a. [Morrissett, Algernon S.] "A Confederate Soldier's Eye-Witness Account of the 'Merrimack' Battle." Edited by Leondra D. Parish and Camillus J. Dismukes. Georgia Historical Quarterly, LIV (Fall 1970), 430-432.
Describes the sinking of the U.S. ships Cumberland and Congress, 1862.

1704. Morse, John T., ed. See Welles, Gideon., no. 2725.

1705. Morton, John W. The Artillery of Nathan Bedford Forrest's Cavalry, "the Wizard of the Saddle." Nashville: M. E. Church, 1909. 374p.
Useful coverage of his success against Union gunboats at Johnsonville in 1864.

1706. -----. "The Battle of Johnsonville." Southern Historical Society Papers, X (1882), 471-488.

1707. -----. "In Memory of the Kearsarge." In George M. Vickers, ed. Under Both Flags. p. 242-247.

1708. Moseley, Cynthia E. "The Naval Career of Henry Kennedy Stevens as Revealed in His Letters,

1839-1863." Unpublished M.A. Thesis, University of North Carolina, 1951.

1709. Moses, Armida. "The Confederate Navy." Confederate Veteran, XXVIII (January-December 1920), 181-182.

1710. Moss, James E., ed. See Cheavens, Henry M., no. 482.

1711. Moury, Duane., Contributor. See Lee, Samuel P., no. 1422.

1712. Mueller, E. A. "Early East Coast Florida Steamboating." Steamboat Bill of Facts, XVIII (Summer 1961), 35-41, 51.

Contains data on war careers of some vessels.

1713. Mullen, Jay C. "Pope's New Madrid and Island Number Ten Campaign." Missouri Historical Review, XLIX (April 1965), 325-343.

1714. -----. "The Turning of Columbus." Kentucky Historical Society Register, LXIV (July 1966), 209-225.

1715. Munden, Kenneth W., Author. See U.S. National Archives, no. 2554.

1716. Murphy, D. F. The Jeff Davis Piracy Cases. Full Report of the Trial of William Smith for Piracy, as One of the Crew of the Confederate Privateer Jeff Davis. Philadelphia: King and Baird, 1861. 100p.

1717. Murphy, John McLeod. American Ships and Shipbuilders. New York: C. W. Baker, 1860. 23p.

By the second skipper of U.S.S. Carondelet.

1718. -----. Nautical Routine and Stowage, with Short Rules in Navigation. By John M. Murphy and W. N. Jeffers. New York: D. Van Nostrand, 1864. 380p.

A standard text used by both sides.

1719. Murray, Paul, Joint Editor. See Bartlett, Stephen C., no. 152.

1720. Murray, Robert B. "The Condemnation of the C.S.S. Georgia." Georgia Historical Quarterly, LII (September 1968), 277-284.

1721. -----. "Mrs. [Elizabeth] Alexander's Cotton." Louisiana History, VI (Fall 1965), 393-400.
Captured by the navy on the Red River Expedition leading to a Supreme Court Case.

1722. Mustard, Edwin C. "The Submarine in the Revolution and Civil War." Social Studies, IIVI (May 1946), 204-210.

1723. Myers, Henry. "Cruising with the Sumter." Confederate Veteran, XXXI (January-December 1923), 452-453.

1724. Nagengast, William E. "The Visit of the Russian Fleet to the United States: Were Americans Deceived?" Russian Review, VIII (January 1949), 46-55.

1725. Nalty, Bernard. "Blue and Gray." Leatherneck, XLIII (November 1960), 54-57.
List of battles in which the two marine organizations were opponets.

1726. -----. "An Escort for Lincoln." Leatherneck, XLIV (February 1961), 78-79.
H. C. Cochran in the Gettysburg honor guard.

1727. -----. The United States Marines in the Civil War. Marine Corps Historical Reference Series, no. 2. Rev. ed. Washington: Historical Branch, U.S. Marine Corps, 1961. 16p.

1728. Narcom, James. "The Eastern Shore of North Carolina in 1861 and 1862." Historical Magazine, New Series IX (November 1870), 301-306.

1729. Nash, Howard P., Jr. "A Civil War Legend Examined." American Neptune, XXIII (July 1963), 197-203.
Thesis: Ericsson did not specifically design Monitor to battle Virginia.

1730. -----. "The C.S.S. Alabama: Roving Terror of

the Seas." Civil War Times Illustrated, II (August 1963), 5-8, 34-39.

1731. -----. "The Ignominious Stone Fleet." Civil War Times Illustrated, III (June 1964), 44-49.

1732. -----. "Ironclads, Tinclads, and Cottonclads." Tradition, III (October 1960), 6-16.

1733. -----. "Island No. 10." Civil War Times Illustrated, V (December 1966), 42-50.

1734. -----., Joint Author. See Bearss, Edwin C., no. 204.

1735. National Research Council. Committee on Undersea Warfare. An Annotated Bibliography of Submarine Technical Literature, 1557-1953. Washington: The Council, 1954. 261p.

1736. "A Naval Fight of '62. A Vivid Description of the Destructions of the Frigate Congress by the Merrimac..., Told by an Eyewitness." Quaker, V (April 1899), 84-88.

1737. Naval Historical Foundation. The Battle of Mobile Bay, 5 August 1864; Official Reports of Rear Admiral David Glasgow Farragut. Washington: The Foundation, 1964. 15p.

1738. -----. Captain Raphael Semmes and the C.S.S. Alabama. Washington: The Foundation, 1968. 26p.

1739. -----. The Navy Department: a Brief History Until 1945. Washington: The Foundation, 1970. 26p.

1740. -----. "River Navies in the Civil War." Military Affairs, XVIII (Spring 1954), 29-32.

1741. "Naval Sheet Music of the Civil War." In U.S. Navy Department, Naval History Division. Civil War Naval Chronology. 6 vols. Washington: U.S. Government Printing Office, 1961-1966. Vol. VI, pp. 111-180.

1742. "The Navy in the Defense of Washington." In U.S.

Navy Department, Naval History Division. Civil War Naval Chronology. 6 vols. Washington: U.S. Government Printing Office, 1961-1966. Vol. VI, pp. 11-24.
Including the Potomac Flotilla.

1743. Navy Times, Editors of the. They Fought Under the Sea. Washington: Army Times, 1962. 184p.
Includes a chapter "The Underwater Confederacy."

1744. Neal, Harry E. "Secret Heroine of the Civil War." Caronet, XXVI (May 1949), 148-152.
Anna E. Carroll.

1745. Neblett, Thomas R. "Major Edward C. Anderson and the C.S.S. Fingal." Georgia Historical Quarterly, LII (June 1968), 132-158.
Anderson skippered the vessel.

1746. -----. "The Yacht America: a New Account Pertaining to Her Confederate Operations." American Neptune, XXVII (October 1967), 233-253.

1747. Neeser, Robert W. "American Naval Gunnery--Past and Present." North American Review, CXCVI (December 1912), 780-791.
Includes the Civil War period.

1748. -----. "Historic Ships of the Navy--Benton." United States Naval Institute Proceedings, LII (September 1926), 1758-1764.

1749. -----. "Historic Ships of the Navy--Brooklyn." United States Naval Institute Proceedings, LIV (September 1928), 763-769.

1750. -----. "Historic Ships of the Navy--Congress." United States Naval Institute Proceedings, LXII (March 1936), 345-351.

1751. -----. "Historic Ships of the Navy--Connecticut." United States Naval Institute Proceedings, XLII (March-April 1916), 522.

1752. -----. "Historic Ships of the Navy--Cricket." United States Naval Institute Proceedings, LX

(November 1934), 1543-1544.

1753. -----. "Historic Ships of the Navy--Essex." United States Naval Institute Proceedings, LIX (December 1933), 1707-1714.

1754. -----. "Historic Ships of the Navy--Hartford." United States Naval Institute Proceedings, LIII (May 1927), 558-566.

1755. -----. "Historic Ships of the Navy--Katahdin." United States Naval Institute Proceedings, LXVII (April 1941), 509-513.

1756. -----. "Historic Ships of the Navy--Lexington." United States Naval Institute Proceedings, LII (July 1926), 1339-1349.

1757. -----. "Historic Ships of the Navy--Monadnock." United States Naval Institute Proceedings, LII (December 1926), 2451-2457.

1758. -----. "Historic Ships of the Navy--Monitor." United States Naval Institute Proceedings, LII (December 1926), 2437-2443.

1759. -----. "Historic Ships of the Navy--Montauk." United States Naval Institute Proceedings, LXVII (May 1941), 687-691.

1760. -----. "Historic Ships of the Navy--New Ironsides." United States Naval Institute Proceedings, LII (December 1926), 2443-2451.

1761. -----. "Historic Ships of the Navy--Portsmouth." United States Naval Institute Proceedings, LII (July 1926), 1349-1355.

1762. -----. "Historic Ships of the Navy--Powhatan." United States Naval Institute Proceedings, LXVI (April 1940), 496-501.

1763. -----. Statistical and Chronological History of the United States Navy, 1775-1907. 2 vols. New York: Macmillan, 1909.

1764. Neill, John H., Jr. "Shipbuilding in Confederate

New Orleans." Unpublished M.A. Thesis, Tulane University, 1940.

1765. Nelson, Thomas. Echoes and Incidents from a Gunboat Flotilla. District of Columbia Commandery, Military Order of the Loyal Legion of the United States. War Papers, no. 78. Washington: The Commandery, 1909.
The Potomac Flotilla.

1766. Ness, George T., Jr. "Louisiana Officers of the Confederate Navy." Louisiana Historical Quarterly, XXVII (April 1944), 479-486.

1767. Neuman, Frederick G. The Story of Paducah, Kentucky. Paducah: Young Printing, 1927. 104p.
Captured by Grant, with aid from the Lexington and Tyler, in September 1861.

1768. Neumann, William L. America Encounters Japan: From Perry to MacArthur. Baltimore: Johns Hopkins University Press, 1963. 353p.
Includes the Wyoming's duel with the forts.

1769. Nevins, Allan. Fremont, the West's Greatest Adventurer. 2 vols. New York: Harper, 1928.

1770. -----. The War for the Union. 8 vols. New York: Scribner, 1959-1971.

1771. New Hampshire. Governor. Official Proceedings at the Dedication of the Statue of Commodore George Hamilton Perkins at Concord, New Hampshire. Concord: Published by Order of the Governor and Council, 1903. 48p.

1772. New York. Chamber of Commerce. Proceedings on the Burning of the Ship Brilliant, by the Rebel Pirate Alabama, October 21, 1862. New York: The Chamber, 1862 22p.

1773. ----- -----. Report of the Special Committee on Testimonials to the Captain, Officers, and Crew of the United States Sloop-of-War Kearsarge. New York: The Chamber, 1865. 22p.

1774. New York City. Public Library. A Selected List

of Works Relating to Naval History, Naval Administration, etc. New York: The Library, 1904. 145p.
References to the Civil War.

1775. "New York Harbor was Defenseless." New York State and the Civil War, I (January 1962), 24-26.
Against the Virginia.

1776. "New York's Nautical Freak." New York State and the Civil War, I (January 1962), 2-15.
The Monitor.

1777. Newcomb, Mary A. Four Years of Personal Reminiscences of the War. Chicago: H. S. Mills, 1893. 131p.
A hospital worker who saw Union army and navy casualties in the Western theatre.

1778. Newcomer, Lee N. "The Battle of the Rams." American Neptune, XXV (April 1965), 128-139.
On the Mississippi in June 1862.

1779. -----. "The [Naval] Battle of Memphis." West Tennessee Historical Society Papers, XII (1958), 40-57.

1780. Newell, Isaac D., Joint Author. See Crandall, Warren D., no. 620.

1781. Newell, Robert R. "Capture and Burning of the Ship Anna F. Schmidt by Alabama." American Neptune, XXV (January 1965), 18-28.

1782. Newman, Ralph G., Joint Author. See Eisenschiml, Otoo., no. 788.

1783. -----, and E. B. Long. The Civil War Digest. New York: Grosset and Dunlap, 1960. 274p.

1784. Newsome, Edmund. Experience in the War of the Great Rebellion. Carbondale, Ill.: The Author, 1879. 137p.
By a soldier of the 81st Illinois who saw the plight of the gunboats on the Red River, 1864.

1785. [Newton, James K.] A Wisconsin Boy in Dixie: The

Selected Letters of James K. Newton. Edited by Stephen E. Ambrose. Madison: University of Wisconsin Press, 1961. 188p.

A soldier of the 14th Wisconsin who saw the defeat of the Yankee ironclads at Grand Gulf, Mississippi, in April 1863.

1786. Newton, Virginius. "The Confederate Navy." Southern Historical Society Papers, XXII (1894), 87-98.

1787. -----. The Confederate States Ram Merrimac or Virginia, Her Engagements with the United States Fleet March 8 and 9, 1862. Richmond: Hermitage, 1907. 25p.

1788. -----. "The Merrimac or Virginia." Southern Historical Society Papers, XX (1892), 1-26.

1789. Nichols, George W. "Down the Mississippi." Harper's New Monthly Magazine, XLI (November 1870), 836-845.

Useful for the flavor of the river only a few years after the conflict.

1790. Nichols, James L. The Confederate Engineers. Confederate Centennial Studies, no. 5. Tuscaloosa, Ala.: Confederate Publishing Company, 1957. 122p.

Includes their parts in building defenses to withstand Union naval attack.

1791. Nichols, Roy. "Fighting in North Carolina Waters." North Carolina Historical Review, XL (Winter 1963), 79-82.

1792. Nicolay, John G. and John Hay. Abraham Lincoln; a History. 10 vols. New York: Century, 1890.

1793. Niles, Blair. The James. Rivers of America. New York: Farrar and Rinehart, 1939. 349p.

1794. Nimitz, Chester W., Joint Author. See Potter, E. B., no. 1938.

1795. Noll, Arthur H. General Kirby Smith. Sewanee, Tenn.: Press of the University of the South,

1907. 293p.

1796. Nordhoff, Charles. "Two Weeks at Port Royal." Harper's New Monthly Magazine, XXVII (June 1863), 110-118.
Events in the spring of 1863.

1797. Norman, N. Philip. "The Red River of the South." Louisiana Historical Quarterly, XXV (April 1942), 397-535.

1798. Norrell, H. D. "Running the Blockade." Confederate Veteran, XXI (January-December 1913), 591-592.

1799. Norris, William. The Story of the Confederate States Ship Virginia (once Merrimac). Her Victory Over the Monitor. Born March 7th, Died May 10th, 1862. N. p., n. c. 25p.

1800. ----- -----. Southern Historical Society Papers, XLII (1917), 216-217.
By the Chief of the Signal Corps and Secret Service Bureau, C. S. Army, who was a witness.

1801. North Carolina. Confederate Centennial Committee. A Guide to Military Organizations and Installations, North Carolina, 1861-1865. Compiled by Louis H. Manarin. Raleigh: The Committee, 1961.
Incomplete.

1802. O'Brien, Lillian., Joint Editor. See Barnes, John S., no. 135.

1803. "Obstructing Federal Gunboats." Confederate Veteran, XXXIV (January-December 1926), 221.
Discovery of the great chain at Columbus, Ky., designed to reach across the Mississippi and hold Federal craft. This Rebel attempt, Fall 1861, did not work.

1804. O'Connell, John C., Joint Author. See Brother, Charles., no. 347.

1805. "Officially, There's a K in Merrimac." Civil War

History, VII (March 1961), 89.

1806. O'Flaherty, Daniel C. "The Blockade that Failed." American Heritage, VI (August 1955), 38-41, 104-105.

1807. Oliver, Frederick L. "The Officers of the Monitor and Merrimack." Shipmate, XXVI (August 1963), 6-7.

1808. Oliver, R. D. "The Destruction of Sea-Borne Commerce: Some Lessons of the American Civil War." Journal of the Royal United Service Institute, LXXXV (February 1938), 103-118.

1809. Olmstead, Charles H. "Reminiscences of Service in Charleston Harbor in 1863." Southern Historical Society Papers, XI (1883), 118-125, 158-171.

1810. Olmstead, Frederick L. Hospital Transports: a Memoir of the Embarkation of the Sick and Wounded from the Peninsular of Virginia in the Summer of 1862. Boston: Ticknor and Fields, 1863. 167p.

1811. O'Neill, Charles. "Engagement Between the Cumberland and Merrimack." United States Naval Institute Proceedings, XLVIII (June 1922), 863-893.

By a sailor on the Union ship who later achieved flag rank.

1812. "Operations of the Confederate States Navy." Southern Historical Society Papers, II (1876), 240-244.

1813. "The Opposing Forces in the Operations at New Orleans, La." In Robert U. Johnson and Clarence C. Buell, eds. B & L. Vol. II, pp. 73-75.

1814. [Orme, William W.] "The Civil War Letters of Brigadier General William W. Orme, 1862-1866." Edited by Harry E. Pratt. Journal of the Illinois State Historical Society, XXIII (July 1930), 246-315.

Tells of the damage caused inside Vicksburg by Union army and navy artillery as viewed after its surrender.

1815. Orth, Michael. "The C.S.S. Stonewall." Civil War Times Illustrated, V (April 1966), 44-48.

1816. Orvin, Maxwell C. In South Carolina Waters, 1861-65. Charleston: 1961. 196p.
Accounts from newspapers and local color.

1817. Osbon, Bradley S. Hand book of the United States Navy: Being a Compilation of all the Principal Events in the History of Every Vessel of the U.S. Navy. New York: D. Van Nostrand, 1864. 277p.

1818. -----. A Sailor of Fortune; Personal Memoirs of Captain B. S. Osbon. [Edited] by Albert Bigelow Paine. New York: McClure, Philips, 1906. 332p.
Osbon saw service as a signal officer aboard the Hartford; as a part-time journalist, many of his battle accounts were published in leading Northern newspapers throughout the war.

1819. -----., ed. See Holton, William C., no. 1182.

1820. Osborn, George C., ed. See Swan, Samuel., no. 2332.

1821. Osborn, P. R. "The American Monitors." United States Naval Institute Proceedings, LXIII (February 1937), 235-238.

1822. Ould, Robert. "Captain Irving and the Steamer Convoy." Southern Historical Society Papers, X (1882), 320-328.

1823. Our Cruise in the Confederate States War Steamer Alabama: the Private Journal of an Officer. London: A. Schulz [1863?] 64p.

1824. "Our Torpedo Boat." Southern Historical Society Papers, XXIX (1901), 292-295.
David.

1825. Owsley, Frank L. "America and the Freedom of the Seas, 1861-1865." In Avery Craven, ed. Essays in Honor of William E. Dodd, by His Former Students at the University of Chicago. Chicago: University of Chicago Press, 1935. p. 194-256.

1826. -----. King Cotton Diplomacy; Foregin Relations of the Confederate States of America. 2nd ed., rev. Chicago: University of Chicago Press, 1959. 614p.
Useful coverage of Southern attempts to obtain foreign-built commerce raiders and supplies via blockade running.

1827. -----. "Local Defense and the Overthrow of the Confederacy: A Study of States Rights." Mississippi Valley Historical Review, XI (March 1925), 490-525.
Nowhere better illustrated than in the lack of co-operation between Louisiana and Confederate naval forces at New Orleans in 1862.

1828. Owsley, Frank L., Jr. The C.S.S. Florida: Her Building and Operations. Philadelphia: University of Pennsylvania Press, 1965. 208p.

1829. -----. "The Capture of the C.S.S. Florida." American Neptune, XXII (January 1962), 45-54.
By Union captain Napoleon Collins in neutral Brazil.

1830. -----., Joint Editor. See Cary, Clarence., no. 457.

1831. Page, Richard L. "The Defense of Fort Morgan." In Robert U. Johnson and Clarence C. Buell, eds. B & L. Vol. IV, pp. 408-409.
Against Farragut's fleet in Mobile Bay, 1864.

1832. Page, Thomas J. "Autobiographical Sketch of Thomas Jefferson Page; Submitted by Commander R. S. Crenshaw, U.S. Navy." United States Naval Institute Proceedings, XLIX (October 1923), 1661-1691.

1833. -----. "The Career of the Confederate Cruiser Stonewall." Southern Historical Society Papers, VII (1879), 263-280.
By her skipper.

1834. Paine, Albert B., ed. See Osbon, Bradley S., no. 1818.

1835. Painter, John S., ed. See Colby, Carlos W., no. 524.

1836. Paist, Paul H. "Monitors--Ships that Changed War." United States Naval Institute Proceedings, LXXXVII (June 1961), 76-89.
A pictorial.

1837. Palfrey, John C. "Port Hudson." In Publications of the Military History Society of Massachusetts. 14 vols. Boston: The Society, 1895-1918. Vol. VIII, pp. 21-64.

1838. Palmer, Sir Roundell. A Speech Delivered in the House of Commons on the Alabama Question, March 11, 1863. London: Macmillan, 1863. 28p.

1839. -----. A Speech Delivered in the House of Commons on the North American Blockade, March 7, 1862. London: J. Ridgway, 1862. 29p.

1840. Pancake, Frank. "Matthew Fontaine Maury." Huguenot, XVI (April 1954), 110-119.

1841. Paris, Louis Philippe, Count of. History of the Civil War in America. Edited by Henry Copee. 4 vols. Philadelphia: Coates, 1875-1888.

1841a. Parish, Leondra D., jt. editor. See Morrissett, Algernon S., no. 1703a.

1842. Parker, Foxhall A. "The Battle of Mobile Bay." In Publications of the Military History Society of Massachusetts. 14 vols. Boston: The Society, 1895-1918. Vol. XII, pp. 209-244.

1843. -----. The Battle of Mobile Bay and the Capture of Forts Powell, Gaines, and Morgan. Boston: A. Williams, 1878. 136p.

1844. -----. "The Monitor and Merrimac." United States Naval Institute Proceedings, I (1874), 155-162.

1845. -----. The Naval Howitzer Afloat. New York: D. Van Nostrand, 1866. 34p.

1846. -----. The Naval Howitzer Ashore. New York: D. Van Nostrand, 1865. 64p.

1847. -----. Squadron Tactics Under Steam. New York: D. Van Nostrand, 1864. 172p.

1848. Parker, James. The Case of Captain Henry Erben, U.S.N. New York: Polkemus, 1880. 8p.
A request to be restored to his original position on the active list.

1849. -----. "The Navy in the Battles and Capture of Fort Fisher." In Personal Recollections of the War of the Rebellion; Papers Read Before the New York Commandery, Military Order of the Loyal Legion of the United States. 4 vols. New York: The Commandery, 1891-1912. Vol. II, pp. 104-117.

1850. Parker, John C. "Admiral David Dixon Porter." In War Papers and Personal Reminiscences, 1861-65; Read Before the Missouri Commandery, Military Order of the Loyal Legion of the United States. St. Louis: Bechtold, 1892. p. 434-442.

1851. -----. "A Night With Farragut." In War Papers and Personal Reminiscences, 1861-65; Read Before the Missouri Commandery, Military Order of the Loyal Legion of the United States. St. Louis: Bechtold, 1892. p. 132-145.
The passage of Port Hudson, 1863.

1852. -----. "With Farragut at Port Hudson." Civil War Times Illustrated, VII (November 1968), 42-49.

1853. Parker, Theodore H. "The Federal Gunboat Flotilla on the Western Rivers During Its Administration By the War Department to October 1, 1862." Unpublished PhD. Dissertation, University of Pittsburgh, 1938.

1854. -----. "Western Pennsylvania and the Naval War on Inland Rivers, 1861-63." Pennsylvania History,

XVI (July 1949), 221-229.

1855. -----. "William J. Kountz, Superintendent of River Transportation under McClellan, 1861-1862." Western Pennsylvania Historical Magazine, XXI (December 1938), 237-254.

1856. Parker, William H. "The Confederate States Navy." In Vol. XII of Clement A. Evans, ed. Confederate Military History; a Library of Confederate States History. 12 vols. Atlanta: Confederate Publishing Company, 1899.

1857. -----. Elements of Seamanship; Prepared as a Text for the Midshipmen of the C. S. Navy. Richmond: MacFarlane and Fergusson, 1864. 189p.

1858. -----. Instructions for Naval Light Artillery, Afloat and Ashore. Annapolis: R. F. Bonsall, 1861. 63p.

1859. ----- -----. 2nd ed., rev. by Stephen B. Luce. Newport: J. Atkinson, 1862. 120p.

1860. -----. The Merrimac and Monitor. Southern Historical Society Papers, XI (1883), 34-40.
By a witness.

1861. -----. Questions on Practical Seamanship; Together with Harbor Routine and Evolutions. Prepared for the Midshipmen of the C. S. Navy by William H. Parker, Commanding the C. S. School-Ship Patrick Henry. Richmond: Macfarlane and Fergusson, 1863. 92p.

1862. -----. Recollections of a Naval Officer, 1841-65. New York: Scribners, 1883. 372p.

1863. Parks, Joseph H. "A Confederate Trade Center Under Federal Occupation: Memphis, 1862 to 1865." Journal of Southern History, VII (August 1941), 289-314.
Captured by the Western Flotilla, June 1862.

1864. -----. General Edmund Kirby-Smith, C. S. A. Baton Rouge: Louisiana State University Press, 1954.

537p.
Includes a good sketch of the Red River Campaign.

1865. -----. General Leonidas Polk, the Fighting Bishop. Baton Rouge: Louisiana State University Press, 1962. 408p.

1866. -----. "Memphis Under Military Rule, 1862 to 1865." East Tennessee Historical Society Publication, XIV (1942), 31-58.

1867. Parks, W. M. "Building a Warship in the Southern Confederacy." United States Naval Institute Proceedings, XLIX (August 1923), 1299-1307.
Including the many difficulties of materials.

1868. Parrott, Enoch G. Description and Cruise of the U.S.S. Augusta. New York: McCarten, 1876.

1869. Parson, Lewis B., Author of Report. See U.S. War Department. Quartermaster Department., no. 2625.

1870. Partin, Robert., ed. See Powers, J. W., no. 1944.

1871. Partin, Robert L., ed. "Confederate Sergeant's Report to His Wife During the Bombardment of Fort Pillow." Tennessee Historical Quarterly, XV (September 1956), 243-252.

1872. Patriotic League of the Revolution. Memorial to the Fifty-Seventh Congress of the United States for the Recognition of the Services Rendered by Theodore R. Timby, the Inventor of the Revolving Turret as Used on the Monitor and all Battleships from the Civil War to the Present Time. Brooklyn: Eagle Press, 1902. 28p.

1873. Patterson, H. K. W. War Memories of Fort Monroe and Vicinity. Containing an Account of the Memorable Battle Between the Merrimac and Monitor, the Incarceration of Jefferson Davis, and Other Topics. Fort Monroe, Va.: Pool and Deuschle, 1885. 102p.

1874. Paullin, Charles O. American Voyages to the Orient,

1690-1865. Annapolis: U.S. Naval Institute, 1970. 182p.

1875. -----. Paullin's History of Naval Administration, 1775-1911; a Collection of Articles from the United States Naval Institute Proceedings. Annapolis: U.S. Naval Institute, 1968. 485p.

1876. -----. "President Lincoln and the Navy." American Historical Review, XIV (January 1909), 284-303.

1877. Payne, Peter and Frank J. Merli. "A Blockade Running Chapter, Spring 1862." American Neptune, XXVI (April 1966), 134-137.
For the steamer Memphis.

1878. Pearce, Charles E. "The Expeditions Against Fort Fisher." In War Papers and Reminiscences; Read Before the Missouri Commandery, Military Order of the Loyal Legion of the United States. St. Louis: Bechtold, 1892. p. 354-381.

1879. Pearsall, Uri B., comp. The Official Reports of Building the "Red River Dam" at Alexandria, La., May 1864, Which Saved the Mississippi Flotilla, Under Admiral Porter, from Destruction. From ...the "History of the Union and Confederate Armies" Published by the War Department. Lansing, Kansas: The Compiler, 1896. 14p.

1880. Peck, Taylor. Round-Shot to Rockets. Annapolis: U.S. Naval Institute, 1949. 267p.
History of the Washington Navy Yard; includes the Civil War years.

1881. Peck, W. F. G. "Four Years Under Fire at Chaleston." Harper's New Monthly Magazine, XXXI (August 1865), 358-366.

1882. Pegram, John C. Recollections of the United States Naval Academy During the Civil War. Personal Narratives of Events in the War of the Rebellion, Being Papers Read Before the Rhode Island Soldiers and Sailors Historical Society. 4th Series, no. 14. Providence: N. B. Williams, 1891.

1883. Pegram, Robert B. "The Cruise of the C.S.S.

Nashville: the Report of Lt. Robert B. Pegram." Virginia Magazine of History and Biography, LXVI (July 1958), 345-350.

1884. -----., Author of Report. See C. S. Congress., no. 553.

1885. Pemberton, John C. Pemberton, Defender of Vicksburg. Chapel Hill: University of North Carolina Press, 1942. 350p.

1886. Pemberton, John C., Author of Report. See C. S. Army. Department of Mississippi and East Louisiana., no. 546.

1887. Penton, Henry. "The U. S. S. Michigan, Now Called Wolverine." Society of Naval Architects and Marine Engineers Proceedings, XVI (1908), 8-12.

1888. Perkins, George H. Letters of Captain Geo. Hamilton Perkins, U. S. N. Edited and arranged [by Susan G. Perkins.] Also a Sketch of His Life, by Commodore George E. Belknap, U. S. N. Concord, N. H.: I. C. Evans, 1886. 257p.

1889. Perkins, Susan G., ed. See Perkins, George H., no. 1888.

1890. Perry, Milton F. Infernal Machines; the Story of Confederate Submarine and Mine Warfare. Baton Rouge: Louisiana State University Press, 1965. 230p.

1891. Peters, Thelma. "Blockade Running in the Bahamas During the Civil War." Tequesta: Journal of the Historical Association of Southern Florida. V (1945), 16-30.

1892. Peterson, Clarence S. Admiral John A. Dahlgren, Father of U. S. Naval Ordnance. New York: Hobson, 1945. 92p.

1893. Peterson, Harold L. Notes on Ordnance of the American Civil War. Washington: American Ordnance Association, 1959. 20p.
Includes naval cannon.

1894. Philadelphia. Board of Trade. Statements Relating to a Navy Yard in the Delaware, for the Construction and Equipment of Iron-clad Steamships of War, Proposed to be Established at League Island. Philadelphia: Collins, 1862. 27p.

1895. Phillimore, John G. Case of the Seizure of the Southern Envoys. Reprinted, with Additions, from the "Saturday Review." London: J. Ridgway, 1861. 26p.
The Trent Affair.

1896. Phillips, Dinwiddie B. "The Career of the Iron-Clad Virginia (Formerly the Merrimac), Confederate States Navy, March-May, 1862." Collections of the Virginia Historical Society, New Series VI (1887), 193-231.

1897. -----. "The Career of the Merrimac." Southern Bivouac, V (March 1887), 598-608.

1898. -----. "Notes on the Monitor-Merrimac Fight." In Robert U. Johnson and Clarence C. Buell, eds. B & L. Vol. I, p. 718.

1899. Phister, George. New York in the War of the Rebellion. 5 vols. Albany: L. B. Lyon, 1912.
Includes naval episodes and personnel.

1900. Piers, Charles. "The Sunflower Expedition: Vicksburg, March 1863." Army Quarterly, XI (January 1926), 395-399.
Porter and Sherman in Steele's Bayou.

1901. Pirtle, John B. "The Defence of Vicksburg in 1862 and the Battle of Baton Rouge." Southern Historical Society Papers, VIII (1880), 324-332.
The last run of the Arkansas.

1902. Pitkin, William A. "When Cairo was Saved for the Union." Illinois State Historical Society Journal, LI (Autumn 1958), 284-305.
Stresses the value of the town to the North, a value later realized in the location there of the base for the Mississippi Squadron.

1903. Pitzman, Julius. "Vicksburg Campaign Reminiscences."

Military Engineer, XV (March 1923), 112-115.

1904. Plummer, E. C. "Running the Gauntlet." New England Magazine, XIV (May 1896), 282-285.
Also known as the "Yankee Blockade."

1905. Plummer, Leonard B., ed. See Hander, Christian W., no. 1054.

1906. Polk, Leonidas. General Polk's Report of the Battle of Belmont. Columbus, Ky.: 1861. 8p.

1907. Polk, William M. "General Polk and the Battle of Belmont." In Robert U. Johnson and Clarence C. Buell, eds. B & L. Vol. I, pp. 348-357.

1908. -----. Leonidas Polk, Bishop and General. 2 vols. New York: Longmans, Green, 1893.

1909. Pollard, Edward A. The First Year of the War. Richmond: West and Johnston, 1862. 406p.

1910. -----. The Second Year of the War. Richmond: West and Johnston, 1863. 326p.

1911. -----. Southern History of the War: the Third Year of the War. New York: C. B. Richardson, 1865. 391p.

1912. -----. Southern History of the War: The Last Year of the War. New York: C. B. Richardson, 1866. 363p.
Pollard includes naval events.

1913. Polley, J. B. "The Gunboat General Taylor Failed to Get." Confederate Veteran, XV (January-December 1907), 281-232.
An unsuccessful plot to deliver one of the Yankee ironclads to "Dick" Taylor, January 1865.

1914. Pomeroy, Earl S. "The Myth After the Russian Fleet, 1863." New York History, XXXI (April 1950), 169-176.

1915. Poolman, Kenneth. The Alabama Incident. London: W. Kimber, 1958. 203p.

Her "escape" and ravages on Union commerce.

1916. Poor, Charles H. Defense of Lt. Cmdr. Charles H. Poor Before the General Court Martial Assembled at Washington, November 18, 1861. Washington: H. Polkinhorn [1861?] 12p.

While in command of the Brooklyn off New Orleans, Poor allowed the Sumter to escape to sea.

1917. Pope, Jennie B., Joint Author. See Albion, Robert G., no. 41.

1918. Pope, R. P. "Coast Defense Service." Confederate Veteran, XXXIII (January-December 1925), 263-264.

1919. Porter, David Dixon. Answer to Misrepresentations. Washington: Chronicle Publishing, 1872. 28p.

On Butler's charges of cowardice.

1920. -----. "A Famous Naval Exploit." North American Review, CXLIX (September 1891), 296-303.

Cushing and the Albemarle.

1921. -----. "The Federal Ironclads and Monitors in Action." Nautical Magazine, (March 1865), 165-168.

At Fort Fisher.

1922. -----. "First Meeting with Sherman." Magazine of American History, XXV (January-June 1891), 298-300.

1923. -----. "The Fort Fisher and Wilmington Campaign: Letters from Rear Admiral David Dixon Porter." Edited by James M. Merrill. North Carolina Historical Review, XXXV (October 1958), 461-475.

1924. -----. Incidents and Anecdotes of the Civil War. New York: D. Appleton, 1885. 357p.

1925. -----. The Naval History of the Civil War. Illustrated from Original Sketches Made by Rear Admiral [Henry] Walke and Others. New York: Sherman, 1886. 843p.

Slim on those events in which he did not participate.

1926. -----. "The Opening of the Lower Mississippi." In Robert U. Johnson and Clarence C. Buell, eds. B & L. Vol. II, pp. 22-55.

1927. -----. "Our Navy." United Service, I (January 1879), 1-9.

1928. -----., Author of General Orders. See U.S. Navy Department. Mississippi Squadron., no. 2593.

1929. Porter, J. D. Tennessee. Vol. VIII of Blement A. Evans, ed. Confederate Military History; a Library of Confederate States History. 12 vols. Atlanta: Confederate Publishing Company, 1899.

1930. Porter, John W. H. "The Confederate States Navy and a Brief History of What Became of It." Southern Historical Society Papers, XXVIII (1900), 125-134.

1931. -----. "Origin of an Ironclad: How the Merrimac Came to be Transformed--the Original Plans Still in Existence." Confederate Veteran, XXIII (January-December 1915), 219-220.

Gives the credit for the idea to his father, John L. Porter.

1932. -----. A Record of Events in Norfolk County, Virginia, from April 19th, 1861, to May 10th, 1862, with a History of the Soldiers and Sailors of Norfolk County, Norfolk City and Portsmouth, who Served in the Confederate States Army or Navy. Portsmouth, Va.: W. A. Fiske, 1892. 366p.

Largely a history of the Virginia.

1933. -----., Joint Author. See Brooke, John M., no. 344.

1934. Porter, Thomas K. "Capture of the Confederate Steamer Florida." Southern Historical Society Papers, XII (1884), 39-45.

1935. Porter, William D. Defense of Commodore W. D.

Porter Before the Naval Retiring Board, Convened at Brooklyn Navy Yard, November 1863. New York: J. A. Gray and Green, 1863. 18p.

1936. -----. and J. L. Jones. Plate Armor Impenetrable to Shot. Washington: The Authors, 1863.

1937. Post, Charles A. "A Diary on the Blockade in 1863." United States Naval Institute Proceedings, XLIV (October-November 1918), 2333-2350, 2567-2594.

Off Wilmington, N. C., aboard the U. S. S. Florida.

1938. Potter, E[lmer] B. and Chester W. Nimitz. Sea Power: a Naval History. Englewood Cliffs, N. J.: Prentice Hall, 1960. 932p.

Includes the Civil War.

1939. Powell, Samuel W. "Blockading Memories of the [West] Gulf [Coast Blockading] Squadron." Magazine of History, VIII (July 1908), 1-11.

1940. Powell, William Henry, ed. Officers of the Army and Navy (Volunteer) Who Served in the Civil War. Philadelphia: L. R. Hamersly, 1893. 419p.

1941. -----. Officers of the Army and Navy (Regular) Who Served in the Civil War. Edited by William H. Powell and Edward Shippen. Philadelphia: L. R. Hamersly, 1892. 487p.

Only Union officers are included.

1942. Powell, William T. "Some Early History Regarding the Double-Turreted Monitors Minatonomah and Class. Society of Naval Architects and Marine Engineers Transactions, XV (1907), 205-210.

Fate of the vessels laid down during the war.

1943. Powells, James M. "The Hunley Sinks the Housatonic." Navy, VIII (January 1965), 23-25.

1944. [Powers, J. Wesley.] "Report of a Corporal of the Alabama First Infantry on Talk and Fighting Along the Mississippi, 1862-63." Edited by Robert Partin. Alabama Historical Quarterly,

XX (October 1958), 583-594.

1945. [Pratt, Albert H.] Search for Fortune Along the Mississippi: The Pratt Letters, 1860-61." Edited by Dorothy J. Ernst. Mid-America, XLII (January 1960), 44-52.

1946. Pratt, Fletcher. The Civil War on Western Waters. New York: Holt, 1958. 255p.
The exploits of the gunboats.

1947. -----. "The Man Who Got There First." Military Engineer, XL (April-May 1948), 149-153, 207-211.
General James H. Wilson and the Red River Dam.

1948. -----. The Navy: The Story of a Service in Action. New York: Garden City Publishing, 1941. 496p.
Includes the Civil War.

1949. -----. A Short History of the Civil War. Rev. ed. New York: W. Sloane, 1948. 426p.
Includes the navies.

1950. -----. "Starvation Blockade." American Mercury, XXXVI (November 1935), 334-342.

1951. Pratt, Harry E., ed. See Orme, William W., no. 1814.

1952. Pratt, Julius W. "Naval Operations on the Virginia Rivers in the Civil War." United States Naval Institute Proceedings, XLV (February 1919), 185-195.

1953. Pratt, Marion D., Joint Editor. See Lincoln, Abraham., no. 1454.

1954. Pray, May M. (Brewer). Dick Dowling's Battle; an Account of the War Between the States in the Eastern Gulf Coast Region of Texas. San Antonio: Naylor, 1936. 143p.
Battle of Sabine Pass.

1955. Preble, George H. The Chase of the Rebel Steamer Oreto, Commander J. N. Maffitt, C.S.N., into the Bay of Mobile, by the United States Steam Sloop Oneida, Commander Geo. Henry Preble, U. S. N., September 4, 1862. Cambridge: Priv. Print., 1862. 60p.

Useful and unusual details on the unsuccessful pursuit of the unarmed C. S. S. Florida.

1956. -----. Henry Knox Thatcher, Rear Admiral U. S. Navy. Boston: Williams, 1882. 20p.

Last commander of the West Gulf Coast Blockading Squadron.

1957. -----. History of the United States Navy Yard, Portsmouth, N. H. Washington: Government Printing Office, 1892. 219p.

1958. -----. Memorial of Captain Geo. Henry Preble, U. S. N., to the Forty Third Congress; with an Appendix Containing the Action of Congress and Extracts from Congratulatory Letters. Boston: D. Clapp, 1874. 50p.

A petition for promotion to the rank of commodore and a defense of the Florida's escape into Mobile in 1862.

1959. -----. "Notes for a History of Steam Navigation." United Service, VI (May 1882), 555-560.

Includes data on the Monitor.

1960. -----. "Notes on Early Shipbuilding in Massachusetts. Vessels of War Built in and about Boston, Mass. from 1778 to 1872, Inclusively; also, Vessels Purchased in Boston for the U. S. Navy Department from 1861 to 1871, Inclusive." New England Historical and Genealogical Register, XXVI (July 1872), 37-50.

1961. -----. "Rear Admiral John Adolphus Dahlgren, U. S. N." United Service, VIII (January 1883), 67-86.

1962. -----. "Ships of the 19th Century." United Service, X (August 1884), 130-137.

Includes the Merrimack.

1963. -----. Vessels of War Built at Portsmouth, New Hampshire, 1690-1868. Boston: The Author,

1868. 10p.

1964. -----., Author. See U.S. Treasury Department, no. 2620.

1965. Prence, Katherine. "The Confederate Mines--1862-1865." Magazine of History, IX (January 1909), 13-16.

1966. Prentice, E. Parmalee. "An American Battle in Foreign Waters." Harper's Monthly Magazine, CXXI (November 1910), 873-88-.

The Alabama and the Kearsarge.

1967. Preston, Anthony. "The Raider that Never Made it." United States Naval Institute Proceedings, XCIV (March 1968), 140-141.

The C.S.S. Rappahannock.

1968. Preston, Francis W. Port Hudson: a History of the Investment, Siege, and Capture. Brooklyn: The Author, 1892. 71p.

1969. Preston, Robert L. "Did the Monitor or Merrimac Revolutionize Naval Warfare? William & Mary Quarterly, XXIV (July 1915), 58-66.

Verdict: the Merrimac was guilty; the Monitor, innocent.

1970. Preu, James A. "The First Phase of Naval Action Against Mobile." Florida State University Studies, XIV (1954), 41-69.

1971. Price, Charles L. and Claude C. Sturgill. "Shock and Assault in the First Battle of Fort Fisher." North Carolina Historical Review, XLVII (Winter 1970), 24-39.

December 1864.

1972. Price, Marcus W. "Blockade Running as a Business in South Carolina During the War Between the States, 1861-1865." American Neptune, IX (January 1949), 31-62.

1973. -----. "Four From Bristol." American Neptune, XVII (October 1957), 249-261.

The blockade runners Calypso, Juno, Flora,

and Old Dominion.

1974. -----. "Masters and Pilots Who Tested the Blockade of the Confederate Ports, 1861-1865." American Neptune, XXI (April 1961), 81-106.
Officer lists.

1975. -----. "Ships that Tested the Blockade of the Carolina Ports, 1861-1865." American Neptune, VIII (April 1948), 196-241.

1976. -----. "Ships that Tested the Blockade of the Georgia and East Florida Ports, 1861-1865." American Neptune, XV (April 1955), 97-132.

1977. -----. "Ships that Tested the Blockade of the Gulf Ports, 1861-1865." American Neptune, XI (October 1951), 262-290; XII (January-July 1952), 52-59, 154-161, 229-238.

1978. Prinz, Andrew K., Joint Editor. See Gardner, Henry R., no. 911.

1979. [Pryor, J. P. and Thomas Jordan.] Gunboats and Cavalry; the Story of Forrest's 1864 Johnsonville Campaign, as told by J. P. Pryor and Thomas Jordan. Edited by E. F. Williams and H. K. Humphreys. Memphis: Nathan Bedford Forrest Trail Committee, 1965. 24p.

1980. Puleston, William D. Mahan: the Life and Works of Captain Alfred T. Mahan, U.S.N. New Haven: Yale University Press, 1939. 380p.

1981. Pullar, Walter S. "Abe Lincoln's Brown Water Navy." Naval War College Review, XXI (April 1969), 71-88.
Emphasis on the over-all strategy of the Federals on the Western rivers.

1982. Purifoy, John. "Capture and Destruction of the Queen City." Confederate Veteran, XXXII (January-December 1924), 178-179.
In the White River, June 1864.

1983. Quarles, Benjamin. "The Abduction of the Planter." Civil War History, IV (March 1958), 5-10.

1984. -----. *The Negro in the Civil War*. Boston: Little Brown, 1953. 379p.
Many saw service afloat, particularly aboard Federal vessels.

1985. Rae, Thomas W. "The Little *Monitor* Saved our Lives." *American History Illustrated*, I (July 1966), 32-39.
Letter by the 3rd Assistant Engineer aboard U. S. S. *Minnesota*.

1986. Rains, Gabriel J. "Torpedoes." *Southern Historical Society Papers*, III (1877), 255-260.

1987. Rains, George W. *History of the Confederate Powder Works*. Augusta, Ga.: Chronicle and Constitutional Printing, 1882. 30p.
A powder mill moved to New Orleans in December 1861.

1988. Ramsay, Frank H. "Confederate Marines." *Leatherneck*, XXXVIII (November 1955), 38-39.

1989. Ramsay, H. Ashton. "Most Famous of Sea Duels: the *Merrimac* and *Monitor*." *Harper's Weekly*, LVI (February 10, 1912), 11-12.

1990. -----. "Wonderful Career of the *Merrimac*." *Confederate Veteran*, XV (January-December 1907), 310-313.

1991. -----., Joint Author. *See* Worden, John L., no. 2828.

1992. Randall, James G. *Lincoln the President*. 4 vols. New York: Dodd, Mead, 1945-1955.
Includes his relations with the navy and particularly Gideon Welles.

1993. -----. and David Donald. *The Civil War and Reconstruction*. 2nd ed., rev. Lexington, Mass.: Heath, 1969. 866p.

1994. Rankin, Robert H. "The Saga of the Ill-Starred U. S. S. *Keokuk*." *Our Navy*, LV (January 1960), 11-12.

1995. -----. "The Story of the First Idaho." United States Naval Institute Proceedings, LXXXVI (June 1960), 173-174.
Launched in 1864 as a Union counter to the Alabama.

1996. -----. "U. S. S. Dunderberg--Old Thundering Mountain." United States Naval Institute Proceedings, LXXXVI (November 1960), 158-159.

1997. -----., ed. See Blades, Henry S., no. 270.

1998. -----., ed. See Weimer, John., no. 2179.

1999. Ranson, George M. "Some Incidents of the Passing of Forts Jackson and St. Philip." United Service, II (May 1880), 608-612.
By the commander of the U. S. S. Kineo.

2000. Ranson, Thomas. "The Monitor and Merrimac at Hampton Raods." Edited by Doris H. Hamilton. Hobbies, LXIV (September 1959), 110-111, 119.
Letter from a soldier posted at Hampton Roads.

2001. "Raphael Semmes." Confederate Veteran, XXIV (January-December 1916), 374.

2002. -----. Confederate Veteran, XXX (January-December 1922), 178.

2003. -----. In Gamaliel Bradford. Confederate Portraits. Boston: Houghton, Mifflin, 1914. p. 219-246.

2004. Ratliff, Mary. "The City of Vicksburg." Confederate Veteran, XXXVI (January-December 1927), 385, 398.

2005. Rawson, Edward K. Twenty Famous Naval Battles. 2 vols. New York: Thomas Y. Crowell, 1900.
Includes Monitor and Merrimac, Alabama and Kearsarge, and Mobile Bay.

2006. Read, Charles W. "Reminiscences of the Confederate States Navy." Southern Historical Society Papers, I (1876), 333-362.
Basic to any study of his exploits.

2007. Reaney, Henry. "How the Gunboat Zouave Aided the Congress." In Robert U. Johnson and Clarence C. Buell, eds. B & L. Vol. I, p. 714.
Against the Merrimac; by a Master's Mate aboard the Zouave.

2008. -----. "The Monitor and Merrimac." In War Papers; Read Before the Commandery of the State of Michigan, Military Order of the Loyal Legion of the United States. 2 vols. Detroit: J. H. Stone, 1893-1898. Vol. II, pp. 167-172.

2009. "Rear Admiral Henry Walke, U. S. N." United Service, New Series VII (March 1898), 319-320.

2010. Rear Admiral John Rogers, United States Navy, Chairman of the Lighthouse Board, 1878-1882. Washington: Government Printing Office, 1882. 13p.

2011. The Rebel Pirates' Fatal Prize; or, the Bloody Tragedy of the Prize Schooner Waring Enacted as the Rebels were Attempting to Run Her into Charleston, S. C., July 7, 1861. By a Passenger on the Waring and an Eye-witness to the Bloody Scenes. Philadelphia: Reechner, 1862. 46p.
Fate of a capture of the privateer Jeff Davis.

2012. "Reconstruction of Farragut's Flagship, the U. S. S. Hartford." Scientific American, LXXXII (January 27, 1900), 53-54.

2013. "The Red River Campaign." United States Service Magazine, II (November 1864), 417-431.
Includes the role of the Yankee navy.

2014. Redmond, R. A. "The Revenue Steamer E. A. Stevens in the Civil War." American Neptune, XX (July 1960), 155-166.

2015. Reed, Samuel W. The Vicksburg Campaign, and the Battles about Chattanooga Under the Command of General U. S. Grant, in 1862-63; an Historical Review. Cincinnati: R. Clarke, 1882. 201p.

2016. Reingold, Nathan. "Science in the Civil War: the Permanent Commission of the Navy Department."

ISIS, XLIX (September 1958), 307-318.

2017. -----., comp. See U.S. National Archives., no. 2559.

2018. [Remington, Ambert O.] "The Occupation of Southeast Louisiana: Impressions of a New York Volunteer, 1862-63." Edited by L. Moody Sims, Jr. Louisiana Studies, VII (Spring 1968), 83-91.

2019. Remington, Jesse A. "The Brown's Ferry 'Cracker Line,' 1863." Military Engineer, LV (January-February 1963), 22-23.

2020. Rentfrow, Frank H. "An Incident at Fort Fisher." Leatherneck, XXI (November 1938), 10-11.
How Pvt. Henry Wasmuth saved the life of Ensign, later Admiral, Robley D. Evans.

2021. -----. "On to Richmond." Leatherneck, XXII (January 1939), 10-11, 52.
An account of the U.S. Marines aboard the Galena during the 1862 Drewry's Bluff fight.

2022. -----. "We Fight Our Country's Battles." Leatherneck, XIII (February 1930), 4-5.
U.S. Marines at Fort Fisher, 1864-1865.

2023. Rerick, Rowland H. Memoirs of Florida. Edited by Francis P. Fleming. 2 vols. Augusta, Ga.: Southern Historical Association, 1902.

2024. Reynolds, Donald E., Joint Author. See Scroggs, Jack B., no. 2133.

2025. Reynolds, John G. Defence of Lt. Cd. Jno. Geo. Reynolds, U.S. Marine Corps, Before the Naval Court-Martial, Convened in Washington, May 7, 1862. Washington: H. Polkinhorn, 1862. 21p.

2026. -----. Proceedings of a Marine Court-Martial at Washington City, May 7, 1862, for the Trial of Lt. Cd. John George Reynolds, U.S. Marine Corps, Upon the Charges of "Drunkeness" and "Treating with Contempt His Superior, Being in the Execution of His Office." Washington: H. Polkinhorn, 1862. 86p.

Reynolds was aboard the Governor enroute to Port Royal in 1861 when she sank.

2027. Rhind, A. C. "The Last of the Fort Fisher Powder Boat." United Service, I (April 1879), 227-236.
U. S. S. Louisiana, purposely detonated in an attempt to soften up the post--a failure.

2028. Rhodes, James F. History of the Civil War, 1861-1865. New York: Macmillan, 1917. 454p.

2029. Rich, Joseph W. "The Battle of Shiloh." Iowa Journal of History and Politics, VII (October 1909), 503-581.
Includes the role of the Union gunboats.

2030. Richardson, Albert D. The Secret Service, the Field, the Dungeon, and the Escape. Hartford: American Publishing, 1866. 512p.
Another journalist viewing extensive Yankee gunboat activity in the West.

2031. Riley, Elihu S. "The Passing of the U. S. S. Santee." Navy, VII (March 1913), 100-101.

2032. Riley, Frank L. "Extinct Towns and Villages of Mississippi." Publications of the Mississippi Historical Society, V (1902), 311-383.
Includes such missing places as Grand Gulf.

2033. [Ringgold, Coldwater.] "A Cruise on the U. S. S. Sabine." Edited by James N. Henwood. American Neptune, XXIX (April 1969), 102-105.
In search of the Alabama.

2034. Ripley, C. Peter. "Prelude to Donelson: Grant's January, 1862, March into Kentucky." Kentucky Historical Society Register, LIV (October 1970), 311-318.

2035. Ripley, Warren. Artillery and Ammunition of the Civil War. New York: Van Nostrand Reinhold, 1970. 384p.
Includes naval ordnance.

2036. Ritter, William L. "Incident of the Deer Creek Expedition." Southern Historical Society Papers,

IX (1881), 280-281.
Also known as the Steele's Bayou Campaign.

2037. -----. "Letter [Giving Additional Information Concerning the Capture of the Indianola.] Southern Historical Society Papers, I (1876), 362-363.

2038. -----. "Operations of the 3d Maryland Battery on the Mississippi in 1863." Southern Historical Society Papers, VII (1879), 247-249.

2039. Roberts, A. Sellew. "High Prices and the Blockade in the Confederacy." South Atlantic Quarterly, XXIV (April 1925), 154-163.

2040. Roberts, Captain., pseud. See Hobart-Hampden, Augustus C., no. 1156.

2041. Roberts, E. E. "How Mosquitoes Prevented the Capture of Farragut." Southern Historical Society Papers, XXXV (1907), 174-175.

2042. Roberts, Elliot B., Joint Author. See U.S. Coast and Geodetic Survey., no. 2437.

2043. Roberts, John C. and Richard H. Webber. "Gunboats in the River War, 1861-1865." United States Naval Institute Proceedings, XCI (March 1965), 83-100.
A pictorial.

2044. -----., Joint Author. See Webber, Richard H., no. 2709.

2045. Roberts, Walter A. Semmes of the Alabama. Indianapolis: Bobbs-Merrill, 1938. 320p.

2046. Robertson, James I., Jr. Author. See U.S. Civil War Centennial Commission., no. 2436.

2047. -----., ed. See Glazier, James E., no. 948.

2048. Robertson, William B. "The Water-battery at Fort Jackson." In Robert U. Johnson and Clarence C. Buell, eds. B & L. Vol. II, pp. 99-100.

2049. Robinson, George H. "Recollections of Ericsson."

United Service, New Series XIII (January 1895), 10-26.

2050. Robinson, R. H. "The Boston Economy During the Civil War." Unpublished PhD. Dissertation, Harvard University, 1958.

2051. Robinson, William M., Jr. "The Alabama-Kearsarge Battle; a Study in Original Sources." Essex Institute Historical Collections, LX (April-July 1924), 97-120, 209-218.

2052. -----. The Confederate Privateers. New Haven: Yale University Press, 1928. 372p.

2053. -----. "Drewry's Bluff: Naval Defense of Richmond, 1862." Civil War History, VII (June 1961), 167-175.

2054. Robinton, Madeline (Russell). An Introduction to the Papers of the New York Prize Court, 1861-1865. New York: Columbia University Press, 1945. 203p.

2055. Rochell, James H. "The Confederate Steamship Patrick Henry." Southern Historical Society Papers, XIV (1886), 126-136.

2056. -----. Life of Rear Admiral John Randolph Tucker. Washington: Neale, 1903. 112p.
Confederate Flag Officer; skipper of the C. S. S. Chicora.

2057. Rock, George H. "The Organization of the Navy Department." In Society of Naval Architects and Marine Engineers. Historical Transactions, 1893-1943. New York: The Society, 1945. p. 245-248.

2058. Rockwell, Alfred P. "The Operations Against Charleston." In Publications of the Military History Society of Massachusetts. 14 vols. Boston: The Society, 1895-1918. Vol. IX, pp. 159-195.

2059. Roddis, Louis H. "The Bureau of Medicine and

Surgery: A Brief History." United States Naval Institute Proceedings, LXXV (April 1949), 457-467.
Includes the Civil War years.

2060. -----. "The U. S. Hospital Ship Red Rover." Military Surgeon, LXXXVII (1935), 91-98.

2061. Rodenbough, Theophilus F. Uncle Sam's Medal of Honor; Some of the Noble Deeds for which the Medal has been Awarded, Described by Those Who have won it. New York: Putnam, 1886. 424p.
Includes naval personnel; entirely Civil War.

2062. Rodimon, William. "The Confederate Cruiser Florida." Unpublished M. A. Thesis, University of Alabama, 1939.

2063. Roe, Francis A. "The Naval Battle Between the Sassacus and the Albemarle." Army and Navy Journal, (August 25, 1906), 26-27.

2064. -----. Naval Duties and Discipline, with the Policy and Principles of Naval Organization. New York: D. Van Nostrand, 1865. 223p.

2065. -----. "Running the Gauntlet of Rebel Batteries." United Service, New Series VI (August 1891), 151-153.
By the executive officer of the U. S. S. Pensacola at New Orleans.

2066. Rogers, C. R. P. "DuPont's Attack at Charleston." In Robert U. Johnson and Clarence C. Buell, eds. B & L. Vol. IV, pp. 32-46.

2067. Rogers, W. L. "A Study of Attacks on Fortified Harbors." United States Naval Institute Proceedings, XXX (December 1904), 708-744.
Part of a series, this issue covers the various bombardments of the Civil War.

2068. Rogers, William. "The Loss of the Monitor." In War Papers, Read before the Commandery of the State of Maine, Military Order of the Loyal Legion of the United States. 3 vols. Portland:

Thurston, 1898-1908. Vol. II, pp. 77-90.

2069. Rogers, William E. The First Battle of the Ironclads as Seen by an Eye Witness; Printed from a Talk by Colonel William E. Rogers to the Mount Pleasant Citizens' Association, Washington, D. C., October 1923. Washington: Haywood, 1923. 18p.
Memories of the Monitor and Merrimac as seen from shore.

2070. Roland, Charles P. "Albert Sidney Johnston and the Loss of Forts Henry and Donelson." Journal of Southern History, XXIII (February 1957), 45-69.

2071. -----. Albert Sidney Johnston, Soldier of Three Republics. Austin: University of Texas Press, 1984. 384p.

2072. Romaine, Laurence B. "A Blockade Runner Who Never Returned; the Story of James Dickson's Diary-Logbook--1861-1862." Manuscripts, VII (Apring 1955), 166-172.
Accidentally killed on the Altamaha River, S. C.

2073. -----., ed. See Bolles, L., Jr., no. 296.

2074. Roman, Alfred. The Military Operations of General Beauregard in the War Between the States, 1861 to 1865. 2 vols. New York: Harper, 1884.

2075. Rombauer, Robert J. The Union Cause in St. Louis in 1861; an Historical Sketch. St. Louis: Nixon-Jones, 1909. 475p.

2076. Root, L. Carroll., ed. See Root, William H., no. 2077.

2077. [Root, William H.] "The Private Journal of William H. Root, Second Lieutenant, Seventy-Fifth New York Volunteers, April 1-June 14, 1863." Edited by L. Carroll Root. Louisiana Historical Quarterly, XIX (July 1936), 635-667.
Port Hudson.

2078. Ropp, Theodore. "Anaconda Anyone?" Military Affairs, XXVII (Summer 1963), 71-76.

Suggests a critical re-evaluation of the accuracy of the term "Anaconda policy," the Union's joint army-navy strategy for the conquest of the South.

2079. -----. *War in the Modern World.* Durham, N. C.: Duke University Press, 1959. 400p.

2080. Roscoe, Theodore. "Naval Pioneers at War." *Saturday Review of Literature*, XXIX (June 9, 1956), 17.

2081. -----., Joint Author. *See* Walesby, Stokes., no. 2665.

2082. Rose, F. P. "The Confederate Ram *Arkansas.*" *Arkansas Historical Quarterly*, XII (Winter 1953), 333-339.

2083. Rose, Willie L. *Rehearsal for Reconstruction; the Port Royal Experiment.* Indianapolis: Bobbs-Merrill, 1964. 442p.

Fate of the island after Union capture.

2084. Roske, Ralph J. and Charles Van Dorn. *Lincoln's Commando; the Biography of Commander William B. Cushing*, U. S. N. New York: Harper, 1957. 310p.

2085. Ross, Frank E. "The American Naval Attack on Skimonoseki in 1863." *Chinese Social and Political Science Review*, XVIII (April 1934), 146-155.

By U. S. S. *Wyoming*.

2086. Ross, Isabel. *Rebel Rose: the Life of Rose O'Neal Greenhow, Confederate Spy.* New York: Harper, 1954. 294p.

Details of how she met her death in the grounding of a blockade runner.

2087. Rossell, H. E. "Types of Naval Ships." *In* Society of Naval Architects and Marine Engineers. *Historical Transactions, 1893-1943.* New York: The Society, 1945. p. 248-330.

2088. Rowan, S. C. "Notes on Old Sea Cannon."

Mariner, VI (April 1962), 35-47.
Includes Civil War ordnance.

2089. Rowland, Kate M. "The Alabama and the Kearsarge." Confederate Veteran, VIII (January-December 1900), 528-529.

2090. -----., ed. See Waitz, Julia., no. 2664.

2091. Ruggles, Daniel. "Fight with the Gunboats at Mathias Point [Virginia]." Southern Historical Society Papers, IX (1881), 496-500.
The action in which Commander James Ward, first CO of the Potomac Flotilla, was killed, 1861.

2092. "Running the Blockade." Southern Historical Society Papers, XXIV (1896), 225-229.

2093. -----. Confederate Veteran, XVII (January-December 1909), 410-411; XXIV (January-December 1911), 392-393.

2094. Rush, Richard., ed. See U.S. Navy Department, no. 2610.

2095. Russell, Charles E. A-Rafting on the Mississippi. New York: Century, 1928. 357p.

2096. Russell, William H. The Civil War in America. Boston: Gardner A. Fuller, 1861. 189p.
A collection of his letters to the London Times; after speaking with Porter and Dahlgren, he concluded: "it will run hard against the Confederates when they [the Federals] get such men at work on the rivers and coasts."

2097. -----. My Diary North and South. 2 vols. London: Bradbury and Evans, 1863.

2098. -----. Pictures of Southern Life, Social, Political and Military. New York: Gregory, 1861. 143p.
Based on his 1861 trip from Charleston to Cairo via New Orleans and the Mississippi.

2099. Rutledge, Archibald. "Abraham Lincoln Fights the

Battle of Fort Sumter." South Atlantic Quarterly, XXXIV (October 1935), 368-383.

2100. Ryan, Daniel J. The Civil War Literature of Ohio: A Bibliography. Cleveland: Burrows Brothers, 1911. 518p.
Some references to naval events.

2101. Ryan, Paul B. "The Puritan and the Cavalier." Shipmate, XXXIV (January 1971), 5-11.
Raphael Semmes vs. John A. Winslow.

2101. Ryden, George H. "How the Monitor Helped the Army in the Peninsular Campaign of 1862." American-Swedish Monthly, XXXI (March 1937), 6-9.
Thesis: Neutralization of the Merrimac.

2103. Sackett, Francis R. Dick Dowling. Houston: Gulf Printing, 1937. 80p.
Sabine Pass Campaign.

2104. Saint Louis Shipbuilding-Federal Barge, Inc. St. Louis: 1964. 33p.
A house organ which proudly hails the company's location on the site of Ead's 1861 Carondelet boatyard.

2105. Salter, William. The Life of James W. Grimes. New York: D. Appleton, 1876. 398p.

2106. Saltonstall, William G. "Personal Reminiscences of the War, 1861-1865." In Publications of the Military History Society of Massachusetts. 14 vols. Boston: The Society, 1895-1918. Vol. XI, pp. 269-304.

2107. Sandburg, Carl. Abraham Lincoln; the War Years. 4 vols. New York: Harcourt, Brace and World, 1939.

2108. Sandefer, H. L. and Archie P. McDonald. "Sabine Pass: David and Goliath." Texana, VII (1969), 177-188.

2109. Sanders, Robert W. "Efforts to Capture Charleston, S. C., and the Evacuation of the City." Confederate Veteran, XXXIII (January-December 1925), 142-143.

2110. Sands, Benjamin F. From Reefer to Rear Admiral. New York: Frederick A. Stokes, 1899. 308p.
Useful discussion of the Gosport destruction, and the Union blockade off Cape Fear and Galveston.

2111. Sands, Francis P. B. The Brilliant Career of Lt. Roswell H. Lamson, U.S. Navy. District of Columbia Commandery, Military Order of the Loyal Legion of the United States. War Papers, no. 76. Washington: the Commandery, 1909.
Skipper of the U.S.S. Nansemond on the North Carolina blockade.

2112. -----. The Last of the Blockade and the Fall of Fort Fisher. District of Columbia Commandery, Military Order of the Loyal Legion of the United States. War Papers, no. 40. Washington: the Commandery, 1902.

2113. -----. Lest We Forget; Memories of Service Afloat from 1862 to 1866. District of Columbia Commandery, Military Order of the Loyal Legion of the United States. War Papers, no. 73. Washington: the Commandery, 1908.
By a former master's mate on the North Carolina blockade.

2114. -----. "Lt. Roswell H. Lamson, U.S.N." United States Naval Institute Proceedings, XXXV (March 1909), 137-152.

2115. -----. My Messmates and Shipmates Who are Gone, 1862 to 1865. District of Columbia Commandery, Military Order of the Loyal Legion of the United States. War Papers, no. 83. Washington: the Commandery, 1911.

2116. -----. A Volunteer's Reminiscences of Life in the North Atlantic Blockading Squadron, 1862 to 1865. District of Columbia Commandery, Military Order of the Loyal Legion of the United States. War Papers, no. 20. Washington: the Commandery, 1894.

Accounts of the various shore raids by Cushing and Lamson.

2117. Sanger, Donald B. "Red River Mercantile Expedition." Tylers Quarterly Historical and Genealogical Magazine, XVII (October 1933), 70-81.
Thesis: Federal campaign for plunder, not military gain.

2118. -----. "Some Problems Facing Joseph E. Johnston." In Avery Carven, ed. Essays in Honor of William E. Dodd, by His Former Students at the University of Chicago. Chicago: University of Chicago Press, 1935. p. 257-290.
In the West from November 1862 to July 1863.

2119. Sargent, Epes. "Ericsson and His Inventions." Atlantic Monthly, X (July 1862), 68-81.

2120. Sass, H. R. "Story of the Little David; First Successful Torpedo Boat." Harper's Magazine, CLXXXVI (May 1943), 620-625.

2121. Savage, Carlton. Policy of the United States Toward Maritime Commerce in War. 2 vols. Washington: Government Printing Office, 1934-1936.

2122. Say, Harold B. "Let the Monitor Steam Again." True, the Man's Magazine, XXII (January 1948), 104-108.

2123. Scales, D. M. "Cruise of the Shenandoah." Confederate Veteran, XII (January-December 1904), 489-490.

2124. Scharf, J. Thomas. History of St. Louis City and County, from the Earliest Periods to the Present Day. 2 vols. Philadelphia: L. H. Everts, 1883.
Includes the Civil War.

2125. -----. History of the Confederate States Navy from its Organization to the Surrender of its Last Vessel. New York: Rogers and Sherwood, 1887. 824p.

2126. Scheips, Paul J. "Signaling at Port Hudson, 1863."

Civil War History, II (December 1956), 106-113.

2127. Scheliha, Viktor E. R. von. A Treatise on Coast Defence Based on the Experience Gained by Officers of the Corps of Engineers of the Army of the Confederate States. London: E. & F. N. Spon, 1868. 326p.

This Prussian's weak batteries held Foote above Island No. 10 for 45 days.

2128. Schmidt, Jay H. "The Trent Affair." Civil War Times Illustrated, I (January 1963), 10-17.

2129. Schroeder, Seaton. A Half Century of Naval Service. New York: D. Appleton, 1922. 443p.

2130. Scott, James B., ed. See Carnegie Endowment for International Peace., no. 446.

2131. Scott, John. Story of the Thirty Second Iowa Infantry Volunteers. Nevada, Ga.: the Author, 1896. 526p.

Accounts of the Red River campaign, including the role of the gunboats.

2132. Scott, Robert N., ed. See U.S. War Department, no. 2623.

2133. Scroggs, Jack B. and Donald E. Reynolds. "Arkansas and the Vicksburg Campaign." Civil War History, V (December 1959), 390-402.

2134. Sears, Louis M. John Slidell. Durham, N.C.: Duke University Press, 1925. 252p.

2135. Seaton, John. "The Battle of Belmont." In War Talks in Kansas; a Series of Papers Read Before the Kansas Commandery, Military Order of the Loyal Legion of the United States. Kansas City: Franklin Hudson, 1906. p. 305-320.

2136. Seifert, E. M. "Evolution of the Torpedo." Ordnance, XXXIX (March-April 1955), 720-724.

2137. "Selected Quotations Relating to Seapower in the Civil War." In U.S. Navy Department, Naval History Division. Civil War Naval Chronology.

6 vols. Washington: U. S. Government Printing Office, 1961-1966. Vol. VI, pp. 385-390.

2138. Selfridge, Thomas O., Jr. The Cumberland. District of Columbia Commandery, Military Order of the Loyal Legion of the United States. War Papers, no. 67. Washington: the Commandery, 1907.

2139. -----. Memoirs of Thomas O. Selfridge, Jr., Rear Admiral, U. S. N., with an Introduction by Captain Dudley W. Knox. New York: Putnam, 1924. 288p.
Useful for the Western theatre and Fort Fisher.

2140. -----. "The Merrimac and the Cumberland." Cosmopolitan, XV (June 1893), 176-184.

2141. -----. "The Navy at Fort Fisher." In Robert U. Johnson and Clarence C. Buell, eds. B & L. Vol. IV, pp. 655-660.

2142. -----. "The Navy in the Red River." In Robert U. Johnson and Clarence C. Buell, eds. B & L. Vol. IV, pp. 362-365.

2143. -----. "The Story of the Cumberland." In Publications of the Military History Society of Massachusetts. 14 vols. Boston: the Society, 1895-1918. Vol. XII, pp. 101-126.

2144. Semmes, Raphael. The Confederate Raider Alabama. Edited with an introduction by Philip Van Dorn Stern. Civil War Centennial Series. Bloomington: Indiana University Press, 1962. 464p.

2145. -----. The Cruise of the Alabama and the Sumter. From the Private Journals and Other Papers of Commander Raphael Semmes, C. S. N., and Other Officers. 2 vols. in 1. New York: Carleton, 1864.

2146. -----. The Log of the Alabama and the Sumter. From the Private Journals and Other Papers of Raphael Semmes and Other Officers. London: Saunders, Otley, 1864. 297p.

2147. -----. Memoirs of Service Afloat, During the War Between the States. Baltimore: Kelly, Piet, 1869. 833p.

2148. -----. My Adventures Afloat: a Personal Memoir of My Cruises and Services in the Sumter and Alabama. 2 pts. London: Bentley, 1869.

2149. -----. "The Prison Diary of Raphael Semmes." Edited by Edward E. Bethel. Journal of Southern History, XXII (November 1956), 498-509.
The period following the war when the admiral was held as a Federal prisoner.

2150. -----. Rebel Raider; Being an Account of Raphael Semmes' Cruise in the C. S. S. Sumter; Composed in Large Part of Extracts from Semmes' Memoirs of Service Afloat, written in the Year 1869. Selected and Supplemented by Harper Allen Gosnell. Chapel Hill: University of North Carolina Press, 1948. 218p.

2151. -----. Service Afloat; or, the Remarkable Career of the Confederate Cruisers Sumter and Alabama. Baltimore: Baltimore Publishing, 1887. 833p.

2152. -----. "The Sumter Runs the Mississippi Blockade." Confederate Veteran, XXIV (January-December 1916), 502-503.

2153. Semmes, S. Spencer. "Admiral Raphael Semmes." Southern Historical Society Papers, XXXVIII (1910), 28-40.

2154. Sevier, Charles F. "Reminiscences of the Confederate Navy." Confederate Veteran, XXXII (January-December 1924), 219-220.

2155. Shanks, W. F. G. "The Brooklyn Navy-Yard." Harper's New Monthly Magazine, XLII (December 1870), 1-13.

2156. Sharkey, H. Clay. "Confederate Floating Mines." Confederate Veteran, XXIII (January-December 1915), 167-168.

2157. Shaw, Arthur M., ed. See Heartsill, William W.,

no. 1113.

2158. Shaw, Frederick J. Anglo-American Relations, 1861-1865. By Brougham Villers, pseud. London: Unwin, 1919. 214p.
The Trent and Alabama.

2159. Shaw, W. R. "The Red River Campaign." Confederate Veteran, XXV (January-December 1917), 116-117.

2160. "Shears that Built the Merrimac." American Machinist, LXXXV (May 14, 1941), 428.
Machines used to punch and trim her armor.

2161. Shepard, Frederick J. "Burleigh--and Johnson's Island." Magazine of History, I (May-June 1905), 306-315; 378-384.
Bennet Burleigh in the plot to capture the U. S. S. Michigan.

2162. Shepherd, Charles H. B. Under Fire with Farragut: the Signal Boy's Story. By Charles H. Bodder, pseud. New York: Signal Boy Publications, 1919. 210p.

2163. Sherman, William T. "General Sherman's Letters Home." Edited by M. A. DeWolfe Howe. Scribner's Monthly, XLV (April-June 1909), 397-415, 532-547, 737-752.

2164. -----. Memoirs of General W. T. Sherman, Written by Himself. 2 vols. New York: D. Appleton, 1875.

2165. -----. Sherman's Civil War. Selected and Edited from His Personal Memoirs, with a Foreword by Earl Schenck Miers. Collier Civil War Classics. New York: Collier Books, 1962. 509p.

2166. Shewmaker, Kenneth E., Joint Editor. See Gardner, Henry R., no. 911.

2167. "Shipboard Life in the Civil War." In U. S. Navy Department, Naval History Division. Civil War Naval Chronology. 6 vols. Washington: U. S. Government Printing Office, 1961-1966. Vol. VI, pp. 99-110.

2168. Shipp, J. F. "The Famous Battle of Hampton Roads." Confederate Veteran, XXIX (January-December 1916), 305-307.

2169. Shippen, Edward. Naval Battles of America. Philadelphia: J. C. McCurdy, 1898. 484p.
Includes the Civil War.

2170. -----. "Notes on the Congress-Merrimac Fight." Century Illustrated Magazine, XXX (August 1885), 642.

2171. -----. "Two Battle Pictures (a Reminiscence of the First Ironclad Fight)." United Service, IV (January 1881), 53-78.

2172. -----., Joint Editor. See Powell, William, no. 1941.

2173. Shively, Joseph W. The U.S.S. Mississippi at the Capture of New Orleans, 1862. District of Columbia Commandery, Military Order of the Loyal Legion of the United States. War Papers, no. 15. Washington: the Commandery, 1893.

2174. Shorey, Henry A. The Story of the Maine Fifteenth; Being a Brief Narrative of the More important Events in the History of the Fifteenth Maine Regiment; Together with a Complete Roster of the Regiment. Bridgton, Me.: Bridgton News, 1890. 178p.
One of the "lumberjack" regiments that worked on the Red River dam, May 1864.

2175. Short, Lloyd M. The Steamboat-Inspection Service; its History, Activities, and Organization. Institude for Government Research. Service Monographs of the United States Government, no. 8. New York: D. Appleton, 1922. 130p.
Reported disasters on the Western rivers such as that overtaking the Ruth.

2176. Shortridge, Wilson P. "Kentucky Neutrality in 1861." Mississippi Valley Historical Review, IX (March 1923), 283-301.

2177. Simmons, Edwin R. "The Federals and Fort Fisher."

Marine Corps Gazette, XXXV (January-February 1951), 52-59, 46-53.

2178. [Simmons, William B.] "Civil War Naval Activities in the Pacific; an Extract from the Autobiography of William B. Simmons. Edited by Brainerd Dyer. Pacific Historical Review, VII (September 1938), 254-266.

2179. Simon, John Y., ed. See Grant, U.S., no. 976.

2180. Simpson, Amos E., Joint Author. See Cassidy, Vincent H., no. 461.

2181. Simpson, Edward. "Ironclads." In Lewis R. Hamersly, ed. A Naval Encyclopedia. p. 398-401.

2182. -----. "The Monitor Passaic." United Service, II (April 1880), 413-423.
By her 1863-1864 commander.

2183. Simpson, Evan J. Atlantic Impact, 1861. By Evan John, pseud. London: Heinemann, 1952. 296p.
Very analytical account of the Trent Affair.

2184. Sims, L. Moody., ed. See Bartlett, Samuel J., no. 151.

2185. -----., ed. See Ginder, Henry., no. 945.

2186. -----., ed. See Remington, Ambert O., no. 2018.

2187. Sims, Lydel. "The Submarine that Wouldn't Come Up." American Heritage, IX (April 1958), 48-51, 107-111.
The Hunley.

2188. Simms, Joseph M. Personal Experiences in the Volunteer Navy During the Civil War. District of Columbia Commandery, Military Order of the Loyal Legion of the United States. War Papers, no. 50. Washington: the Commandery, 1903.
By an ensign aboard the Minnesota at Fort Fisher.

2189. Sinclair, Arthur. "How the Monitor Fought the

Merrimac." Hearst's Magazine, XXIV (December 1913), 884-894.

2190. -----. Two Years on the Alabama. Boston: Lee and Shepard, 1895. 344p.
Includes small biographical sketches of officers and muster rolls.

2191. Sinclair, G. Terry. "The Eventful Cruise of the Florida." Century Illustrated Magazine, LVI (July 1898), 417-427.

2192. Sinclair, Harold. The Port of New Orleans. Garden City, N. Y.: Doubleday, Doran, 1942. 335p.

2193. Singletary, Donald. "The Battle of Belmont, Mo." Confederate Veteran, XV (January-December 1907), 564-565.

2194. "The Sinking of the Mississippi." Confederate Veteran, XXXII (January-December 1924), 181-182.

2195. Sketch of the Public Services of Rear Admiral Samuel F. DuPont. Wilmington, Del.: H. Eckel, 1865. 12p.

2196. Skipwith, Henry. East Feliciana, Louisiana: Past and Present. New Orleans: Hopkins, 1892. 39p.
Useful description of Port Hudson.

2197. Sloan, Benjamin. The Merrimac and the Monitor. Bulletin of the University of South Carolina, no. 189. Columbia, S. C.: Bureau of Publications, University of South Carolina, 1926. 16p.
Witness of a former Confederate major ashore.

2198. Sloan, Edward W., III. B. F. Isherwood, Naval Engineer: the Years as Engineer in Chief, 1861-1869. Annapolis: U. S. Naval Institute, 1965. 299p.

2199. Smith, Alan C. "The Monitor-Merrimac Legend." United States Naval Institute Proceedings, XLVI (March 1940), 385-389.

2200. Smith, Arthur D. H. Old Fuss and Feathers; the Life and Exploits of Lt. General Winfield Scott. New York: Greystone, 1937. 386p.
Author of the "Anaconda Plan."

2201. Smith, C. Alphonso. Matthew Fontaine Maury. Charlottesville, Va.: University of Virginia Press, 1924. 10p.

2202. Smith, C. Carter., ed. See Brother, Charles, no. 347.

2203. -----., Joint Editor. See Smith, Sidney A., no. 2236.

2204. Smith, Coleman. "Capture of the Gunboat Queen City." Confederate Veteran, XXII (January-December 1914), 120-121.

2205. Smith, Daniel P. Company K, First Alabama Regiment; Three Years in the Confederate Service. Prattsville, Ala.: Published by the Survivors, 1885. 135p.
Most useful for the passage of Farragut's fleet past Port Hudson, March 1863, and the loss of U.S.S. Mississippi in the process.

2206. Smith, David R. The Monitor and the Merrimac: a Bibliography. U.C.L.A. Library Occasional Papers, no. 15. Los Angeles: University of California Library, 1968. 35p.

2207. Smith, E. Kirby. "The Defense of the Red River." In Robert U. Johnson and Clarence C. Buell, eds. B & L. Vol. IV, pp. 369-373.

2208. Smith, Edward D. The Peterhoff. Arguments Addressed to the United States Court at New York, in the Case of the Prize Steamer Peterhoff, 1863. New York: J. W. Amerman, 1863. 25p.

2209. Smith, Frank E. The Yazoo River. Rivers of America. New York: Rinehart, 1954. 362p.

2210. Smith, Franklin W. The Conspiracy of the U.S. Navy Department Against Franklin W. Smith of

Boston, 1861-1865. New York: American Publishing, 1890. 100p.

2211. -----. Naval General Court-Martial. Navy-Yard, Charleston, Massachusetts. The United States Against Franklin W. Smith. Arguments of the Judge-Advocates. Boston: Farwell and McGlennen, 1865. 139p.

Smith was not in the navy, but was accused in a swindle of supplies for the navy yard. Provides useful understanding of the Union Navy's justice system and the contract-pricing practices.

2212. -----. The United States Versus Franklin W. Smith. Argument for the Defence by Benjamin F. Thomas. Boston: Alfred Mudge, 1865. 127p.

2213. -----. The United States Versus Franklin W. Smith. Memorials of Senators and Representatives from Massachusetts to the President of the United States. Testimonial of Merchantile and Manufacturing Houses. Boston: Alfred Mudge, 1865. 11p.

2214. Smith, G. "The Confederate Cruiser Alabama." Independent, LIV (April 10, 1902), 849-851.

2215. Smith, George G. Leaves from a Soldier's Diary; the Personal Record of Lt. George Gilbert Smith, Co. C, 1st Louisiana Regiment Infantry Volunteers (White) During the War of the Rebellion; Also a Partial History of the Operations of the Army and Navy in the Department of the Gulf from the Capture of New Orleans to the Close of the War. Putnam, Conn.: the Author, 1906. 151p.

2216. Smith, George W. "The Banks Expedition of 1862." Louisiana Historical Quarterly, XXVI (April 1943), 341-360.

The attack on Baton Rouge.

2217. Smith, George Washington. A History of Southern Illinois: a Narrative Account of its Historical Progress, its People, and its Principal Interests. Chicago: Lewis, 1912.

Includes Cairo as the Yankee naval base, 1862,

and Mound City as the naval station.

2218. Smith, Gustavus W. Confederate War Papers. New York: Atlantic, 1884. 381p.
Includes New Orleans and the operations off the North Carolina coast.

2219. Smith, H. D. "Cutting Out the Underwriter: A Brilliant Exploit in a Southern Harbor." In George M. Vickers, ed. Under Both Flags. p. 153-156.

2220. -----. "The Harriet Lane." United Service, New Series V (January 1891), 55-65.

2221. -----. "With Farragut on the Hartford." In George M. Vickers, ed. Under Both Flags. p. 1-68.
Includes biographical data on the admiral.

2222. Smith, Hanries S. "The Futile Star of the West." Journal of Mississippi History, XIV (January 1952), 63-66.

2223. Smith, Henry W. The Vicksburg Campaign; a Synopsis of Activities from November 1862 to July 4, 1863. Souix Falls, S. D.: Will A. Beach, 1931. 16p.

2224. Smith, Joseph A. An Address Delivered Before the Union League of Philadelphia on Saturday Evening January 20, 1906, at the Presentation by the Art Association of the Painting Representing the Battle Between the Kearsarge and Alabama. Philadelphia: J. B. Lippincott, 1906. 31p.
By last survivor among the Union cruiser's officers; an interesting account.

2225. -----. "The Battle Between the Kearsarge and the Alabama." Magazine of History, V (January 1907), 1-26.

2226. Smith, Marshall J. and James Freret. "The Fortification and Siege of Port Hudson." Southern Historical Society Papers, XIV (1886), 305-348.

2227. Smith, Metancton. "The Mississippi at the Passage of the Forts." Century Illustrated Magazine,

XXX (July 1885), 478.
A letter from her skipper.

2228. Smith, Myron J., Jr. "The Civil War Career of Captain Henry Walke." Unpublished Paper, Files of the Ohio Historical Society, 1970.

2229. -----. "A Construction and Recruiting History of the U.S. Steam Gunboat *Carondelet*." Unpublished M.A. Thesis, Shippensburg State College, 1969.

2230. -----. "The Greenman's Forgotten Gunboat: U.S.S. *Albatross*." Unpublished Paper, Files of the Vicksburg National Military Park, 1971.

2231. -----. "Gunboats in a Ditch: The Steeles Bayou Expedition, March, 1863." Unpublished Paper, Files of the Vicksburg National Military Park, 1971.

2232. -----. "An Indiana Sailor Scuttles Morgan's Raid." *Indiana History Bulletin*, XLVIII (June 1971), 87-98.
Leroy Fitch and the tinclad, U.S.S. *Moose*.

2233. -----. "Mystic Treasure Ship of the Civil War." *Log of Mystic Seaport*, XX (June 1968), 41-45.
The clipper *B. F. Hoxie*, with silver bullion aboard, captured by the C.S.S. *Florida*.

2234. -----. "Notes on the Fate of U.S.S. *Carondelet*." Unpublished Paper, Files of the Vicksburg National Military Park, 1971.

2235. [Smith, N. H.]. "N. H. Smith's Letters from Sabine Pass, 1863." Edited by Alwyn Barr. *East Texas Historical Journal*, IV (October 1966), 140-143.

2236. Smith, Sidney A. and C. Carter., eds. *Mobile: 1861-1865; Notes and a Bibliography*. Chicago: Wyvern Press, 1964. 52p.
Selections from manuscripts present a useful picture of war-time Mobile.

2237. Smith, Washington J. "The Battle of Sabine Pass." *Confederate Veteran*, XXII (January-December

1919), 461-462.

2238. Smith, William F. "Operations Before Fort Donelson." Magazine of American History, XV (January 1886), 20-43.

2239. Smith, Xanthus. "Confederate Ram Raid off Charleston." In George M. Vickers, ed. Under Both Flags. p. 236-239.
January 1863 attack of the Palmetto State and Chicora upon the Yankee blockade; results; U. S. S. Mercedita captured, U. S. S. Keystone State damaged, and the blockade of the inshore lifted.

2240. Snead, Thomas L. "The Conquest of Arkansas." In Robert U. Johnson and Clarence C. Buell, eds. B & L. Vol. III, pp. 441-458.
Includes Arkansas Post.

2241. Snow, Elliot. "The Metamorphosis of the Merrimac." United States Naval Institute Proceedings, LVII (November 1931), 1518-1521.
Her conversion into the ironclad Virginia.

2242. Society of Naval Architects and Marine Engineers. Historical Transactions, 1893-1943. New York: the Society, 1945. 544p.

2243. Soley, James R. Admiral Porter. New York: D. Appleton, 1903. 499p.

2244. -----. The Blockade and the Cruisers. Vol. I of The Navy in the Civil War. New York: Scribner, 1883. 257p.

2245. -----. "Closing Operations in the Gulf and Western Rivers." In Robert U. Johnson and Clarence C. Buell, eds. B & L. Vol. IV, p. 412.

2246. -----. "The Confederate Cruisers." In Robert U. Johnson and Clarence C. Buell, eds. B & L. Vol. IV, pp. 595-599.

2247. -----. "Early Operations in the Gulf." In Robert U. Johnson and Clarence C. Buell, eds. B & L. Vol. II, p. 13.

2248. -----. "Early Operations in the Potomac River." In Robert U. Johnson and Clarence C. Buell, eds. B & L. Vol. II, pp. 143-144.

2249. -----. "Gulf Operations in 1862 and 1863." In Robert U. Johnson and Clarence C. Buell, eds. B & L. Vol. III, p. 571.

2250. -----. Historical Sketch of the United States Naval Academy. Prepared by Direction of Rear Admiral C. R. P. Rodgers. For the Department of Education at the International Exhibition, 1876. Washington: Government Printing Office, 1876. 348p.

2251. -----. "Minor Operations of the South Atlantic [Blockading] Squadron Under DuPont." In Robert U. Johnson and Clarence C. Buell, eds. B & L. Vol. IV, pp. 27-29.

2252. -----. "Naval Operations in the Vicksburg Campaign." In Robert U. Johnson and Clarence C. Buell, eds. B & L. Vol. III, pp. 551-570.

2253. -----. "The Navy in the Peninsular Campaign." In Robert U. Johnson and Clarence C. Buell, eds. B & L. Vol. II, pp. 264-270.

2254. -----. The Sailor Boys of '61. Boston: Estes and Lauriat, 1888. 381p.

2255. -----. "The Union and Confederate Navies." In Robert U. Johnson and Clarence C. Buell, eds. B & L. Vol. I, pp. 611-633.

2256. "Some Further Particulars of the Fight Between the Merrimac and the Monitor." Once A Week, VI (May 17, 1862), 582-584.
Title misleading; Fight involved Congress, Cumberland, and Merrimac, not Monitor.

2257. Somerset, Edward A. S., Duke of. "The Merrimac and Monitor." Southern Historical Society Papers, XVI (1888), 218-222.

2258. "The South Atlantic Blockading Squadron." In Robert U. Johnson and Clarence C. Buell, eds. B & L.

Vol. IV, p. 51.

2259. "Southern Ports." Confederate Veteran, XXIX (January-December 1921), 96-97.

2260. Spaulding, Oliver L. "The Bombardment of Fort Sumter, 1861." In Annual Report of the American Historical Association for the Year 1913. 2 vols. Washington: Government Printing Office, 1915. Vol. I, pp. 179-203.
Note the appendix, "Artillery Material," pp. 199-203.

2261. Spears, John R. David G. Farragut. American Crisis Biographies. Philadelphia: G. W. Jacobs, 1905. 407p.

2262. -----. History of the United States Navy from its Origin to the Present Day, 1775-1897. 5 vols. New York: Scribner, 1897-1899.
The Civil War is covered in Vol. IV.

2263. Speed, Thomas. The Union Cause in Kentucky, 1860-1865. New York: Putnam, 1907. 355p.

2264. Sperry, Andrew F. History of the 33rd Iowa Infantry Volunteer Regiment. Des Moines: Mills, 1866. 237p.
Useful for the Yazoo Pass Expedition and the July 4, 1863 Battle of Helena.

2265. Sprague, A. B. R. "The Burnside Expedition." In Civil War Papers; Read Before the Massachusetts Commandery, Military Order of the Loyal Legion of the United States. 2 vols. Boston: the Commandery, 1890. Vol. I, pp. 427-446.
The capture of Roanoke Island with the support of Goldsborough's fleet, 1862.

2266. Sprunt, James. Chronicles of the Cape Fear River. 2nd ed. Raleigh, N.C.: Edwards and Brougton, 1916. 732p.
Blockade tales by the ex-purser of the C.S.S. Lilian.

2267. -----. Derelicts; an Account of Ships Lost at Sea

in General Commercial Traffic and a Brief History of Blockade Runners Stranded along the North Carolina Coast, 1861-1865. Wilmington, N. C.: 1919. 304p.

2268. -----. "Running the Blockade." Southern Historical Society Papers, XXIV (1896), 157-165.
John Newland Maffitt.

2269. -----. Tales and Traditions of the Lower Cape Fear, 1661-1898. Wilmington, N. C.: LeGwin Brothers, 1896. 215p.
Additional blockade memoiries.

2270. -----. Tales of the Cape Fear Blockade; Being a Turn of the Century Account of Blockade Running. Raleigh, N. C.: Captial Printing, 1902. 134p.

2271. Stackpole, Edouard A. "Mr. Lincoln's Flagship: the River Queen." Yankee, XXXIV (February 1969), 68-71, 104-115.
On his trips to visit Grant at City Point.

2272. Stampp, Kenneth M. "Lincoln and the Strategy of Defense in the Crisis of 1861." Journal of Southern History, XI (August 1945), 297-323.
Provides background to the attempt engineered by Gustavus Fox to reinforce Fort Sumter.

2273. Standing, P. C. "Boarding-Officer of the Alabama." Cornhill Magazine, LXXV (May 1897), 592-603.

2274. Stanton, Oscar F. "A Few Years of the Early Sixties." In Personal Recollections of the War of the Rebellion; Papers Read Before the New York Commandery, Military Order of the Loyal Legion of the United States. 4 vols. New York: the Commandery, 1891-1912. Vol. II, pp. 280-289.
By the commander of the Panola, West Gulf Coast Blockading Squadron, 1864.

2275. Stanton, Samuel W. Nineteenth Century United States Naval Steam Vessels. American Steam Vessels Series, no. 4. Meriden, Conn.: Meriden, Gravure, 1964. 40p.
Includes many used during the Civil War.

2276. Starbuck, Alexander. "History of the American Whale Fishery from its Earliest Inception to the Year 1870." In Report of the Commissioner of Fish and Fisheries for 1875-1876. Washington: Government Printing Office, 1878. 779p.
Includes a list of the whalers taken by the Alabama and Shenandoah.

2277. Starr, Louis M. Bohemian Brigade; Civil War Newsmen in Action. New York: Alfred A. Knopf, 1954. 367p.

2278. "The State Honored the Monitor's Captain." New York State and the Civil War, I (January 1962), 27-29.
John L. Worden.

2279. [Steedman, Charles.] Memoir and Correspondence of Charles Steedman, with His Autobiography and Private Journals. Edited by Augustus L. Mason. Cambridge: Priv. Print. at the Riverside Press, 1912. 556p.
Union commander in the attacks on St. John's Bluff and River, Florida.

2280. Steele, Matthew F. American Campaigns. 2 vols. Washington: B. S. Adams, 1909.
Includes Vicksburg in the text and atlas.

2281. Stephen, Walter W. "The Brooke Guns from Selma." Alabama Historical Quarterly, XX (Fall 1958), 462-475.
Manufactured at the Selma Naval Gun Factory.

2282. Stern, Philip Van Doren. The Confederate Navy; a Pictorial History. Garden City, N. Y.: Doubleday, 1962. 252p.

2283. -----., ed. See Grant, Ulysses S., no. 977.

2284. -----., ed. See McMaster, John B., no. 1534.

2285. -----., ed. See Semmes, Raphael., no. 2144.

2286. Sternlight, Sanford V. "Ninety Nine Years in the Navy." United States Naval Institute Proceedings, LXXXV (May 1959), 150-152.

Fate of the U. S. S. Hartford.

2287. Stevens, Hazard. "Military Operations in South Carolina in 1862, Against Charleston, Port Royal Ferry, James Island, Secessionville." In Publications of the Military History Society of Massachusetts. 14 vols. Boston: the Society, 1895-1918. Vol. IX, pp. 111-158.

2288. Stevens, Paul., Joint Author. See Coleman, S. B., no. 527.

2289. Stevens, Thomas H. "The Battle of Port Royal." United Service, 3rd Series IV (February 1904), 175-177.

2290. -----. "The Boat Attack on Sumter." In Robert U. Johnson and Clarence C. Buell, eds. B & L. Vol. IV, pp. 47-50.

2291. Stevens, William O. David Glasgow Farragut: Our First Admiral. New York: Dodd, Mead, 1942. 241p.

2292. Stevenson, Charles S. "Abraham Lincoln and the Russian Fleet Myth." Military Review, L (August 1970), 35-37.

2293. Stevenson, Daniel. "Blockade Running." Confederate Veteran, IV (January-December 1896), 210-211.

2294. Steward, Charles W. The Blockade and Cruisers of the Confederacy. Washington: Navy League of the United States, 1917. 14p.

2295. -----. "Lion-Hearted [Charles W.] Flusser, Naval Hero of the Civil War." United States Naval Institute Proceedings, XXXI (June 1905), 275-238.

Commander of the Union naval forces who lost Plymouth, North Carolina, to the Albemarle and Rebel troops after a gallant action with his wooden vessels, 1864.

2296. -----. "William Barker Cushing." United States Naval Institute Proceedings, XXXVIII (August-September 1912), 425-491, 913-939.

A very complete biography.

2297. Stewart, Edwin. "An Address on Admiral Farragut." In Personal Recollections of the War of the Rebellion; Papers Read Before the New York Commandery, Military Order of the Loyal Legion of the United States. 4 vols. New York: the Commandery, 1891-1912. Vol. IV, pp. 162-170.

2298. Stick, David. Graveyard of the Atlantic; Shipwrecks of the North Carolina Coast. Chapel Hill: University of North Carolina Press, 1952. 276p.
Includes unlucky blockade runners.

2299. -----. The Outer Banks of North Carolina, 1584-1958. Chapel Hill: University of North Carolina Press, 1958. 352p.
Includes two chapters on Federal amphibious operations in the area.

2300. Stiles, Israel N. "The Monitor and the Merrimac." In Military Essays and Recollections; Papers Read Before the Illinois Commandery, Military Order of the Loyal Legion of the United States. 4 vols. Chicago: A. C. McClurg, 1891-1912. Vol. I, pp. 185-210.
By an officer of the 20th Indiana Infantry who witnessed the battle from the shore.

2301. Stiles, John C. "For Distinguished Valor and Skill." Confederate Veteran, XXXII (January-December 1924), 348-349.
Promotions in the Confederate Navy.

2302. Still, John S. "Blitzkrieg, 1863: Morgan's Raid and Rout." Civil War History, III (September 1957), 291-307.

2303. Still, William N., Jr. "The Career of the Confederate Ironclad Neuse." North Carolina Historical Review, XLIII (January 1966), 1-13.

2304. -----. "The Confederate Ironclad Missouri." Louisiana Studies, IV (Summer 1965), 101-110.

2305. -----. "Confederate Naval Strategy: the Ironclad." Journal of Southern History, XXVII (August 1961), 330-343.

2306. -----. Confederate Shipbuilding. Athens: University of Georgia Press, 1969. 204p.

2307. -----. "Confederate Shipbuilding in Mississippi." Journal of Mississippi History, XXX (November 1968), 291-303.

2308. -----. "The Confederate States Navy at Mobile, 1861 to August 1864." Alabama Historical Quarterly, XXX (Fall-Winter 1968), 127-144.

2309. -----. "The Construction and Fitting Out of Iron-clad Vessels-of-War Within the Confederacy." Unpublished PhD. Dissertation, University of Alabama, 1964.

2310. -----. "Facilities for the Construction of War Vessels in the Confederacy." Journal of Southern History, XXXI (August 1965), 285-304.

2311. -----. Iron Afloat: the Story of the Confederate Armorclads. Nashville: Vanderbilt University Press, 1971. 312p.

2312. -----. "Selma and the Confederate States Navy." Alabama Review, XV (January 1961), 19-37.

2313. [Stimers, Alban C.] "Aboard the Monitor." Edited by John D. Milligan. Civil War Times Illustrated, IX (April 1970), 28-35.

2314. -----. "Aboard the Monitor in Hampton Roads." Niagra Frontier, III (Summer 1956), 47-50.

2315. [Stodder, Louis N.] Aboard the U.S.S. Monitor." Edited by Albert S. Crockett. Civil War Times Illustrated, I (January 1963), 31-36.

2316. Stokesberry, James. U.S.S. Tecumseh: Treasure in Mobile Bay." United States Naval Institute Proceedings, XCIV (August 1968), 147-149.

2317. Stotherd, Richard H. Notes on Torpedoes, Offensive and Defensive. Washington: Government Printing Office, 1872. 318p.

2318. Stretch, Tom., Joint Author. See Wondrus, H.,

no. 2819.

2319. Strickland, Alice. "Blockade Runners." Florida Historical Quarterly, XXXVI (October 1957), 85-93.
On the Florida coast.

2320. Strode, Hudson. Jefferson Davis. 3 vols. New York: Harcourt, Brace, 1955-1964.

2321. Stryker, William S. "The 'Swamp Angel': the Gun Used in Firing on Charleston in 1863." Magazine of American History, XVI (December 1886), 553-560.
An 8-inch Parrott rifle which exploded on the 36th shot.

2322. Stubbs, Jane. "Virginians Run the Sea Blockade." Virginia Cavalcade, IX (Autumn 1960), 17-22.

2323. Sturgill, Claude C., Joint Author. See Price, Charles L., no. 1971.

2324. Stuyvesant, Moses S. "How the Cumberland Went Down." In War Papers and Reminiscences, 1861-65; Read Before the Missouri Commandery, Military Order of the Loyal Legion of the United States. St. Louis: Bechtold, 1892. p. 204-210.
By a junior officer aboard.

2325. -----. Navy Record of M. S. Stuyvesant. St. Louis: Perrin and Smith, 1906. 26p.
Author also served aboard Weehawken.

2326. Sulivane, Clement. "The Arkansas at Vicksburg in 1862." Confederate Veteran, XXV (January-December 1917), 490-491.

2327. Sullivan, James R. Chickamauga and Chattanooga Battlefields: Chickamauga and Chattanooga National Military Park, Georgia-Tennessee. National Park Service Historical Handbook Series, no. 25. Washington: U.S. Government Printing Office, 1956. 60p.
Background to the famous "Cracker Line."

2328. Summersell, Charles G. "The Career of Raphael

Semmes Prior to the Cruise of the Alabama." Unpublished PhD. Dissertation, Vanderbilt University, 1940.
Includes the voyage of the Sumter.

2329. -----. The Cruise of the C. S. S. Sumter. Confederate Centennial Studies, no. 27. Tuscaloosa, Ala.: Confederate Publishing Company, 1965. 187p.

2330. Sumner, Charles. A Speech on Maritime Rights; Delivered in the Senate, January 9, 1862. Washington: Congressional Globe, 1862. 13p.

2331. "Survivors of the Confederate Navy." Confederate Veteran, XII (January-December 1904), 373-374.

2332. [Swan, Samuel A. R.] "A Tennesseean at the Siege of Vicksburg." Edited by George C. Osborn. Tennessee Historical Quarterly, XIV (December 1955), 353-372.

2333. Swanberg, W. A. First Blood: the Story of Fort Sumter. New York: Scribner, 1957. 373p.

2334. Swann, Leonard. John Roach: Maritime Entrepreneur: the Years as Naval Contractor, 1862-1886. Annapolis: U.S. Naval Institute, 1965. 301p.

2335. Swartz, Oretha D. "Franklin Buchanan: a Study in Divided Loyalties." United States Naval Institute Proceedings, LXXXVIII (December 1962), 61-71.

2336. Sweet, F. H. "Chasing a Blockade Runner." Americana, V (February 1910), 194-200.

2337. Swift, Lester L. "Letters from a Sailor on a Tinclad." Civil War History, X (March 1961), 48-62.

2338. Swinton, William. "The Monitor and the Merrimac." In his Twelve Decisive Battles of the War: a History of the Eastern and Western Campaigns in Relation to the Actions that Decided Their Issue. New York: Dick and Fitzgerald, 1867. p. 226-261.

2339. Switzer, David C. "Down-East Ships of the Union Navy." United States Naval Institute Proceedings, XC (November 1964), 82-88.
Warships built in Maine.

2340. Switzler, William P. See U.S. Congress. House of Representatives., no. 2473.

2341. "T. H. Stevens, U.S.N." United Service, New Series V (May 1891), 545-548.

2342. Talkington, Robert. "A Survivor from the Sultana." Indiana History Bulletin, XXXII (July 1955), 123-125.

2343. Tawresey, John G. "The Portsmouth, New Hampshire, Navy Yard." In Society of Naval Architects and Marine Engineers. Historical Transactions, 1893-1943. New York: the Society, 1945. p. 28-31.

2344. Tayler, Jessee. "The Defense of Fort Henry." In Robert U. Johnson and Clarence C. Buell, eds. B & L. Vol. I, pp. 368-372.
Against Foote's gunboats, February 1862.

2345. Taylor, Asher. Notes of Conversations with a Volunteer Officer, on the Passage of the Forts Below New Orleans. New York: Priv. Print., 1868. 29p.
The movements of Gorham C. Taylor and the Yankee gunboat Sciota.

2346. Taylor, Joseph H. The American Negro Soldier in the Civil War; a Pictorial Documentary. [Durham, N.C.: J. S. C. & A. Publishers] 1960. 2p.
Includes Blacks aboard the Kearsarge.

2347. Taylor, Richard. "A Chapter of History." Southern Historical Society Papers, XXXI (1903), 48-52.

2348. -----. Destruction and Reconstruction; Personal Experiences of the Late War. New York: D. Appleton, 1879. 274p.
Especially useful for the Red River Campaign.

2349. ----- -----. Edited by Richard B. Harwell. New York: Longmans, Green, 1955. 274p.

2350. -----. "Operations in the Trans-Mississippi Department." Southern Historical Society Papers, VII (1879), 442-444, 497-502.

2351. [Taylor, Thomas E.] "Blockade-Buster--1863." All Hands, No. 461 (July 1955), 59-63.

2352. -----. Running the Blockade: A Personal Narrative of Adventure, Risks, and Escapes During the American Civil War. With an Introduction by Julian Corbett. 3rd ed. London: J. Murray, 1897. 180p.
By the bold skipper of the Banshee.

2353. Temple, Wayne C., ed. See Bear, Henry C., no. 186.

2354. Tenney, William J. The Military and Naval History of the Rebellion in the United States. New York: D. Appleton, 1865. 843p.
Too early for accuracy.

2355. [Terrell, "Spot" F.] "A Confederate Private at Fort Donelson, 1862." Edited by Walter F. Meier. American Historical Review, XXXI (April 1926), 477-484.
Includes the repulse of Foote's gunboats.

2356. Thom, J. C. "Unity of Command in the Civil War." United States Naval Institute Proceedings, LVIII (March 1932), 371-374.

2357. Thomas, Benjamin P., ed. See Cadwallander, Sylvanua., no. 414.

2358. -----, and Harold M. Hyman. Stanton; the Life and Times of Lincoln's Secretary of War. New York: Alfred A. Knopf, 1952. 642p.

2359. Thomas, David. Arkansas in War and Reconstruction, 1861-1874. Little Rock: United Daughters of the Confederacy, 1926. 446p.
Includes naval events on the state's rivers.

2360. Thomas, Frances P. The Career of John Grimes Walker, U. S. N., 1835-1907. Boston: 1959. 174p.

2361. Thomas, R. S. "The Yankee Gunboat Smith Briggs." Southern Historical Society Papers, XXXIV (1906), 162-169.
A Union army expedition, supported by minor naval elements, was repulsed near Smithfield, Va., with the loss of this army gunboat, February 1864.

2362. "Thomas O. Selfridge, Jr." United Service, New Series VII (May 1892), 529-530.

2363. Thomes, William H. Running the Blockade; or, U. S. Secret Service Adventures. Boston: Lee and Shepard, 1875. 474p.

2364. Thompson, Brooks., Joint Editor. See Cary, Clarence., no. 457.

2365. Thompson, Edgar K. "The U. S. Monitor Patapsco." United States Naval Institute Proceedings, XCIV (December 1968), 148-149.

2366. Thompson, Egbert. Petition of Lieutenant Egbert Thompson, U. S. N., Protesting Against the Action of the Late Advisory Board, and Praying for Relief. Philadelphia: the Author, 1862. 8p.

2367. Thompson, John. A Text-Book of Facts for the Use of Students in Naval History. Washington: J. Shillington, 1877. 48p.
Civil War data.

2368. Thompson, M. S., comp. See U. S. Navy Department, no. 2564.

2369. Thompson, Robert M., Joint Editor. See Fox, Gustavus V., no. 897.

2370. Thompson, Samuel B. Confederate Purchasing Operations Abroad. Chapel Hill: University of North Carolina Press, 1935. 137p.
Useful data on the means for Bullock's naval purchases.

2371. Thomson, David W. "Three Confederate Submarines; Operations at New Orleans, Mobile, and Charleston, 1862-1864." United States Naval Institute Proceedings, LXVII (January 1941), 39-47.

2372. Thornberry, Ruby S. "The Alabama." Confederate Veteran, XXXI (January-December 1923), 250-251.

2373. Thrasher, Mary. "The Cruiser Shenandoah." United Daughters of the Confederacy Magazine, XIII (August-September 1950), 12-13, 9, 24.

2374. Throne, Mildred., ed. See Turner, William H., no. 2411.

2375. Thruston, Jason. "Capture of the Indianola." Confederate Veteran, VI (January-December 1898), 573-574.

2376. Tiemann, William F. The 159th Regiment Infantry, New York State Volunteers, in the War of the Rebellion, 1862-1865. Brooklyn: the Author, 1891. 135p.

Story of men who worked on the Red River dam.

2377. "Timby's Claim as Turret Inventor." New York State and the Civil War, I (January 1962), 30-31.

2378. Tindall, William. The True Story of the Virginia and the Monitor; the Account of an Eyewitness. Richmond, Va.: Old Dominion Press, 1923. 90p.

2379. ----- -----. With an Introduction by Milledge L. Bonham. Virginia Magazine of History and Biography, XXXI (January-April 1923), 1-38, 89-145.

2380. Tobin, M. F., comp. A List of the Survivors of Farragut's Fleet. N. p.: 1900.

Not a great number were left by the turn of the century.

2381. Tod, G. M. S. "Farewell Hartford." Motor Boating, CVII (January 1961), 114-115.

2382. Todd, Herbert H. "The Building of the Confederate States Navy in Europe." Unpublished PhD. Dissertation, Vanderbilt University, 1940.

2383. Tolbert, Frank X. Dick Dowling at Sabine Pass: A Texas Incident in the War Between the States. New York: McGraw Hill, 1962. 159p.

2384. Tomb, James H. "Incidents of Naval Service." Confederate Veteran, XXXIV (January-December 1926), 129-130.
Aboard the C. S. S. McRae at New Madrid, Mo.

2385. -----. "The Last Obstructions in Charleston Harbor, 1863." Confederate Veteran, XXXII (January-December 1924), 98-99.

2386. -----. "Naval Operations at Charleston." Confederate Veteran, XXXIV (January-December 1926), 259-260.

2387. -----. "Submarines and Torpedo Boats, C. S. N." Confederate Veteran, XXII (January-December 1914), 168-169.

2388. -----. "When Farragut Passed the Forts." Confederate Veteran, XXXIV (January-December 1926), 50-51.
At New Orleans.

2389. Totten, Benjamin J. Naval Text-Book and Dictionary. Rev. Ed. New York: D. Van Nostrand, 1862. 430p.
Data from the title page of the 1841 1st edition shows what midshipmen at the U. S. Naval Academy were studying: Masting, rigging, managing vessels of war, stationing tables, and naval gun exercises. The glossary is extremely useful for "sea terms" of the time.

2390. Town, Franklyn. "The 'Expeditionary Corps' of 1861." Marine Corps Gazette, LIX (January 1933), 20-23.
At Port Royal.

2391. Townsend, Leah. "The Confederate Gunboat Pedee." South Carolina Historical Magazine, XL (April

1959), 66-73.
Also spelled Peedee; built by John L. Porter, the brain behind the conversion of the Merrimack.

2392. Trapier, James H. "Report of the Battle of Apl. 7, 1863." Southern Historical Society Papers, VI (1878), 125-127.
The naval attack upon Charleston.

2393. Traver, Lorenzo. The Burnside Expedition in North Carolina; the Battles of Roanoke Island and Elizabeth City. Personal Narratives of Events in the War of the Rebellion; Being Papers Read Before the Rhode Island Soldiers and Sailors Historical Society. 2nd Series, no. 5. Providence: N. B. Williams, 1880.

2394. "A Treasury of Early Submarines (1775-1903)." United States Naval Institute Proceedings, XCIII (May 1967), 97-116.
A pictorial; includes the Rebel craft.

2395. Treat, Payson J. The Early Diplomatic Relations Between the United States and Japan, 1853-1865. Baltimore: Johns Hopkins University Press, 1917. 459p.
Includes the Wyoming's battles with the forts.

2396. [Trenchard, Edward and Stephen D.] Reminiscences of the Old Navy, From the Journals and Private Papers of Captain Edward Trenchard and Rear Admiral Stephen Decatur Trenchard. Edited by Edgar S. Maclay. New York: Putnam, 1898. 362p.
The admiral commanded the supply vessel Rhode Island during the conflict; his journals indicate it was a very dull duty.

2397. Trexler, Harrison A. "Coaling the Confederate Commerce Raiders." Georgia Historical Quarterly, XVII (March 1933), 13-25.

2398. -----. The Confederate Ironclad Virginia (Merrimac). Chicago: University of Chicago Press, 1938. 95p.

2399. -----. "The Confederate Navy Department and the

Fall of New Orleans." Southwest Review, XIX (Autumn 1933), 88-102.

2400. -----. "The Harriet Lane and the Blockade of Galveston." Southwest Historical Quarterly, XXXV (October 1931), 109-123.
The vessel was taken from the Yankees when the Confederates retook the town in 1863.

2401. Trowbridge, J. R. "David Dixon Porter." In Charles F. Horne, ed. Great Men and Famous Women. 3 vols. New York: Selmar Hess, 1894. Vol. I, pp. 387-390.

2402. "Troy Ironmen Paraded in Pride." New York State and the Civil War, I (January 1962), 22-23.
On the building and "victory" of the Monitor.

2403. Truesdale, John. The Blue Coats, and How They Lived, Fought and Died for the Union. With Scenes and Incidents in the Great Rebellion. Philadelphia: Jones Brothers, 1867. 510p.
Part IV: "The Blue Coats Afloat."

2404. Trumbull, H. Clay. "Four Naval Officers Whom I Knew." United Service, I (January 1879), 32-44.
George Rogers, E. P. Williams, S. W. Preston, and Benjamin H. Porter.

2405. Truskitt, Peter., pseud. See Lewis, Samuel, no. 1452.

2406. Trussell, John B. B., Jr. "The Saga of 'Whistling Dick.'" Antiaircraft Journal, XCV (March-April 1952), 22-23.

2407. Tucker, John. Reply to the Report of the Select Committee of the Senate on Transports for the War Department. Philadelphia: Moss, 1863. 57p.
By an ex-Assistant Secretary of War.

2408. Tucker, Louis L. Cincinnati During the Civil War. Publications of the Ohio Civil War Centennial Commission, no. 9. Columbus: Ohio State University Press, 1962. 42p.
Includes the outfitting of gunboats.

2409. Tucker, Philip C. "The United States Gunboat Harriet Lane." Southwest Historical Quarterly, XXI (April 1918), 360-380.
Includes the Battle of Galveston, 1863.

2410. Tunnard, Will H. "Running the Mississippi Blockade." Confederate Veteran, XXIV (January-December 1916), 27-28.

2411. [Turner, William H.] "The Diary of William H. Turner, M. D., 1863." Edited by Mildred Throne. Iowa Journal of History, XLVII (July 1950), 267-282.
Journal of the Assistant Surgeon of the 2nd Iowa Infantry cruising between St. Louis and Vicksburg, March-May 1863.

2412. Twain, Mark., pseud. See Clemens, Samuel L., no. 507.

2413. Twiggs, Hansford D. D. "The Defense of Battery Wagner." Southern Historical Society Papers, XX (1892), 166-184.
Charleston, 1863.

2414. Twisleton, Edward. "The Trent Affair." Massachusetts Historical Society Proceedings, XLVII (1914), 107-109.
Printing of a December 1861 letter.

2415. "Two Gallant Young Seamen." Confederate Veteran, XXI (January-December 1913), 226.
Includes Midshipman John F. Holden of the C. S. S. Sumter.

2416. Tyler, Lyon G. "Lincoln and Fort Sumter." Tylers Quarterly Historical and Genealogical Magazine, III (January 1921), 208-214.

2417. -----. "Thornton Alexander Jenkins." In his Encyclopedia of Virginia Biography. 5 vols. New York: Lewis, 1915. Vol. III, pp. 294-295.
Farragut's one-time fleet captain.

2418. -----. "Virginia, Founder of the World's Navies."

Tylers Quarterly Historical and Genealogical Magazine, III (October 1921), 84-106.
Thesis: the "Victory" of the Merrimack changed naval warfare.

2419. Tyler, Willard C. "The Wyoming at Shimonoseki; the Story of a Very Gallant Naval Action." United States Naval Institute Proceedings, LVIII (October 1932), 1464-1477.

2420. Ulasek, Henry T., comp. See U.S. National Archives., no. 2560.

2421. Ulibarri, George S., comp. See U.S. National Archives., no. 2556.

2422. Underwood, E. Rebellion Record of the Town of Quincy. An Alphabetically Arranged Record of Each Resident of Qunicy who has Served in the Army and Navy of the United States During the Late Rebellion. Boston: J. E. Farrell, 1866. 37p.

2423. Underwood, E. B. "Wolverine neé Michigan." United States Naval Institute Proceedings, L (April 1924), 597-602.

2424. Union and Emancipation Society [Great Britain]. Report of the Sub-Committee on the Building of Vessels of War in Great Britain for the "So-Styled" Confederate States of North America. Manchester: the Society, 1863. 4p.
An anti-Confederate document.

2425. "Union Vessels in the Vicksburg Operations." In Robert U. Johnson and Clarence C. Buell, eds. B & L. Vol. III, p. 581.

2426. United States of America. Army. Historical Register and Dictionary of the United States Army. From its Organization, September 29, 1789, to March 2, 1903. Edited by Francis B. Heitman. 2 vols. Washington: Government Printing Office, 1903.

2427. ----- -----. Coast Artillery School, Committee No. 6. "Campaigns Against Forts Henry and Donelson,

February 1862." Coast Artillery Journal, LXVII (November 1927), 389-404.
The role of the Confederate batteries in loosing or securing victory over Foote's ironclads.

2428. ----- -----. Department of Research, Infantry School. Camp Benning, Ga. The Battle of Belmont. Fort Benning, Ga.: Infantry School Press, 1921. 108p.

2429. ----- -----. General Service Schools. Fort Leavenworth, Kansas. Donelson Campaign Sources, Supplementing Volume 7 of the Official Records of the Union and Confederate Armies in the War of the Rebellion. Compiled by Arthur L. Conger. Fort Leavenworth, Kansas: General Service Schools Press, 1912. 244p.

2430. ----- ----- -----. Fort Henry and Fort Donelson Campaigns, February 1862: Source Book. Fort Leavenworth, Kansas: General Service Schools Press, 1923. 1488p.

2431. ----- ----- -----. Source Book of the Peninsula Campaign in Virginia, April to July, 1862. Fort Leavenworth, Kansas: General Service Schools Press, 1921. 996p.

2432. -----. Circuit Court. Southern District of New York. Reports of Cases in Prize, Argued and Determined in the Circuit and District Courts of the United States, for the Southern District of New York, 1861-65. Reported by Samuel Blatchford. New York: Baker, Voorhis, 1866. 729p.
An invaluable printed source for data on ships taken by the Yankee blockade.

2433. ----- ----- -----. Trial of the Officers and Crew of the Privateer Savannah, on the Charge of Piracy, in the United States Circuit Court of New York, the Hon. Judges Nelson and Shipman, Presiding. Reported by A. F. Warburton. New York: Baker and Goodwin, 1862. 385p.
A precedent-setting case and the last trial of letter-of-marque seamen; when Jefferson Davis threatened retaliation should anything happen to the men, the Lincoln government,

also trying the prize crew from the Jeff Davis at Philadelphia, backed down and later released the men.

2434. ----- ----- -----. The United States vs. the Schooner Stephen Hart and Her Cargo. In Prize. Opinion. Reported by Samuel R. Betts. New York: J. W. Amerman, 1863. 58p.

2435. ----- ----- -----. The United States vs. the Steamer Peterhoff and Her Cargo. In Prize. Opinion. With the Opinions... in the Cases of the Dolphin and the Pearl. New York: J. W. Amerman, 1864. 116p.

2436. -----. Civil War Centennial Commission. The Civil War. By James I. Robertson, Jr. Washington: U. S. Government Printing Office, 1963. 63p.

2437. United States of America. Coast and Geodetic Survey. The Coast and Geodetic Survey, 1807-1957; 150 Years of History. By Joseph Wraight and Elliott B. Roberts. Washington: U. S. Government Printing Office, 1957. 89p.

Men of the Survey gave invaluable service, especially in setting cannon ranges, to the Union Navy.

2438. ----- -----. Military and Naval Service of the United States Coast Survey, 1861-65. Washington: Government Printing Office, 1916. 72p.

Includes much correspondence.

2439. -----. Coast Guard. Brief Sketch of the Naval History of the United States Coast Guard, with Citations of Various Statutes Defining its Military Status from 1790 to 1922. Washington: B. S. Adams, 1922. 16p.

2440. -----. Congress. House of Representatives. Communication from the Board of Trade of Philadelphia in Relation to Maritime Defences. House. Misc. Doc. 17, 37th Cong., 2nd Sess., 1861. 2p.

2441. ----- ----- -----. Communication from the Secretary of War on the Subject of an Armed Flotilla on Western Rivers. House. Misc. Doc. 17, 37th Cong., 2nd Sess., 1862. 2p.

2442. ----- ----- -----. The Court-Martial of Commodore Charles Wilkes. House. Ex. Doc. 102, 38th Cong., 1st Sess., 1864. See no. 2416.

2443. ----- ----- -----. Evidence Taken by the Board of Navy Officers for Investigating the Condition of the Navy Yards. House. Ex. Doc. 71, 36th Cong., 1st Sess., 1860. 316p.

2444. ----- ----- -----. Letter from Acting Volunteer Lieutenant-Commander Edward F. Devens, in Relation to the Treatment of the U.S. Steamer Houqua, at Halifax, in June [1863]. House. Ex. Doc. 21, 38th Cong., 1st Sess., 1864. 2p.

2445. ----- ----- -----. Letter from the Secretary of the Navy in Regard to the Rebel Ram [Albemarle] Which Recently Participated in the Rebel Attack on Plymouth. House. Ex. Doc. 83, 38th Cong., 1st Sess., 1864. 12p.

2446. ----- ----- -----. Letter from the Secretary of the Navy, in Relation to the Appointments to the Naval Academy. House. Ex. Doc. 6. 37th Cong., 3rd Sess., 1862. 4p.

2447. ----- ----- -----. Letter from the Secretary of the Navy in Relation to the Propriety of An Appropriation for Testing Durfee's Submarine Gun. House. Ex. Doc. 126. 37th Congress, 2nd Sess., 1862. 2p.

2448. ----- ----- -----. Letter from the Secretary of the Navy, in Relation to Transportation of Naval Supplies, Munitions of War, etc., to the Pacific Coast. House. Ex. Doc. 73, 37th Cong., 2nd Sess., 1862. 4p.

2449. ----- ----- -----. Letter from the Secretary of War Relative to the Apportionment of Naval Recruits Among the Different Enrollment Districts. House. Ex. Doc. 30, 38th Cong., 2nd Sess., 1865. 2p.

2450. ----- ----- -----. Letter from the Secretary of the Navy Relative to the Case of Rear Admiral L. M. Goldsborough. House. Ex. Doc. 27, 40th Cong., 1st Sess., 1867. 27p.

2451. ----- ----- -----. Letter from the Secretary of the Navy Relative to the Contracts Made With Bureaus Connected with the Navy Department. House. Ex. Doc. 150, 37th Cong., 2nd Sess., 1862.

2452. ----- ----- -----. Letter from the Secretary of the Navy Relative to the Number of Vessels in the Navy, Jan. 1, 1861, Number of Officers, Expense of the Navy, etc. House. Ex. Doc. 159. 40th Cong., 2nd Sess., 1868. 2p.

2453. ----- ----- -----. Letter from the Secretary of the Navy Transmitting a Statement of all Ordnance and Ordnance Stores on Hand. House. Ex. Doc. 16. 39th Cong., 2nd Sess., 1866. 48p.

2454. ----- ----- -----. Letter from the Secretary of the Navy Transmitting Reports of the Wreck of the Transport Steamer Governor and the Search for the U.S. Ship Vermont by the Frigate Sabine. House. Ex. Doc. 139, 37th Cong., 2nd Sess., 1862. 23p.

2455. ----- ----- -----. Letter from the Secretary of the Navy Transmitting the Proceedings of the Court-Martial which Tried Commodore Charles Wilkes. House. Ex. Doc. 102, 38th Cong., 1st Sess., 1864. 301p.

Some material on the Trent Affair and naval administration not printed elsewhere.

2456. ----- ----- -----. Letters of Gideon Welles, Secretary of the Navy, Vindicating the Appointment of His Relative George D. Morgan, of New York, to Purchase Vessels for the Government. House. Ex. Doc. 15, 37th Cong., 2nd Sess., 1862. 2p.

2457. ----- ----- -----. List of all Vessels, Once Foreign, which have Received American Registers in the Year 1865. House. Ex. Doc. 28, 39th Cong., 1st Sess., 1865. 3p.

2458. ----- ----- -----. Message from the President of the United States in Relation to the Collision Between the U. S. War Steamer San Jacinto and the French Brig Jules et Marie. House. Ex. Doc. 4, 37th Cong., 3rd Sess., 1862. 2p.

2459. ----- ----- -----. Message from the President of the United States on Insurgent Privateers in Foreign Ports. House. Ex. Doc. 104, 37th Cong., 2nd Sess., 1862. 211p.

2460. ----- ----- -----. Message from the President of the United States Recommending a Vote of Thanks of Congress to Captain A. H. Foote of the U. S. Navy, for His Eminent Services in Organizing the Western Flotilla, etc. House. Ex. Doc. 141, 37th Cong., 2nd Sess., 1862. 1p.

2461. ----- ----- -----. Message from the President of the United States Recommending a vote of Thanks of Congress to Captains Lardner, Davis, and Stringham, and Commanders Dahlgren, Rowan, and Porter, for Distinguished Services. House. Ex. Doc. 147, 37th Cong., 2nd Sess., 1862. 1p.

2462. ----- ----- -----. Message from the President of the United States Recommending a Vote of Thanks of Congress to Commander J. L. Worden for His Skill and Gallantry Exhibited in the Battle Between the U. S. Iron-Clad Steamer Monitor and the Rebel Steamer Merrimac. House. Ex. Doc. 8, 37th Cong., 3rd Sess., 1862. 1p.

2463. ----- ----- -----. Message from the President of the United States Recommending a Vote of Thanks of Congress to Lt. Cmdr. Geo. U. Morris for His Valor and Heroism in the Defence of the U. S. Sloop-of-War Cumberland. House. Ex. Doc. 9, 37th Cong., 3rd Sess., 1862. 1p.

2464. ----- ----- -----. Message from the President of the United States Recommending a Vote of Thanks of Congress to Samuel Francis DuPont for His Services and Gallantry Displayed in the Capture of Various Points on the Coast of Georgia and Florida. House. Ex. Doc. 82, 37th Cong., 2nd Sess., 1862. 1p.

2465. ----- ----- -----. Message from the President of the United States Recommending that Captain Louis M. Goldsborough Receive a Vote of Thanks of Congress for His Services and Gallantry Displayed in the Attack of Roanoke Island, March 4, 1862. House. Ex. Doc. 66, 37th Cong., 2nd Sess., 1862.

2466. ----- ----- -----. Message from the President of the United States Relative to the Reported Surrender of the Rebel Pirate Shenandoah. House. Ex. Doc. 36, 39th Cong., 1st Sess., 1866. 25p.

2467. ----- ----- -----. Message from the President of the United States Transmitting Correspondence Concerning the Case of the Danish Bark Jurgen Dorentzen, Seized on Her Voyage from Rio Janeiro to Havanna by the U.S. Ship Morning Light. House. Ex. Doc. 78, 37th Cong., 2nd Sess., 1862. 9p.

2468. ----- ----- -----. Report by the Quartermaster General Relative to the Number of Vessels Bought, Sold, and Chartered by the United States Since April, 1861. House. Ex. Doc. 337, 40th Cong., 2nd Sess., 1868. 227p.

2469. ----- ----- -----. Report of Admiral Foote in Relation to a Naval Depot on Western Waters. House. Ex. Doc. 48, 38th Cong., 1st Sess., 1864. 3p.

2470. ----- ----- -----. Report of Captain James B. Eads on the Ironclads of Europe and This Country. House. Ex. Doc. 327, 40th Cong., 2nd Sess., 1868.

Most of those seen by Eads in America were left from the recent War Between the States.

2471. ----- ----- -----. Report of the Advisory Board in Relation to the Grade of Line Officers of the Navy. House. Ex. Doc. 56, 38th Cong., 1st Sess., 1864. 19p.

2472. ----- ----- -----. Report of the Secretary of the Navy Transmitting the Instructions Issued to Officers of the Several Depots for the Enlistment of Seamen. House. Ex. Doc. 7, 37th Cong., 1st Sess., 1861. 4p.

2473. ----- ----- -----. Report on the Internal Commerce of the United States, by William P. Switzler, Chief of the Bureau of Statistics, Treasury Department. House. Ex. Doc. 6, Part II, 50th Cong., 1st Sess., 1888.

2374. ----- ----- -----. Resolutions of the Legislature of Ohio in Relation to the Establishment of a Naval Depot on the Western Lakes. House. Misc. Doc. 45, 37th Cong., 2nd Sess., 1862. 1p.

2475. ----- ----- -----. Telegrams, Letters, and Affidavits of Paymaster Thomas H. Looker, U.S. Navy, in Relation to the Questioned Letter of Admiral Farragut of January 29, 1869. House. Ex. Doc. 184, 41st Cong., 2nd Sess., 1870. 6p.
Seeking prize money for the capture of New Orleans in 1862.

2476. ----- ----- -----. Commission on War Claims at St. Louis. War Claims at St. Louis. House. Ex. Doc. 94, 37th Cong., 2nd Sess., 1862.
Among the claims were some for materials and stores for the Western Flotilla.

2477. ----- ----- -----. Committee on Commerce. Trade with the Rebellious States. House. Rept. 24, 38th Cong., 2nd Sess., 1864.

2478. ----- ----- -----. Committee on Naval Affairs. Letter from the Secretary of the Navy in Relation to Iron-Clad Ships, Ordnance, etc. House. Misc. Doc. 82, 37th Cong., 2nd Sess., 1862. 6p.

2479. ----- ----- ----- -----. Prize-Money to the Officers and Crew of the United States Steamer Monitor. House. Rept. 144, 47th Cong., 1st Sess., 1882. 8p.

2480. ----- ----- ----- -----. Report Concerning Payment to the Warrant Officers and Sailors of the Farragut Fleet, the Balance of the Bounty Due Them for Destroying the Enemy's Vessels at

New Orleans. House. Rept. 313, 46th Congress, 3rd Sess., 1881. 1p.
A favorable report rendered 11 years after Paymaster Looker assembled his evidence.

2481. ----- ----- ----- -----. Report on Tendering the Thanks of Congress to Lieutenant John Henry Russell, the Officers, Seamen and Marines of the Boat Expedition from the United States Steam Frigate Colorado, for Their Gallantry at Pensacola. House. Rept. 38, 38th Cong., 1st Sess., 1864. 1p.
An unfavorable report.

2482. ----- ----- ----- -----. Report on the Establishment of a New Yard for the Construction, Docking, etc., of Iron, Iron-Clad Vessels, etc. House. Rept. 100, 38th Cong., 1st Sess., 1864. 54p.
League Island vs. New London, Conn.

2483. ----- ----- ----- -----. Report on the Payment of 125,000 dollars from the Japanese Indemnity Fund to the Officers and Crew of the Wyoming, and the Officers and Crew Detached from the United States Ship Jamestown, who Manned the Ta-Kiang. House. Rept. 343, 43rd Cong., 1st Sess., 1874. 5p.
A favorable report growing out of the 1863 Shimonoseki Affair.

2484. ----- ----- ----- -----. Report on the Petition for the Relief of the Widow of Rear Admiral Dahlgren. House. Rept. 133, 43rd Cong., 1st Sess., 1875. 2p.
A favorable report.

2485. ----- ----- ----- -----. Report on the Prosecution of the Claims of the Captors of the Ram Albemarle, Before the Court of Claims. House. Rept. 461, 46th Cong., 2nd Sess., 1880. 14p.
A favorable report.

2486. ----- ----- ----- -----. Report that the President be Authorized to Nominate for Advancement, and, by and with the Consent of the Senate, to Advance Captain Thomas H. Stevens not Exceeding Twenty-One Numbers on the Active List of the Navy.

House. Rept. 22, 40th Cong., 2nd Sess., 1868. 1p.

2487. ----- ----- -----. Select Committee. Report on that Part of the Message of the President Relating to the Naval Force of the United States. House. Ex. Doc. 87, 36th Cong., 2nd Sess., 1861. 102p.

2488. ----- ----- ----- -----. Report to Inquire into the Contracts of the Government. House. Rept. 2, 37th Cong., 2nd Sess., 1862.

2489. ----- -----. Joint Committee on the Conduct of the War. Report... at the Second Session, Thirty-Eighth Congress. 3 vols. Washington: Government Printing Office, 1865.

Reports of interest include those on the Red River and Fort Fisher expeditions, Heavy Ordnance, and Monitor-class warships.

2490. ----- -----. Senate. Centennial of the United States Naval Academy, 1845-1945; a Sketch Containing the History, the Growth, the Daily Routine, and the Activities of the United States Naval Academy. Senate. Doc. 91, 79th Cong., 1st Sess., 1945. 27p.

2491. ----- ----- -----. Certain War Vessels Built in 1862-1865. Senate. Doc. 1942, 57th Cong., 1st Sess., 1902.

Includes some built for use on the Western rivers.

2492. ----- ----- -----. Letter from the Secretary of the Navy Communicating Extracts from Reports in Relation to the Accident on Board the Steam-Battery Passaic. Senate. Ex. Doc. 15, 37th Cong., 3rd Sess., 1863. 4p.

2493. ----- ----- -----. Letter from the Secretary of the Navy Communicating Information as to what Congressional District has more than two Midshipmen at the Naval Academy, Under what Law Appointed, and by Whom Recommended. Senate. Ex. Doc. 8, 37th Cong., 3rd Sess., 1862. 4p.

2494. ----- ----- -----. Letter from the Secretary of the Navy Communicating Information in Relation to the Construction of the Iron-Clad Monitor. Senate. Ex. Doc. 86, 40th Cong., 2nd Sess., 1868. 10p.

2495. ----- ----- -----. Letter from the Secretary of the Navy in Explanation of the Course of that Department in Recommending to the President the Appointment of Midshipmen in the Naval Academy. Senate. Ex. Doc. 31, 37th Cong., 3rd Sess., 1863. 2p.

2496. ----- ----- -----. Letter from the Secretary of the Navy in Relation to the Appointment of Rear Admirals Since the Last Session of Congress. Senate. Ex. Doc. 13, 37th Cong., 3rd Sess., 1863. 2p.

2497. ----- ----- -----. Letter from the Secretary of the Navy in Relation to the Construction of Iron-Clad Steamers, etc. Senate. Misc. Doc. 70, 37th Cong., 2nd Sess., 1862. 3p.

2498. ----- ----- -----. Letter from the Secretary of the Navy in Relation to the Number of Captains and Commanders on the Active List in the Navy, and by the Virtue of what Law any were Appointed in Excess of the Number Authorized by the Law of July 16, 1862. Senate. Ex. Doc. 12, 37th Cong., 3rd Sess., 1863. 2p.

2499. ----- ----- -----. Letter from the Secretary of the Navy in Relation to the Removal of the Academy from Annapolis, Maryland, to Newport, R.I. Senate. Ex. Doc. 35, 37th Cong., 2nd Sess., 1862. 4p.

2500. ----- ----- -----. Letter from the Secretary of the Navy in Relation to the Transfer of Seamen from the Army to the Navy. Senate. Ex. Doc. 33, 38th Cong., 1st Sess., 1864. 6p.

This procedure was of great importance on the Western rivers.

2501. ----- ----- -----. Letter from the Secretary of the Navy in Relation to the War Steamers Ossipee and Pensacola. Senate. Ex. Doc. 45, 37th

Cong., 3rd Sess., 1863. 11p.

2502. ----- ----- -----. Letter from the Secretary of the Navy Relative to the Employment of George D. Morgan of New York, to Purchase Vessels for the Government. Senate. Ex. Doc. 15, 37th Cong., 2nd Sess., 1862. 2p.

2503. ----- ----- -----. Letter from the Secretary of the Navy Transmitting the Official Reports and Documents Connected with the Recent Engagements on the Mississippi River, which Resulted in the Capture of Fort Jackson, St. Philip, and the City of New Orleans, the Destruction of the Rebel Flotilla, etc. Senate. Ex. Doc. 56, 37th Cong., 2nd Sess., 1862. 107p.

2504. ----- ----- -----. Letter of the Secretary of War in Relation to the Vessels Purchased or Chartered for the use of the War Department. Senate. Ex. Doc. 37, 37th Cong., 2nd Sess., 1862.

Includes some Western ships such as those in the Mississippi Marine Brigade, or used by Ellet as rams.

2505. ----- ----- -----. Letter of the Secretary of War Transmitting Information in Relation to the Steamer Niagara, Chartered for the Banks Expedition in 1862. Senate. Ex. Doc. 12, 38th Cong., 1st Sess., 1864. 8p.

2506. ----- ----- -----. List of Officers of the Navy and of the Marine Corps, who, Between 1 December 1860, and 1 December 1863, Left the Service, with the Grade and Rank of Each. Senate. Ex. Doc. 3, 38th Cong., 1st Sess., 1864. 12p.

For any number of reasons, e.g., to "go South" as in the case of Admiral Buchanan, or most often, illness or wounds, such as the case of Acting Volunteer Lieutenant John M. Murphy of the Carondelet.

2507. ----- ----- -----. List of the Naval Officers who Commanded Vessels Engaged in the Recent Drill Operations of the Squadron Commanded by Flag-Officer Farragut. Senate. Ex. Doc. 49, 37th Cong., 2nd Sess., 1862. 2p.

The capture of New Orleans.

2508. ----- ----- -----. Memorial of E. W. Hinman of New York [on] the Employment by the Government of Vessels Employed in Fisheries, as Particularly Adapted to aid in Maintaining an Effective Blockade. Senate. Misc. Doc. 20, 37th Cong., 2nd Sess., 1862. 3p.

2509. ----- ----- -----. Memorial of the Legislature of Wisconsin in Favor of the Establishment of a Naval Depot, etc., in Said State. Senate. Misc. Doc. 82, 37th Cong., 2nd Sess., 1862. 3p.

2510. ----- ----- -----. Message from the President of the United States Concerning the Imprisonment of Lieut. John L. Worden. Senate. Ex. Doc. 6, 37th Cong., 1st Sess., 1862. 1p.

2511. ----- ----- -----. Message From the President of the United States Recommending that Captain D. G. Farragut Receive a Vote of Thanks of Congress for his Services and Gallantry Displayed in the Capture, since the 21st December 1861, of Forts Jackson and St. Philip and the City of New Orleans, and the Destruction of Various Rebel Gunboats, Rams, etc. Senate. Ex. Doc. 48, 37th Cong., 2nd Sess., 1862. 1p.

2512. ----- ----- -----. Message from the President of the United States Recommending that some Suitable Acknowledgment be made to Cornelius Vanderbilt for His Valuable Present to the United States of the Steamer Vanderbilt. Senate. Ex. Doc. 71, 37th Cong., 2nd Sess., 1862. 1p.

2513. ----- ----- -----. Message from the President of the United States Transmitting Correspondence Between the Minister from Austria and the Secretary of State of the United States, in Relation to the Taking of Certain Citizens of the U.S. from on board the British Steamer Trent, by order of Captain Wilkes, U.S.N. Senate. Ex. Doc. 14, 37th Cong., 2nd Sess., 1862. 2p.

2514. ----- ----- -----. Message from the President of the United States Transmitting Correspondence

Between the Minister from Prussia and the Secretary of State of the United States, in Relation to the Taking of Certain Citizens of the U. S. from on board the British Steamer Trent, by order of Captain Wilkes, U. S. N. Senate. Ex. Doc. 18, 37th Cong., 2nd Sess., 1862. 3p.

2515. ----- ----- -----. Message from the President of the United States Transmitting Correspondence Between the Secretary of State and Authorities of Great Britain and France, in Relation to the Recent Removal of Certain Citizens of the U... from the British Mail Steamer Trent. Senate. Ex. Doc. 8, 37th Cong., 2nd Sess., 1862. 16p.

2516. ----- ----- -----. Names of all Officers on the Retired List of the United States Navy, Their Present Rank, Rank When Retired, Pay, etc. Senate. Misc. Doc. 126, 47th Cong., 1st Sess., 1882. 9p.

2517. ----- ----- ----- -----. Senate. Misc. Doc. 111, 49th Cong., 1st Sess., 1886. 11p.
Includes many Civil War officers, eg. Walke.

2518. ----- ----- -----. Navy Yard, Washington. History from its Organization, 1799, to the Present Date, by Henry B. Hibben. Senate. Ex. Doc. , 51st Sess., 1890. 22p.

2519. ----- ----- -----. Number and Character of Ships in Commission, with Their Batteries and Their Stations for and During Each Year from 1840 to 1860, Inclusive. Senate. Ex. Doc. 4, 36th Cong., 2nd Sess., 1861. 29p.

2520. ----- ----- -----. Record of the Proceedings of the Advisory Board Appointed Under the Act of July 16, 1862, Entitled "An Act to Establish and Equalize the Grade of Line Officer of the United States Navy." Senate. Ex. Doc. 23, 38th Cong., 1st Sess., 1864. 19p.

2521. ----- ----- -----. Report of a Board of Navy Officers Appointed to Inquire into and Determine How Much the Vessels-of-War and Steam Machinery Contracted for by the Department in the Years

1862 and 1863 Cost the Contractors Over and Above the Contract Price and Allowance for Extra Work. Senate. Ex. Doc. 18, 39th Cong., 1st Sess., 1866. 64p.

Civil War "cost over-run."

2522. ----- ----- -----. Report of a Committee Appointed by the Court of Common Council of the City of New London, Conn., in Favor of the Location of a Naval School at that Place. Senate. Misc. Doc. 61, 37th Cong., 1st Sess., 1861. 6p.

2523. ----- ----- -----. Report of the Board of Examiners of the Naval School at Newport, R.I. Senate. Ex. Doc. 61, 37th Cong., 2nd Sess., 1862. 8p.

2524. ----- ----- -----. Report of the Committee to Select the Most Approved Site for a Navy Yard or Naval Station on the Mississippi River or Upon one of its Tributaries. Senate. Ex. Doc. 19, 38th Cong., 2nd Sess., 1865.

Headed by Rear Admiral C. H. Davis, who once commanded the Western Flotilla, the Committee recommended Carondelet, Mo., for the yard and Mound City, Illinois, for the station.

2525. ----- ----- -----. Report of the Secretary of the Navy, in Relation to the Erection of a Naval Hospital at Kittery, Me. Senate. Ex. Doc. 45, 38th Cong., 1st Sess., 1864. 31p.

2526. ----- ----- -----. Report of the Secretary of the Navy, on Various Subjects Pertaining to the Naval Establishment. Senate. Ex. Doc. 4, 36th Cong., 2nd Sess., 1861. 65p.

2527. ----- ----- -----. Report of the Secretary of State Relating to the Naval Force to be Maintained Upon the American Lakes. Senate. Ex. Doc. 6, 38th Cong., 2nd Sess., 1865. 1p.

2528. ----- ----- -----. Resolution of the Legislature of Pennsylvania in Favor of the Construction of one or more Iron-Clad Gunboats, for the Protection of Philadelphia. Senate. Misc. Doc. 80, 37th Cong., 2nd Sess., 1862. 2p.

When it was feared in the North that the Virginia would steam up the coast sinking all Yankee vessels before her.

2529. ----- ----- -----. Resolution of the Legislature of Rhode Island, in Favor of the Location of the Naval Academy of the United States at Newport. Senate. Misc. Doc. 41, 37th Cong., 2nd Sess., 1862. 2p.

2530. ----- ----- -----. Stephen Russell Mallory, Late a Senator from Florida. Memorial Addresses. Senate. Doc. 762, 60th Cong., 2nd Sess., 1908. 86p.

Once the Confederate Secretary of the Navy.

2531. ----- ----- -----. Committee on Armed Services. Historic Naval Vessels. Washington: U.S. Government Printing Office, 1954. 60p.

Includes U.S.S. Hartford.

2532. ----- ----- -----. Committee on Claims. Report [on] the Petition of Fenton & Brother, of Memphis, Tenn., Praying Compensation for the Use and Occupation of Lot. No. 59 of the Memphis Navy Yard from June 6, 1862 to August 20, 1866. Senate. Rept. 330, 44th Cong., 1st Sess., 1876. 4p.

A favorable report.

2533. ----- ----- -----. Committee on Commerce. Report on the Memorial of the Owners of the Ship John H. Jarvis, Praying that Provision be made by which the Said Vessel, Captured by the Rebels and Recaptured by the United States, may be Restored to the Owners. Senate. Rept. 57, 37th Cong., 2nd Sess., 1862. 7p.

2534. ----- ----- -----. Committee on Foreign Relations. Letter from the Secretary of State Transmitting Papers Relating to the Case of the Norwegian Bark Admiral P. Tordenskiold. Senate. Misc. Doc. 6, 37th Cong., 3rd Sess., 1863. 11p.

2535. ----- ----- -----. Committee on Labor and Public Welfare. Subcommittee on Veteran's Affairs. Medal of Honor, 1863-1968: "In the Name of

the Congress of the United States." Washington: U.S. Government Printing Office, 1968. 1058p.
Includes Civil War sailors awarded.

2536. ----- ----- -----. Committee on Naval Affairs. Letter of the Secretary of the Navy to the Hon. J. P. Hale, Chairman, Granting Compensation to the Officers and Crew of the Gunboat Essex for the Destruction of the Rebel Ram Arkansas. Senate. Misc. Doc. 113, 38th Cong., 1st Sess., 1864. 2p.

2537. ----- ----- ----- -----. Report [Concerning Enlistments in the Navy]. Senate. Rept. 44, 38th Cong., 1st Sess., 1864. 2p.

2538. ----- ----- ----- -----. Report on Bill for the Relief of Rear Admiral Thomas Turner. Senate. Rept. 132, 42nd Cong., 2nd Sess., 1872. 2p.
A favorable report.

2539. ----- ----- ----- -----. Report on Bill for the Relief of the Officers and Crew of the United States Steamer Monitor, who Participated in the Action with the Rebel Iron-Clad Merrimac, on the 9th Day of March, 1862. Senate. Rept. 394, 47th Cong., 1st Sess., 1882. 8p.
A favorable report on a very controversial issue.

2540. ----- ----- ----- -----. Report on Memorials, etc., Praying the Establishment of Naval Depots in Michigan and Ohio. Senate. Rept. 22, 37th Cong., 2nd Sess., 1862. 2p.

2541. ----- ----- ----- -----. Report [on] Resolution of Senate... to "Inquire if the Superintendent of the Officers Connected with the Government or Instruction Thereof, have Allowed or Countenanced in the Young Men Under Their Charge any Manifestation or Exhibition of Feelings of Sentiments Hostile to the Government of the United States, and Whether any of the Officers of Said Academy have Manifested any Sentiments of like Character." Senate. Rept. 68, 37th Cong., 2nd Sess., 1862. 19p.

2542. ----- ----- ----- -----. Report Relative to the Employment of George D. Morgan of New York, to Purchase Vessels for the Government. Senate. Rept. 9, 37th Cong., 2nd Sess., 1862. 7p.

2543. ----- ----- ----- -----. Report to Authorize the President to Restore Capt. George Henry Preble, now a Captain in the Navy, to His Original Position on the Navy Register, and Promote Him to the Rank of Commodore on the Active List. Senate. Rept. 148, 43rd Cong., 1st Sess., 1874. 3p.

Despite this unfavorable report, Preble was eventually advanced.

2544. ----- ----- ----- -----. Report to Compensate the Officers and Crew of the Kearsarge for the Destruction of the Rebel Piratical Vessel Alabama. Senate. Rept. 250. 41st Cong., 2nd Sess., 1870. 4p.

2545. ----- ----- -----. Select Committee. Report on Chartering of Transport Vessels for the Banks Expedition, and Also in Regard to the Employment of Transports Generally. Senate. Rept. 75, 32nd Sess., 1863. 127p.

2546. ----- ----- ----- -----. Report on the Surrender of the Navy Yard at Pensacola and the Destruction of Property, Norfolk Navy Yard. Senate. Rept. 37, 37th Cong., 2nd Sess., 1862. 250p.

2547. -----. Interior Department. Census Office. Tenth Census. 22 vols. Washington: Government Printing Office, 1883-1888.

Henry Hall's excellent report on the "Shipbuilding Industry" appears in Vol. VIII.

2548. -----. Laws, Statutes, Etc. The Statutes at Large of the United States, Vols. XII-XV, December 5, 1859-March 1869. 3 vols. Washington: Government Printing Office, 1859-1869.

2549. ----- -----. The Statutes Relating to the Navy of the United States, as Revised, Simplified, Arranged, and Consolidated by the Commission Appointed for that Purpose, from the Various

Acts of Congress now in Force, in Whole or in Part. Washington: Government Printing Office, 1869. 92p.

Of particular interest is the fundamental navy law of July 16, 1862.

2550. -----. Marine Corps. One Hundred Eighty Landings of the United States Marines, 1800-1934; a Brief History. By Harry A. Ellsworth. 2 vols. Washington: 1934.

Vol. I covers the Civil War.

2551. ----- -----. Historical Branch, G-3. A Chronology of the United States Marine Corps. 2 vols. Washington: U. S. Government Printing Office, 1965.

2552. ----- ----- -----. The United States Marines in the Civil War, by Bernard C. Nalty. Rev. ed. Washington: 1962. 16p.

2553. -----. National Archives. Guide to the Archives of the Confederate States of America. By Henry P. Beers. Publication, no. 68-15. Washington: U. S. Government Printing Office, 1968. 536p.

2554. ----- -----. Guide to the Federal Archives Relating to the Civil War. By Kenneth W. Munden and Henry P. Beers. Publication, no. 63-1. Washington: U. S. Government Printing Office, 1962. 721p.

Records of the Union Navy Department described on p. 439-498.

2555. ----- -----. Preliminary Checklist of the Naval Records Collection of the Office of Naval Records and Library, 1775-1910 (Record Group 45). Compiled by James R. Masterson. Preliminary Checklist, 30. Publication, no. 46-19. Washington: 1945. 149p.

An extremely useful guide to manuscripts.

2556. ----- -----. Preliminary Inventory of Records Relating to Civil War Claims: the United States and Great Britain (Record Group 76). Compiled by George S. Ulibarri and Daniel T. Goggin. Preliminary Inventory, 135. Publication, no.

62-6. Washington: 1962. 21p.

2557. ----- -----. Preliminary Inventory of the Records of the Bureau of Naval Personnel (Record Group 24). Compiled by Virgil E. Baugh. Preliminary Inventory, 123. Publication, no. 60-14. Washington: 1960. 135p.

2558. ----- -----. Preliminary Inventory of the Records of the Bureau of Ships (Record Group 19). Compiled by Elizabeth Bethel et al. Preliminary Inventory, 133. Publication, no. 61-11. Washington: 1961. 241p.

2559. ----- -----. Preliminary Inventory of the Records of the Coast and Geodetic Service (Record Group 23). Compiled by Nathan Reingold. Preliminary Inventory, 105. Publication, no. 59-3. Washington: 1958. 83p.

2560. ----- -----. Preliminary Inventory of the Records of the U. S. District Court for the Eastern District of Pennsylvania (Record Group 21). Compiled by Marion M. Johnson, Mary Jo Grotenrath, and Henry T. Ulasek. Preliminary Inventory, 124. Publication, no. 60-15. Washington: 1960. 44p.

2561. ----- -----. Preliminary Inventory of the Records of the U. S. District Court for the Southern District of New York (Record Group 21). Compiled by Henry T. Ulasek and Marion Johnson. Preliminary Inventory, 116. Publication, no. 60-3. Washington: 1959. 68p.

2562. ----- -----. Preliminary Inventory of the War Department Collection of Confederate Records (Record Group 109). Compiled by Elizabeth Bethel. Preliminary Inventory, 101. Publication, no. 58-3. Washington: 1957. 310p.

2563. -----. National Waterways Commission. A Traffic History of the Mississippi River System. By Frank Haigh Dixon. Document, no. 11. Washington: Government Printing Office, 1909. 70p.

2564. -----. Navy Department. General Orders and

Circulars Issued by the Navy Department, from 1863 to 1887. With an Alphabetical Index of Subjects; Also, an Index of Bureau and Marine Corps Circulars, General Court-Martial Orders, and Special Death Notices. Compiled by M. S. Thompson. Washington: Government Printing Office, 1887. 353p.

2565. ----- -----. List of Nautical Books Furnished to all U. S. Vessels-of-War. Washington: Government Printing Office, 1866. 14p.
Volumes on navigation and sailing directions issued to the navigation departments of various ships late in the war.

2566. ----- -----. List of Rear-Admirals, Commodores, Captains, and Commanders, Showing the Dates on which They Retire and the Promotions Consequent. Washington: Government Printing Office, 1870. 15p.
Includes Civil War officers of the regular navy still on active duty by said date.

2567. ----- -----. Naval Court-Martial of Commander Henry Walke. Washington: 1861. 25p.

2568. ----- -----. Proceedings of a Naval Court of Inquiry in the Case of Acting Master L. L. D. Voornees, Commanding the U. S. Steamer Marigold, Charged with Violating the Maritime Jurisdiction of Spain, by Firing at the British Merchant Vessel Belle While Entering the Port of Ravana. Washington: 1864. 10p.

2569. ----- -----. Record of the Medal of Honor Issued to Blue Jackets of the United States Navy, 1862-1888. Washington: Government Printing Office, 1888. 72p.

2570. ----- -----. Register of the Commissioned and Warrant Officers of the Navy of the United States and of the Marine Corps. Vols. XLVII-LIII. Washington: Government Printing Office, 1861-1865.

2571. ----- -----. Regulations for the Government of the United States Navy. Washington: Government

Printing Office, 1865. 345p.

2572. ----- -----. Regulations for the Uniform and Dress of the Navy and Marine Corps of the United States. Washington: C. Alexander, 1852. 38p.

2573. ----- ----- -----. Boston: 1862. 7p.

2574. ----- -----. Report of the Secretary of the Navy. Washington: Government Printing Office, 1861-1865.

Prior to the publication of the Navy's "Official Records," this was the standard source for documents relating to naval battles, etc.

2575. ----- -----. Report of the Secretary of the Navy and the Commission by him Appointed on the Proposed New Iron Navy Yard at League Island. Philadelphia: Collins, 1863. 56p.

2576. ----- -----. Report of the Secretary of the Navy in Relation to Armored Vessels. Washington: Government Printing Office, 1864. 607p.

Useful.

2577. ----- -----. Report to the Navy Department, by John A. Dahlgren, on the Condition of the United States Navy. Washington: Government Printing Office, 1862. 16p.

2578. ----- -----. Report to the Navy Department on the Eads Steam Turret, by James W. King. N.p.: 1864.

Interestingly, an Eads Turret and an Ericsson Turret were installed aboard the river monitor Winnebago.

2579. ----- -----. Bureau of Naval Personnel. The History of the Chaplain Corps, United States Navy, 1778-1945. By Clifford M. Drury. 6 vols. Washington: U.S. Government Printing Office, 1949-1960.

2580. ----- ----- -----. Medal of Honor, 1861-1949: the Navy. Washington: U.S. Government Printing Office, 1950. 327p.

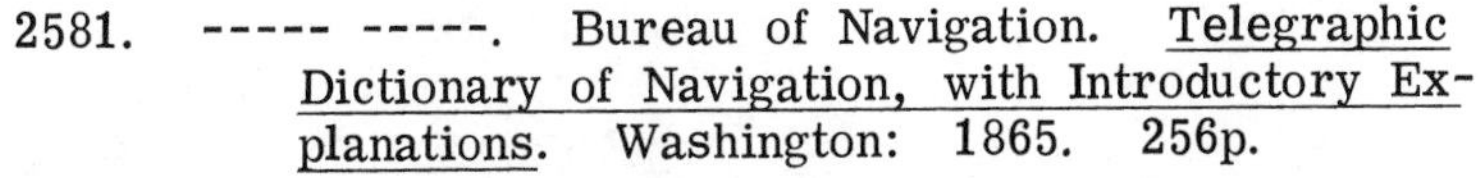

2581. ----- -----. Bureau of Navigation. *Telegraphic Dictionary of Navigation, with Introductory Explanations*. Washington: 1865. 256p.

2582. ----- -----. Bureau of Ordnance and Hydrography. *Code of Flotilla and Boat Squadron Signals for the United States Navy*. Prepared by Commander Thorton A. Jenkins. Washington: Government Printing Office, 1861. 191p.

2583. ----- ----- -----. *Exercises in Small Arms and Field Artillery: Arranged for the Naval Service*. Philadelphia: T. K. and P. G. Collins, 1852. 103p.

Possibly the volume Lt. H. Erben used to refresh his howitzer battery prior to the Battle of Antietam.

2584. ----- ----- -----. *Ordnance and Armor*. Washington: 1865. 892p.

2585. ----- ----- -----. *Ordnance Instruction for the United States Navy, Relating to the Preparation of Vessels-of-War for Battle; to the Duties of Officers and Others when at Quarters; to Ordnance and Ordnance Stores; and to Gunnery*. 2nd ed. Washington: George W. Bowman, 1860. 171p.

2586. ----- ----- -----. *Report by John A. Dahlgren on the Drill of the Pivot 11-inch Gun as Practiced on board the U. S. Ship Plymouth*. Washington: 1861. 16p.

2587. ----- -----. Bureau of Provisions and Clothing. *Instructions for the Government of Inspectors in Charge of Stores, Naval Storekeepers, Paymasters, and Assistant Paymasters*. Washington: 1862. 123p.

2588. ----- ----- -----. *Pay and Tax Tables for the Use of Paymasters and Others in the Navy*. Washington: 1862. 68p.

2589. ----- -----. Bureau of Ships. "The Boston Naval Shipyard." *Bureau of Ships Journal*, II (January 1954), 13-18.

2590. ----- ----- -----. "The New York Naval Shipyard; a Record of Progressive Achievement in Shipbuilding Since 1801." Bureau of Ships Journal, II (April 1954), 22-26.

2591. ----- ----- -----. "The Philadelphia Naval Shipyard." Bureau of Ships Journal, III (June 1954), 8-13.

2592. ----- -----. Bureau of Steam Engineering. Regulations, Circulars, Orders and Decisions Relating to the U.S. Naval Engineer Corps from its Organization Until March 1865. Washington: 1865. 75p.

2593. ----- -----. Mississippi Squadron. General Orders. Rear Adm. D. D. Porter, Commanding, From Oct. 16th 1862 to Oct. 26th 1864. St. Louis: R. P. Studley, 1864.

2594. ----- ----- -----. General Orders. Rear Adm. S. P. Lee, Commanding, From Nov. 1st 1864 to April 24th 1865. St. Louis: R. P. Studley, 1865. 52p.

2595. ----- -----. Naval Academy. Routine and Orders for the United States Naval Academy. Newport: J. Atkinson, 1862. 16p.

2596. ----- -----. Naval Amphibious School, Little Creek, Va. Monitor and Merrimack; Re-enactment--April 20-25, 1964. N. P.: 1964. 7p.
By use of a computer.

2597. ----- -----. Naval History Division. American Ships-of-the-Line. Washington: U.S. Government Printing Office, 1969. 44p.
During the Civil War, the few remaining served as receiving ships.

2598. ----- -----. Civil War Naval Chronology. 6 vols. Washington: U.S. Government Printing Office, 1961-1966.

2599. ----- ----- -----. Rev. ed. 6 vols. in 1. Washington: U.S. Government Printing Office, 1971.

2600. ----- ----- -----. Civil War Naval Ordnance, by Eugene B. Canfield. Washington: U.S. Government Printing Office, 1969. 25p.

2601. ----- ----- -----. Dictionary of American Naval Fighting Ships. Vol. I--. Washington: U.S. Government Printing Office, 1959--.
Includes "biographies" of individual Civil War vessels.

2602. ----- ----- -----. Historic Ship Exhibits in the United States. Washington: U.S. Government Printing Office, 1969. 71p.
Includes such Civil War vessels as the Cairo.

2603. ----- ----- -----. Monitors of the U.S. Navy, 1861-1937. Washington: U.S. Government Printing Office, 1969. 49p.

2604. ----- ----- -----. Riverine Warfare: the U.S. Navy's Operations on Inland Waters. Rev. ed. Washington: U.S. Government Printing Office, 1968. 53p.
Includes the Civil War.

2605. ----- ----- -----. United States Naval History: A Bibliography. 5th ed. Washington: U.S. Government Printing Office, 1969. 33p.
Includes entires for the Civil War.

2606. ----- -----. Office of the Chief of Naval Operations. U.S. Naval Communications; a Chronological History. Washington: Defense Printing Service, 1963. 26p.

2607. ----- -----. Office of Naval Records and Library. List of Log Books of U.S. Vessels, 1861-1865, on File in the Navy Department. Office Memoranda. Washington: 1891. 49p.
Most of these are now in National Archives.

2608. ----- ----- -----. List of U.S. Naval Vessels, 1861-1865, Including the Ellet Ram Fleet and the Mississippi Marine Brigade; Appendix, List of U.S. Coast Survey Vessels. Office Memoranda. Washington: 1891. 8p.

2609. ----- ----- -----. Naval Service of Negroes, United States Navy. Office Memoranda. Washington: 1924. 3p.

2610. ----- ----- -----. Official Records of the Union and Confederate Navies in the War of the Rebellion. Edited by Richard Rush et al. 31 vols. Washington: Government Printing Office, 1894-1922.

Perhaps the single most important printed source for naval actions.

2611. ----- ----- -----. Register of Officers of the Confederate States Navy, 1861-1865. Office Memoranda. Washington: 1898. 157p.

2612. -----. Norfolk Naval Shipyard. A Brief History of the Norfolk Naval Shipyard, Portsmouth, Virginia. By Marshall W. Butt. Rev. ed. Portsmouth: Public Information Office, 1956. 28p.

2613. -----. President (Abraham Lincoln). General Order Respecting the Observance of the Sabbath Day in the Army and Navy. Washington: 1862. 1p.

2614. United States of America. State Department. Correspondence Concerning the Claims Against Great Britain. 7 vols. Washington: Government Printing Office, 1869-1871.

Much data on the Confederate cruisers and their victims.

2615. ----- -----. Foreign Relations of the United States. Diplomatic Papers. Washington: Government Printing Office, 1861--.

Also known as Diplomatic Correspondence, 1862-1868; Contains non-confidential dispatches between the Department and U. S. ministers abroad. Covers many subjects; especially useful on the U. S. and Confederate naval operations in foreign waters and the blockade.

2616. ----- -----. Mixed Commission on British and American Claims Under Article XII of the Treaty of Washington, 1871. British and American

Claims. 34 vols. Washington: Government Printing Office, 1873.

2617. -----. Supreme Court. United States Reports... Cases Adjudged in the Supreme Court. Vols. LXVI-LXXI. Washington: 1861-1866.
Includes such important prize cases as that of the Peterhoff.

2618. -----. Treasury Department. Commercial Intercourse with, and in, States Declared in Insurrection, and the Collection of Abandoned and Captured Propery. Embracing the Treasury Department Circulars and Regulations; the Executive Proclamations and Licenses; and the War and Navy Department Orders Relating to those Subjects. Washington: Government Printing Office, 1863. 56p.
Constantly in demand as "required reading" by officers of the river gunboats.

2619. ----- -----. In Memoriam. Rear Admiral Robert Harris Wyman, U. S. Navy, Chairman of the Lighthouse Board. Washington: 1882. 7p.
Skipper of the U. S. S. Wachusett and Santiago de Cuba in the West Indies, 1862-1863.

2620. ----- -----. Bureau of Statistics. "A Complete List of the Vessels of the United States Navy from 1779 to 1874, Together with Tables Showing the Personnel of the U. S. Navy and Naval Expeditions, etc., etc." By George Henry Preble. In Mercantile Navy List of the United States, 1874. Washington: Government Printing Office, 1874. 33p.

2621. ----- -----. Office of the Fourth Auditor. Regulations for the Payment of Prize Money. N. p.: 1864. 8p.

2622. -----. War Department. Annual Report of the Secretary of War. Washington: Government Printing Office, 1861-1866.

2623. ----- -----. The War of the Rebellion: A Compilation of the Official Records of the Union and Confederate Armies. Edited by R. N. Scott

et al. 128 vols. Washington: Government Printing Office, 1880-1901.
Contains many naval documents later published in the Navy's "Official Records."

2624. ----- -----. The War of the Rebellion Atlas, to Accompany the Official Records of the Union and Confederate Armies. Compiled by Calvin D. Cowles. 3 vols. Washington: Government Printing Office, 1891-1895.
The 175 plates illustrate many adventures, such as Port Royal and Vicksburg, in which the Union navy played important roles.

2625. ----- -----. Quartermaster Department. Reports to the War Department by Brev. Maj. Gen. Lewis B. Parson, Chief of Rail and River Transportation. St. Louis: G. Knapp, 1867. 64p.

2626. -----. Vicksburg National Military Park Commission. Record of the Organizations Engaged in the Campaign, Siege, and Defense of Vicksburg. Compiled by John S. Kountz, Secretary and Historian of the Commission. Washington: Government Printing Office, 1901. 72p.

2627. Upshur, John H. "A Torpedo Attack on the Minnesota." Navy, VII (February 1913), 52-54.
An unsuccessful venture in 1863.

2628. Upton, J. H. "An Alphabetical List of Vessels Captured by Rebel Privateers." Merchant Magazine and Commercial Review, XLIX (November 1863), 349-354.
An early, inaccurate listing.

2629. Vail, Israel E. Three Years on the Blockade: a Naval Experience. New York: Abbey Press, 1902. 171p.
By the Assistant Paymaster of the U. S. S. Massachusetts.

2630. Vallandingham, Edward N. "Piracy or Privateering?" Pearson's Magazine, X (July 1903), 82-88.
Seizure of the Chesapeake, 1863.

2631. Van Alstyne, Laurence. Diary of an Enlisted Man.

New Haven: Tuttle, Morehouse and Taylor, 1910. 348p.

Author served as a sailor on the Red River expedition.

2632. Vandiver, Frank E., ed. Confederate Blockade Running Through Bermuda, 1861-1865; Letters and Cargo Manifests. Austin: University of Texas Press, 1947. 155p.

2633. -----., ed. See Gayle, Richard H., no. 915.

2634. -----., ed. See Gorgas, Josiah., no. 964.

2635. Van Dorn, Charles., Joint Author. See Roske, Ralph J., no. 2084.

2636. Van Dorn, Earl., Author of Report. See C.S.A. War Department., no. 584.

2637. Van Hoose, G. W. "The Confederate States Marine Corps." Marine Corps Gazette, XIII (September 1928), 166-177.

Data on personnel and service conditions; brief accounts of various operations.

2638. Van Ravenswaay, Charles. "New Madrid Reminiscences, 1789-1882." Missouri Historical Society Bulletin, IV (January 1948), 93-96.

2639. Vestal, Stanley. The Missouri. Rivers of America. New York: Farrar and Rinehart, 1945. 368p.

2640. Vickers, George M., ed. Under Both Flags: Tales of the Civil War as Told by the Veterans. Philadelphia: People's Publishing, 1896. 592p.

2641. Viele, Egbert L. "The Port Royal Expedition, 1861: the First Union Victory of the Civil War." Magazine of American History, XIV (October 1885), 329-340.

2642. "Vigilans," pseud. The Foreign Enlistment Acts of England and America. The Alexandra and the Rams. London: Saunders, Otley, 1864. 124p.

2643. Villard, Henry. Memoirs of Henry Villard, Jour-

nalist and Financier, 1835-1900. 2 vols. Boston: Houghton, Mifflin, 1904.
Followed the early river war in the West; with other reporters was invited by Captain Walke to tour the Carondelet after the Battle of Memphis.

2644. Villard, Oswald G. "Submarine and Torpedo in the Blockade of the Confederacy." Harper's Monthly Magazine, CXXXIII (June 1916), 131-137.

2645. Villers, Broughton., pseud. See Shaw, Frederick J., no. 2158.

2646. "The Virginia-Merrimac: Behind the Scenes in the Confederate Navy Department, from the New York Sun." United Service, New Series XIII (May 1895), 493-497.
On the decision to convert the burned hulk at the Gosport Yard into the large ironclad.

2647. Vitz, Carl. "Cincinnati: Civil War Port." Museum Echoes, XXXIV (July 1961), 51-54.

2648. Von Kolnitz, Harry. "The Confederate Submarine." United States Naval Institute Proceedings, LXIII (October 1937), 1453-1457.

2649. -----. "The Keokuk's Guns." United States Naval Institute Proceedings, LXIV (May 1938), 678-679.

2650. Voorhies, Hugh. "Steamboats on the Red River of the South." Steamboat Bill of Facts, I (August 1942), 120-123.

2651. Votaw, Homer C. "The Curious Case of the Camanche." United States Naval Institute Proceedings, LXXXII (July 1956), 792-793.
Monitor sent by ship to be assembled in and for the defense of San Francisco.

2652. "W. S. G." "The Policy of British and American Blockades." United Service Magazine (July 1862), 324-325.
The British view of the period.

2653. Waddell, Alfred M. The Last Year of the War in

North Carolina, Including Plymouth, Fort Fisher, and Bentonville. Richmond: W. E. Jones, 1888. 31p.

2654. Waddell, James I. C. S. S. Shenandoah; the Memoirs of Lieutenant Commanding James I. Waddell. Edited by James D. Horan. New York: Crown, 1960. 200p.

2655. -----. "The Shenandoah." Southern Historical Society Papers, XXXII (1904), 320-328.

2656. Wade, William W. "The Man Who Stopped the Rams." American Heritage, XIV (April 1963), 18-23, 78-81.
Thomas R. Dudley.

2657. Wagner, Scrimshaw. "The Story of the Jane Campbell." Nautical Research Journal, III (January 1951), 1-2, 11.
Brief history of a blockade runner.

2658. Wainwright, Richard. "The Naval Attack Upon Charleston, South Carolina." United Service, New Series IV (November 1890), 433-441.

2659. -----., Joint Editor. See Fox, Gustavus V., no. 897.

2660. Wait, Horatio L. "The Blockade of the Confederacy." Century Illustrated Magazine, LVI (October 1898), 914-928.
By a former Union Navy Paymaster.

2661. -----. "The Blockading Service." In Military Essays and Recollections; Papers Read Before the Illinois Commandery, Military Order of the Loyal Legion of the United States. 4 vols. Chicago: A. C. McClurg, 1891-1912. Vol. II, pp. 211-252.

2662. -----. "Reminiscences of Fort Sumter." In Military Essays and Recollections; Papers Read Before the Illinois Commandery, Military Order of the Loyal Legion of the United States. 4 vols. Chicago: A. C. McClurg, 1891-1912. Vol. I, pp. 185-210.

2663. Waite, M. R. Reply of Mr. Waite, Counsel of the United States, to the Argument of the Counsel of Great Britain, Upon the Special Question as to Supplies of Coal in British Ports to Confederate Ships. Geneva, Switzerland: Carey Brothers, 1872. 20p.

2664. Waitz, Julia E. (Le Grand). The Journal of Julia Le Grand, New Orleans, 1862-1863. Edited by Kate Mason Rowland and Mrs. Morris L. Croxall. Richmond: Everett Waddey, 1911. 318p.
Records the fall of the city.

2665. Walesby, Stokes and Theodore Roscoe. Navy: History and Traditions; Naval Actions of the Civil War. Washington: Stokes Walesby, 1961. 32p.
Illustrated much like a comic book.

2666. Walke, Henry. "The Gun-Boats at Belmont and Fort Henry." In Robert U. Johnson and Clarence C. Buell, eds. B & L. Vol. I, pp. 358-367.

2667. -----. Naval Scenes and Reminiscences of the Civil War in the United States, on the Southern and Western Waters during the Years 1861, 1862, and 1863; with the History of that Period, Compared and Corrected from Authentic Sources. New York: F. R. Reed, 1877. 480p.
Although self-centered, contains many newspaper and unofficial versions not found elsewhere. The hurt tone of writing encountered is not repeated in the author's various articles. Aside from the "Official Records," one of the most rewarding printed sources for the theatre and period covered.

2668. -----. Naval Scenes on the Western Waters. The Gunboats Tyler, Carondelet, and Lafayette. N. p., n. d. 71p.

2669. -----. "Operations of the Western Flotilla." Century Illustrated Magazine, XXIX (January 1885), 419-433.
Contains a few details not carried over to the "Battles and Leaders" series.

2670. -----. "The Western Flotilla at Fort Donelson,

Number Ten, Fort Pillow, and Memphis." In Robert U. Johnson and Clarence C. Buell, eds. B & L. Vol. I, pp. 430-452.

2671. Walker, Eva D. W., ed. See Walker, John., no. 2674.

2672. Walker, Georgiana F. (Gholson). Private Journal, 1862-1865, with Selections from the Post-War Years, 1865-1876. Confederate Centennial Studies, no. 25. Tuscaloosa, Ala: Confederate Publishing Company, 1963. 148p.
Blockade running.

2673. Walker, Jennie M. Life of Capt. Joseph Fry, the Cuban Martyr. Being a Faithful Records of His Remarkable Career from Childhood to the Time of His Heroic Death at the Hands of Spanish Executioners; Recounting His Experiences as an Officer in the U. S. and Confederate Navies, and Revealing Much of the Inner History and Secret Marine Service of the Late Civil War in America. Hartford: J. B. Burr, 1875. 589p.
Fry was a blockade runner and skipper of the Rebel vessels Ivy and Morgan at New Orleans.

2674. [Walker, John L.] Cahaba Prison and the Sultana Disaster. Edited by Eva D. Wilbee Walker. Hamilton, Ohio: Brown and Whitaker, 1910. 33p.

2675. Walker, Peter F. "Building a Tennessee Army; Autumn, 1861." Tennessee Historical Quarterly, XVI (June 1957), 99-116.

2676. -----. "Command Failure; the Fall of Forts Henry and Donelson." Tennessee Historical Quarterly, XVI (December 1957), 335-360.

2677. -----. "Holding the Tennessee Line; Winter, 1861-1862." Tennessee Historical Quarterly, XVI (September 1957), 228-249.

2678. -----. Vicksburg: a People at War, 1860-1865. Chapel Hill: University of North Carolina Press, 1960. 235p.

2679. Walker, R. "Peripatetic Coffin: the Underwater Torpedo Boat H. L. Hunley." South Atlantic Quarterly, XXXIX (October 1940), 438-447.

2680. Walker, Robert M. "Marines in Gray: the Forgotten Service of [the] Confederacy." Civil War Times, II (August 1960), 16-17.

2681. Wallace, Lee A., Jr. "Lieutenant Francis Hawke Cameron, Confederate States Marine Corps." Military Collector and Historian, VI (September 1954), 79.
Discussion of a photograph.

2682. -----. "Seal of the C. S. Navy Department." Military Collector and Historian, XIV (Summer 1962), 60.
Discussion of the symbols thereon.

2683. Wallace, Lew. An Autobiography. 2 vols. New York: Harper, 1906.

2684. -----. "The Capture of Fort Donelson." In Robert U. Johnson and Clarence C. Buell, eds. B & L. Vol. I, pp. 398-428.

2685. Walter, Francis X. "The Naval Battle of Mobile Bay." Alabama Historical Quarterly, XVI (Spring 1952), 5-46.

2686. Walter, H. "The Monitor: History's Strangest Warship." Popular Science, CLXXVII (March 1961), 72-76.

2687. Warburton, A. F., Reporter. See U. S. Circuit Court., no. 2433.

2688. Ward, James H. Elementary Instruction in Naval Ordnance and Gunnery. New ed., rev. and enl. New York: D. Van Nostrand, 1861. 209p.
Based on Navy Department procedures, but highly simplified.

2689. -----. Steam for the Millions. New York: H. Dexter, 1860. 120p.
Ship machinery and propulsion.

2690. Ward, W. S. "How We Ran the Vicksburg Batteries." Magazine of American History, XIV (December 1885), 600-605.

2691. Wardle, A. C. "British-Built Blockade Runners." Steamboat Bill of Facts, XI (December 1954), 77-80.

2692. Warley, A. F. "Notes on the Destruction of the Albemarle." In Robert U. Johnson and Clarence C. Buell, eds. B & L. Vol. IV, p. 641.

2693. -----. "The Ram Mansassas at the Passage of the New Orleans Forts." In Robert U. Johnson and Clarence C. Buell, eds. B & L. Vol. II, pp. 89-90.
By her commander.

2694. Warner, Ezra J. Generals in Blue; Lives of the Union Commanders. Baton Rouge: Louisiana State University Press, 1964. 679p.
Includes partners in join operations.

2695. -----. Generals in Gray; Lives of the Confederate Commanders. Baton Rouge: Louisiana State University Press, 1959. 420p.

2696. Warner, Oliver. Great Sea Battles. New York: Macmillan, 1963. 303p.
Largely pictorial; includes Mobile Bay.

2697. [Warmouth, Henry C.] "The Vicksburg Diary of Henry Clay Warmouth." Edited by Paul H. Haas. Journal of Mississippi History, XXXI (November 1969), 334-347; XXXII (February 1970), 60-74.
Recounts the Battle of Grand Gulf, 1863.

2698. Waterman, George C. "Notable Events of the War." Confederate Veteran, VI (January-December 1898), 59-62, 170-173, 390-394; VII (January-December 1899), 16-21, 449-452, 490-492; VIII (January-December 1900), 21-24, 53-55; IX (January-December 1901), 24-29.

2699. Watson, J. Crittenden. "Admiral Farragut in the Rigging of the Hartford." Navy, VII (March 1913), 81-83.

2700. -----. Farragut and Mobile Bay. District of Columbia Commandery, Military Order of the Loyal Legion of the United States. War Papers, no. 98. Washington: the Commandery, 1916.
By one of the Hartford's lieutenants.

2701. -----. "Farragut and Mobile Bay--Personal Reminiscences." United States Naval Institute Proceedings, LIII (May 1927), 551-557.

2702. -----. "The Lashing of Admiral Farragut in the Rigging." By J. Crittenden Watson and Joseph Marthon. In Robert U. Johnson and Clarence C. Buell, eds. B & L. Vol. IV, pp. 406-407.

2703. Watson, John W. "The Building of the Ship." Harper's New Monthly Magazine, XXIV (April 1862), 608-620.
Popular account of shipbuilding at the time; illustrations make this a useful introduction.

2704. Watson, William. The Adventures of a Blockade Runner; or, Trade in Time of War. New York: Macmillan, 1892. 324p.
By the captain of the swift Rob Roy.

2705. Way, Frederick, Jr. "The Oldest Mississippi Steamboat?" Steamboat Bill of Facts, No. 20 (August 1946), 385-387.
The U.S.S. Goldsboro, which survived the war in various capacities for almost 100 years.

2706. Wayland, John W. The Pathfinder of the Seas; the Life of Matthew Fontaine Maury. Richmond: Garrett and Massie, 1930. 191p.

2707. Webb, William L. Battles and Biographies of Missourians; or, the Civil War Period of Our State. Kansas City: Hudson-Kimberly, 1900. 369p.

2708. Webber, John. "The Monitor and the Merrimac." Collector, XXV (October 1912), 116-117.
A letter dated a few days after the fight.

2709. Webber, Richard and John C. Roberts. "James B. Eads: Master Builder." The Navy, VIII (March

1965), 23-25.
Concentrates on his gunboat construction.

2710. -----., Joint Author. See Roberts, John C., no. 2043.

2711. Weber, Gustavus A. The Coast and Geodetic Survey; Its History, Activities, and Organization. Institute for Government Research. Service Monographs of the United States Government, no. 16. Baltimore: Johns Hopkins University Press, 1923. 107p.
Includes the Civil War Years.

2712. Webster, Donald B. "Rodman's Great Guns." Ordnance, XLVII (July-August 1962), 60-65.
Some of which were fitted aboard Civil War vessels.

2713. Webster, Harrie. "An August Morning with Farragut at Mobile Bay." In U. S. Navy Department, Naval History Division. Civil War Naval Chronology. 6 vols. Washington: U. S. Government Printing Office, 1961-1966. Vol. VI, pp. 85-98.
Includes a useful eye-witness description of the sinking of the monitor Tecumseh.

2714. -----. Personal Experiences on a Monitor at the Battle of Mobile Bay. California Commandery, Military Order of the Loyal Legion of the United States. War Papers, no. 14. San Francisco: the Commandery, 1894.

2715. -----. Some Personal Recollections and Reminiscences of the Battle of Port Hudson. District of Columbia Commandery, Military Order of the Loyal Legion of the United States. War Papers, no. 16. Washington: the Commandery, 1894.
By the Chief Engineer aboard the U. S. S. Genesee.

2716. Weeks, Grenville M. "The Last Cruise of the Monitor." Atlantic Monthly, XI (March 1863), 366-372.
By a rescued member of her crew.

2717. Weigley, Russel F. "Montgomery Meigs--a Person-

ality Profile." Civil War Times Illustrated, III (November 1964), 42-48.
As QMG, he was directly responsible for overseeing and financing the building of Ead's "City Series" gunboats.

2718. -----. Quartermaster General of the Union Army; a Biography of M. C. Meigs. New York: Columbia University Press, 1959. 396p.

2719. [Weimer, John.] The Diary of a Union Soldier, 1864-1865. Edited by Walter H. Rankins. Frankfort, Ky.: Roberts, 1952. 34p.
Serving aboard a Western gunbaot.

2720. Weisberger, Bernard A. Reporters for the Union. Boston: Little, Brown, 1953. 316p.

2721. Well, Thomas H. "The Confederate Navy: A Study in Organization." Unpublished PhD. Dissertation, Emory University, 1963.

2722. Weller, Jac. "Bedford Forrest: Tactical Teamwork was His Secret Weapon." Ordnance, XXXVIII (September-October 1953), 248-251.
A study of the use of his cannon; includes the Johnsonville Affair.

2723. Welles, Gideon. "Admiral Farragut and New Orleans, with an Account of the Origin and Command of the First Three Naval Expeditions of the War." Galaxy, XII (November-December 1871), 669-683, 817-832.

2724. -----. "The Capture and Release of Mason and Slidell." Galaxy, XV (May 1873), 640-651.

2725. -----. The Diary of Gideon Welles, Secretary of the Navy under Lincoln and Johnson. Edited by John T. Morse, Jr. 3 vols. Boston: Houghton, Mifflin, 1911.

2726. ----- -----. New Edition with Foreword and Notes by Howard K. Beale. 3 vols. New York: W. W. Norton, 1960.

2727. -----. "Facts in Relation to the Expedition Ordered

by the Administration of President Lincoln for the Relief of the Garrison in Fort Sumter." Galaxy, X (November 1870), 613-637.

2728. -----. "Facts in Relation to the Reinforcement of Fort Pickens, in the Spring of 1861." Galaxy, XI (January 1871), 92-107.

2729. -----. "The Facts of the Abandonment of the Gosport Navy Yard." Galaxy, X (July 1870), 109-119.

2730. -----. "The First Iron-Clad Monitor." In Annals of the War. p. 17-31.
U.S.S. Monitor and the Department's role in her development.

2731. -----. "Narrative of Events." American Historical Review, XXXI (April 1962), 486-494.

2732. -----. Selected Essays. Compiled by Albert Mordell. 2 vols. New York: Twayne, 1959-1960.
The Galaxy articles in their most available form.

2733. -----. "Two Manuscripts of Gideon Welles." Edited by Muriel Bernett. New England Quarterly, XI (September 1938), 576-605.
One demonstrates the ideas of Welles and Secretary of State Seward on Confederate privateers.

2734. Wells, John G. Wells' Army and Navy Handy Book; or, Every Soldier and Marine His Own Counsellor, Being a Full and Complete Guide to the Soldier and Marine in all Matters Pertaining to His Duties and Obligations, and His Rights and How to Obtain His Rights without Legal Assistance; Together with Everything of Interest Connected with the Army and Navy Departments and a Complete Historical Record of Events Connected with the War. New York: the Author, 1864. 191p.
Not as complete as the title.

2735. Wells, Tom H. The Confederate Navy: A Study in Organization. University, Ala.: University of

Alabama Press, 1971. 182p.
An administrative history.

2736. -----. "The Navies." In Allan Nevins, James I. Robertson, Jr., and Bell I. Wiley, eds. Civil War Books: a Critical Bibliography. 2 vols. Baton Rouge: Louisiana State University Press, 1967-1969. Vol. I, pp. 217-240.

2737. Wells, William S., ed. The Original United States Warship Monitor; Copies of Correspondence Between the Late Cornelius S. Bushnell, Captain John Ericsson, and the Hon. Gideon Welles. New Haven: [C. S. Bushnell National Memorial Association], 1899. 61p.

2738. Werner, H. O. "The Fall of New Orleans, 1862." United States Naval Institute Proceedings, LXXXVIII (April 1962), 78-86.

2739. Wertenbaker, Thomas J. Norfolk: Historic Southern Port. Durham, N.C.: Duke University Press, 1931. 378p.

2740. West, James H. "The New York Navy Yard." In Society of Naval Architects and Marine Engineers. Historical Transactions, 1893-1943. New York: the Society, 1945. p. 17-18.

2741. West, Richard S., Jr. "Admiral Farragut and General Butler." United States Naval Institute Proceedings, LXXXII (June 1956), 634-643.

2742. -----. Gideon Welles, Lincoln's Navy Department. Indianapolis: Bobbs, Merrill, 1943. 379p.

2743. -----. "Gunboats in the Swamps: the Yazoo Pass Expedition." Civil War History, IX (June 1963), 157-166.

2744. -----. "Lincoln's Hand in Naval Matters." Civil War History, IV (June 1958), 175-183.

2745. -----. Lincoln's Scapegoat General. New York: Houghton, Mifflin, 1965. 462p.
Benjamin Butler.

2746. -----. Mr. Lincoln's Navy. New York: Longmans, Green, 1957. 328p.

2747. -----. "The Morgan Purchases." United States Naval Institute Proceedings, LXVI (January 1940), 73-77.

2748. -----. "The Navy and the Press during the Civil War." United States Naval Institute Proceedings, LXIII (February 1937), 33-41.

2749. -----. "(Private and Confidential) My Dear Fox--." United States Naval Institute Proceedings, LXIII (May 1937), 694-698.
Gustavus V. Fox in the Navy Department.

2750. -----. "Relations Between Farragut and Porter." United States Naval Institute Proceedings, LXI (July 1935), 985-996.

2751. -----. The Second Admiral: a Life of David Dixon Porter, 1813-1891. New York: Coward-McCann, 1937. 376p.

2752. Westcott, Allan., Joint Author. See Alden, Carrol S., no. 46.

2753. "What the Alabama Did." Southern Historical Society Papers, XXIV (1896), 249-250.

2754. Whatley, J. H. "The Ironclad U.S.S. Cairo--1862-1864." Daughters of the American Revolution Magazine, XCIX (February 1965), 168, 170, 234.

2755. Wheeler, Francis B. "The Building of the Monitor." Magazine of American History, XIII (January 1885), 59-65.

2756. -----. The First Monitor and Its Builders. Poughkeepsie, N.Y.: Haight and Dudley, 1884. 12p.

2757. -----. John F. Winslow, L.L.D. and the Monitor. [Poughkeepsie, N.Y.: 1893]. 66p.

2758. Wheeler, Joseph. "Alabama." In Vol. VII of Clement A. Evans, ed. Confederate Military History; a Library of Confederate States History.

12 vols. Atlanta: Confederate Publishing Company, 1899.

2759. Wheeler-Bennett, J. "The Trent Affair: How the Prince Consort Saved the United States." History Today, XI (December 1961), 805-816.
The role of Prince Albert in the crisis.

2760. [Wheelwright, Charles H.] The Correspondence of Dr. Charles H. Wheelwright, Surgeon of the United States Navy. Edited by Hildegarde B. Forbes. N. p.: 1958. 350p.
A surgeon aboard the U. S. S. San Jacinto.

2761. Wheless, John F. "The Confederate Treasure." Southern Historical Society Papers, X (1882), 137-141.

2762. White, Ellsberry V. The First Iron-Clad Engagement in the World; History of the Facts of the Great Naval Battle Between the Merrimac-Virginia, C. S. N., and the Ericsson Monitor, U. S. N., Hampton Roads, March 8 and 9, 1862. New York: J. S. Ogilvie, 1906. 24p.
The personal experiences of a participant.

2763. White, Lonnie J. "Federal Operations at New Madrid and Island Number Ten." West Tennessee Historical Society Papers, XVII (1963), 47-67.
Includes the role of the Union Navy.

2764. White, Ruth (Morris). Yankee from Sweden; the Dream and Reality in the Days of John Ericsson. New York: Holt, 1960. 299p.

2765. -----., Joint Editor. See White, William C., no. 2767.

2766. [White, Thomas Benton.] "Down the Rivers: the Civil War Diary of Thomas Benton White." Edited by Charles G. William. Kentucky Historical Society Register, LXVII (April 1969), 134-174.
The Western rivers.

2767. White, William C. and Ruth White. Tin Can on a Shingle. With an Introduction by Henry Steele Commander. New York: Dutton, 1957. 176p.

2768. White, William W., Joint Editor. See Baylen, Joseph O., no. 181.

2769. Whitridge, Arnold. "The *Alabama*, 1862-1864: a Crisis in Anglo-American Relations." *History Today*, V (March 1955), 174-185.

2770. -----. "The *Trent* Affair." *History Today*, IV (June 1954), 394-402.

2771. Whitsell, Robert D. "Military and Naval Activity Between Cairo and Columbus." *Kentucky Historical Society Register*, LXI (April 1963), 107-121.
1861-1862.

2772. Whittle, William C. "The Cruise of the C.S. Steamer *Nashville*." *Southern Historical Society Papers*, XXIX (1901), 207-212; XXXVIII (1910), 334-340.

2773. -----. "The Cruise of the *Shenandoah*." *Southern Historical Society Papers*, XXXV (1907), 235-258.

2774. -----. *Cruises in the Confederate States Steamers Shenandoah and Nashville*. Norfolk, Va.: the Author, 1910.

2775. -----. "The Opening of the Lower Mississippi." *Southern Historical Society Papers*, XIII (1885), 560-572.
By a Rebel navy lieutenant.

2776. Whittlesey, Charles. *War Memoranda: Cheat River to the Tennessee, 1861-1862*. Cleveland: W. W. Williams, 1884. 89p.
By a participant in the early Western campaigns who saw much of the Yankee gunboats.

2777. "Who Planned the *Monitor*?" *Blackwood's Magazine*, CLXXVII (June 1862), 787-789.

2778. *Who Was Who in America. Historical Volume, 1607-1898*. Chicago: Marquis, 1963. 670p.
Capsule biographies of Civil War naval officers included.

2779. Wiard, Norman. Marine Artillery, as Adapted for Service on the Coast, and on Inland Waters. New York: Holman, 1863. 37p.

2780. Wickham, Julia P. "Recovering the Guns of the Keokuk." Confederate Veteran, XXXVII (January-December 1929), 96-97.

2781. [Wilcox, Charles E.] "With Grant at Vicksburg--From the Civil War Diary of Captain Charles E. Wilcox." Edited by Edgar L. Erickson. Journal of the Illinois State Historical Society, XXX (January 1938), 463-497.

2782. Wiley, Bell I., ed. See Dyer, Frederick H., no. 769.

2783. Wilkes, Charles. Defence of Commodore Charles Wilkes, U.S.N., Late Acting Rear Admiral in Command of the West India Squadron. Read Before a General Court Martial. Washington: McGill and Witherow, 1864. 56p.

2784. Wilkie, Franc B. Pen and Powder. Boston: Tickman, 1888. 383p.

New York Times reporter in the West whose articles on the Steele's Bayou Expedition in that sheet make most interesting reading.

2785. Wilkinson, John. The Narrative of a Blockade Runner. New York: Sheldon, 1877. 252p.

The skipper of the Robert E. Lee who sailed his vessel through the Yankee blockade 21 times in only 10 months.

2786. William, Charles G., ed. See White, Thomas B., no. 2766.

2787. William Conway and the Conway Celebration at Camden, Maine, August 30, 1906. Portland: Lefavor-Tower, 1906. 42p.

A "hero" at the Surrender of Pensacola's Navy Yard in 1861.

2788. Williams, E. Cort. "The Cruise of the 'Black Terror.'" In Sketches of War History, 1861-1865; Papers Read Before the Ohio Commandery,

Military Order of the Loyal Legion of the United States. 6 vols. Cincinnati: R. Clarke, 1888-1908. Vol. II, pp. 96-121.
By an ensign aboard one of the gunboats.

2790. Williams, Edward F., III. "The Johnsonville Raid and Nathan Bedford Forrest State Park." Tennessee Historical Quarterly, XXVIII (Fall 1969), 225-251.

2791. -----., Joint Editor. See Pryor, J. P., no. 1979.

2792. Williams, Frances L. Matthew Fontaine Maury, Scientist of the Sea. New Brunswick, N. J.: Rutgers University Press, 1963. 720p.
Although emphasizing his work in oceanography, presents useful coverage of his Civil War career.

2793. Williams, G. M. "The First Vicksburg Expedition and the Battle of Baton Rouge, 1862." In War Papers, Read Before the Wisconsin Commandery, Military Order of the Loyal Legion of the United States. 3 vols. Milwaukee: Burdick, Armitage & Allen, 1891-1903. Vol. II, pp. 52-69.

2794. Williams, (Mrs.) H. Dwight. A Year in China, and a Narrative of Capture and Imprisonment when Homeward Bound on board the Rebel Pirate Florida. New York: Hurd and Houghton, 1864. 362p.

2795. Williams, Harold. "Yankee Whaling Fleets Raided by Confederate Cruisers: the Story of the Bark Jerah Swift, Captain Thomas W. Williams." American Neptune, XXVII (October 1967), 263-267.
Captured and sunk by the Shenandoah.

2796. Williams, Kenneth P. "The Tennessee River Campaign and Anna Ella Carroll." Indiana Magazine of History, XLVI (September 1950), 221-248.

2797. Williams, Richard H. "General Bank's Red River Campaign." Louisiana Historical Quarterly, XXXII (January 1949), 103-144.

2798. Williams, T. Harry. "The Navy and the Committee on the Conduct of the War." United States Naval Institute Proceedings, LXV (December 1939), 1751-1755.

2799. -----. P. G. T. Beauregard; Napoleon in Gray. Baton Rouge: Louisiana State University Press, 1955. 345p.

2800. -----, and A. Otis Herbert, Jr. The Civil War in Louisiana; a Chronology. Baton Rouge: Louisiana Civil War Centennial Commission, 1961. 29p.
Includes naval affairs.

2801. Williams, Thomas. "Letters of General Thomas Williams, 1862." American Historical Review, XIV (January 1909), 309-328.
Yankee field officer killed at the Battle of Baton Rouge.

2802. Williams, Thomas W. Review of the Minority Report on the Navy Yard Question. New London, Conn.: Starr and Farnham, 1864. 36p.
New London vs. League Island, Pa.

2803. Willis, Henry A. The Fifty-Third Regiment of Massachusetts Volunteers, Comprising Also a History of the Siege of Port Hudson. Fitchburg, Mass.: Blanchard and Brown, 1889. 247p.

2804. Willis, V. B. "James Dunwoody Bulloch." Sewanee Review, XXXIV (October 1924), 386-401.

2805. Wills, Charles W. Army Life of an Illinois Soldier, Including a Day to Day Record of Sherman's March to the Sea; Letters and Diary of the Late Charles W. Wills, Private and Sergeant of the 8th Illinois Infantry; Lieutenant and Battalion Adjutant of the 7th Illinois Cavalry, Captain, Major, Lt. Colonel of the 103rd Illinois Infantry. Compiled and Published by His Sister. Washington: Globe Printing, 1906. 383p.
An early participant in the Western theatre, the author recalled the sad fact that when the Navy requested men of the Army, the commander at Cape Girardeau, Mo., chose some

fifty or sixty of "his most worthless men and put them on gunboats."

2806. "Wilmington and the Blockade Runners." Confederate Veteran, XXIX (January-December 1921), 258-259.

2807. Wilson, Herbert W. Ironclads in Action; a Sketch of Naval Warfare from 1855 to 1898, with Some Account of the Development of the Battleship in England. 2 vols. Boston: Little, Brown, 1896.
The Civil War in covered in Vol. I, pp. 1-209.

2808. -----. "Naval Operations of the Civil War (1861-1865)." In The Cambridge Modern History. 14 vols. New York: Macmillan, 1906. Vol. VII, pp. 549-568.

2809. Wilson, James Grant. "The Red River Dam." Galaxy, I (June 1866), 241-245.

2810. -----, and John Fiske, eds. Appleton's Cyclopedia of American Biography. 6 vols. New York: D. Appleton, 1888.
Although some of the biographies of non-Civil War naval officers are fictitious, many lesser naval figures are covered herein, e.g., Leroy Fitch.

2811. -----. -----. In Personal Recollections of the War of the Rebellion; Papers Read Before the New York Commandery, Military Order of the Loyal Legion of the United States. 4 vols. New York: the Commandery, 1891-1912. Vol. I, pp. 78-95.
Includes useful diagrams and sketches.

2812. Wilson, James H. Under the Old Flag; Recollections of Military Operations in the War for the Union, the Spanish War, the Boxer Rebellion, etc. 2 vols. New York: D. Appleton, 1902.
This young cavalry officer had little use for the Navy and blamed Admiral Lee's slowness for the escape of Hood's men after the Battle of Nashville.

2813. Wilson, John M. The Campaign Ending with the Capture of Mobile. District of Columbia Commandery, Military Order of the Loyal Legion of the United States. War Papers, no. 17. Washington: the Commandery, 1894.

2814. Wingfield, J. H. D. "A Thanksgiving Service on the Virginia." Southern Historical Society Papers, XIX (1891), 248-251.

2815. Winks, Robin W. "The Second Chesapeake Affair." American Neptune, XIX (January 1959), 51-72.
The capture of the coasting steamer Chesapeake off the New England coast by Confederate Conspirators led by John Braines; Her Recapture and the ensuing litigation.

2816. Winters, John D. The Civil War in Louisiana. Baton Rouge: Louisiana State University Press, 1963. 534p.
Includes naval actions.

2817. Wolfe, George D. "The Confederate Raider Shenandoah." Nautical Research Journal, IV (February 1952), 19-20.

2818. Wolfe, Simeon K. "The Battle of Corydon." Indiana Magazine of History, LIV (June 1958), 131-140.
Morgan's Raid.

2819. Wondrus, Harry and Tom Stretch. "Brief Notes on the Arms Brought into the Confederacy by Blockade Runners." Hobbies, LV (July 1950), 129-131.

2820. Wood, John T. "The First Fight of Iron-Clads." In Robert U. Johnson and Clarence C. Buell, eds. B & L. Vol. I, pp. 692-711.
Monitor vs. Virginia.

2821. -----. "The Tallahassee's Dash into New York Waters." Century Illustrated Magazine, LVI (July 1898), 408-417.
By her commander.

2822. Wood, William. Captains of the Civil War: a Chronicle of the Blue and the Gray. Vol. XXXI of the Chronicles of America Series. New Haven: Yale University Press, 1921. 424p.

2823. Woods, Helen. "Timby the Forgotten." Harper's Weekly, LV (February 11, 1911), 11, 26.

2824. Woods, Robert H. "Cruise of the Clarence, Taconey, Archer." Southern Historical Society Papers, XXIII (1895), 274-282.

2825. ----- -----. United States Naval Institute Proceedings, XXXV (September 1909), 675-684.

2826. Woodman, John E., Jr. "The Stone Fleet." American Neptune, XXI (October 1961), 233-259.

2827. Woodward, D. "Launching the Confederate Navy." History Today, XII (March 1962), 206-212.

2828. Worden, John L., S. Dana Greene, and H. Ashton Ramsay. The Monitor and the Merrimac. New York: Harper, 1912. 72p.

Includes also "The Last of the Monitor," by Rear Admiral E. W. Watson.

2829. Worley, Theodore R. "Helena on the Mississippi." Arkansas Historical Quarterly, XIII (Spring 1954), 1-15.

2830. Wraight, A. Joseph., Joint Author. See U.S. Coast and Geodetic Survey., no. 2437.

2831. Wright, A. O. "The Destruction of the Fleet." Record of the Confederate Navy, I (January 1925), 8-10.

The James River Squadron blown up by order of Admiral Semmes in 1865.

2832. Wright, Howard G. Port Hudson, its History from an Interior Point of View, as Sketched from the Diary of an Officer, Howard G. Wright, 1863. Baton Rouge: [Committee for the Preservation of Port Hudson Battlefield]. 1961. 62p.

2833. Wright, Marcus J. Arkansas in the War, 1861-65. Batesville, Ark.: Independence City Historical Society, 1963. 104p.

2834. -----. "The Battle of Belmont." Southern Historical Society Papers, XVI (1888), 69-82.

2835. -----. Tennessee in the War, 1861-1865. New York: A. Lee, 1908. 228p.

2836. -----. Texas in the War, 1861-1865. Edited and Notes by Harold B. Sampson. Hillsboro, Texas: Hillsboro Junior College Press, 1965. 246p.

2837. Wright, Robert. "The Sinking of the Jamestown." Southern Historical Society Papers, XXIX (1901), 371-372.
One of the Confederate vessels which assisted the Virginia during the first day at Hampton Roads.

2838. Writings on American History. A Bibliography of Books and Articles on United States History Published During the Year--. New York: Macmillan, 1908-1910; Washington: Government Printing Office, 1911-1913; New Haven: Yale University Press, 1914-1919; Washington: Government Printing Office, 1921-1940, 1948--.
A valuable source for data on Civil War naval writings.

2839. Yeiser, A. R. "The Capture of the Alice Dean." Confederate Veteran, XXII (January-December 1914), 364-365.

2840. Yost, George. "Cabin Boy's Diary of Action Aboard the Cairo." Life Magazine, LVIII (February 12, 1965), 44.

2841. Young, Franklin K. "A Tale of Two Frigates. Unwritten History of One of the Most Peculair and Well-Known Episodes of the Civil War, by an Eyewitness." Told to Franklin K. Young. Nickell Magazine, VII (May 1897), 269-278.
Monitor vs. Virginia.

2842. Young, Jesse Bowman. What a Boy Saw in the Army; a Story of Sight-Seeing and Adventure in the War for the Union. New York: Hunt and Eaton, 1894. 398p.
Western gunboats were among the "sights."

2843. Young, Jo. "The Battle of Sabine Pass." Southwest Historical Quarterly, LII (April 1949), 398-409.

2844. "Yvan." Carrying Despatches to Farragut." In George M. Vickers, ed. Under Both Flags. p. 125-127.
A trip from Donaldsonville, Louisiana, to New Orleans 9 July 1863 with messages from the grounded U. S. S. New London.

2845. -----. "Daring Exploit at Donaldsonville." In George M. Vickers, ed. Under Both Flags. p. 209-210.
Intelligence-gathering at Donaldsonville.

2846. -----. "From Vicksburg to New Orleans, Through the Enemy's Country." In George M. Vickers, ed. Under Both Flags. p. 248-250.
With a message from Grant to Farragut.

2847. Ziemke, P. C. "Powder Boat Fiasco at Fort Fisher; Episode of the American Civil War." Compressed Air Magazine, LXV (October 1960), 23-25.

APPENDIX A

The "Votes of Thanks of Congress" To Naval Officers of the Civil War

The United States Congress established the Medal of Honor for the Navy on December 21, 1861. This highest of the nation's tributes was to be conferred upon gallant "petty officers, seamen, landsmen, and marines." Unlike the Union Army, whose officers were allowed to receive the decoration under a separate act, no provision was made for awarding the Medal to commissioned naval or marine personnel until 1915.

As a Civil War substitute, particularly worthy sea force officers were given a resolution of Congressional appreciation, or "Thanks." These were recorded upon the files of the men involved and almost automatically insured their continued upward promotion.

A total of fifteen "Votes of Thnaks" were passed during the conflict. These are here reproduced in their original form by the session of Congress bestowing the honor.

THE SECOND SESSION OF THE THIRTY-SEVENTH CONGRESS

Resolved by the Senate and House of Representatives of the United States of America in Congress assembled, That the thanks of Congress be and they are hereby tendered to Captain Samuel F. DuPont, and through him to the officers, petty officers, seamen, and marines, attached to the squadron under his command, for the decisive and splendid victory achieved at Port Royal on the seventh day of November last.

Approved February 22, 1862.

Resolved by the Senate and House of Representatives of the United States of America in Congress assembled, That the thanks of Congress are due, and are hereby tendered, to the officers, soldiers, and seamen of the army and navy of the United States, for the heroic gallantry that, under the providence of Almighty God, has won the recent series of brilliant victories over the enemies of the Union and the Constitution.

Approved February 22, 1862.

Resolved by the Senate and House of Representatives of the United States of America in Congress assembled, That the thanks of Congress and of the American people are due, and are hereby tendered, to Captain A. H. Foote, of the United States navy, and to the officers and men of the western flotilla under his command, for the great gallantry exhibited by them in the attacks upon Forts Henry and Donaldson [sic], for their efficiency in opening the Tennessee, Cumberland, and Mississippi rivers to the pursuits of lawful commerce, and for their unwavering devotion to the cause of the country in the midst of the greatest difficulties and dangers.

Approved March 19, 1862.

Resolved by the Senate and House of Representatives of the United States of America in Congress assembled, That the thanks of Congress be, and they are hereby, tendered to Captain Louis M. Goldsborough, and through him to the officers, petty officers, seamen, and marines attached to the squadron under his command, for the brilliant and decisive victory achieved at Roanoke island on the seventh, eighth, and tenth days of February last.

Approved July 11, 1862.

Resolved by the Senate and House of Representatives of the United States of America in Congress assembled, That the thanks of Congress and of the American people are due, and are hereby tendered, to Leiutenant J. L. Worden, of the United States navy, and to the officers and men of the iron-clad gunboat Monitor, under his command, for the skill and gallantry exhibited by them in the late remarkable battle between the Monitor and the rebel iron-clad steamer Merrimack.

Sec. 2. Be it further resolved, That the President of the United States be requested to cause this resolution to be communicated to Lieutenant Worden, and through him to the officers and men under his command.

Approved July 11, 1862.

Resolved by the Senate and House of Representatives of the United States of America in Congress assembled, That the thanks of the people and of the Congress of the United States are due and are hereby tendered to Captain David G. Farragut, of the United States navy, and to the officers and men under his command, composing his squadron in the Gulf of Mexico, for their gallantry displayed in the capture of Forts Jackson and St. Phillip [sic], and the city of New Orleans, and in the destruction of the enemy's gunboats and armed flotilla.

Sec. 2. And be it further resolved, That the Secretary of the Navy be directed to communicate this resolution to Captain Farragut, and through him to the officers and men under his command.

Approved July 11, 1862.

Resolved by the Senate and House of Representatives of the United States of America in Congress assembled, That the thanks of Congress be, and the same are hereby, tendered to Captain Andrew H. Foote, of the United States navy, for his eminent services and gallantry at Fort Henry, Fort Donelson, and Island No. Ten, while in command of the naval forces of the United States.

Sec. 2. And be it further resolved, That the President of the United States be, and he is hereby, requested to transmit a certified copy of the foregoing resolution to Captain Foote.

Approved July 16, 1862.

THE THIRD SESSION OF THE THIRTY-SEVENTH CONGRESS

Resolved by the Senate and House of Representatives of the United States of America in Congress assembled, That in pursuance of the recommendation of the President of the United States, and to enable him to advance Commander John L. Worden one grade, in pursuance of the ninth section of the act of Congress of sixteenth July, eighteen hundred and sixty-two, that the thanks of Congress be, and they are hereby, tendered to Commander John L. Worden for highly distinguished conduct in conflict with the enemy in the Remarkable battle between the United States iron-clad steamer Monitor, under his command, and the rebel iron-clad frigate Merrimac, in March, eighteen hundred and sixty-two.

Approved February 3, 1863.

Resolved by the Senate and House of Representatives of the United States of America in Congress assembled, That the thanks of Congress be and they are hereby given to the following officers of the United States navy, upon the recommendation of the President of the United States, viz: Commodore Charles Henry Davis, for distinguished services in conflict with the enemy at Fort Pillow, at Memphis, and for successful operations at other points in the waters of the Mississippi river; Captain John A. Dahlgren, for distinguished service in the line of his profession, improvements in ordnance, and zealous and efficient labors in the ordnance branch of the service; Captain Stephen C. Rowan, for distinguished services in the waters of North Carolina, and particularly in the capture of Newbern, being in chief command of the naval forces; Commander David D. Porter, for the bravery and skill displayed in tha attack on the post of Arkansas, which surrendered to the combined military and naval forces on the tenth of January, eighteen hundred and sixty-three; Rear Admiral Silas H. Stringham, now on the retired list, for distinguished services in the capture of Forts Hatteras and Clark; and that a copy of this resolution be forwarded to each of the above officers by the President of the United States.

Approved February 7, 1863.

THE FIRST SESSION OF THE THIRTY-EIGHTH CONGRESS

Be it resolved by the Senate and House of Representatives of the United States of America in Congress assembled, That, in pursuance of the recommendation of the President of the United States, and to enable him to advance Captain Rodgers one grade in pursuance of the ninth section of the act of Congress of sixteenth July, eighteen hundred and sixty-two, the thanks of Congress be, and they are hereby, tendered to Captain John Rodgers "for the eminent skill and gallantry exhibited by him in the engagement with the rebel armed iron-clad steamer 'Fingal,' alias 'Atlanta,' whilst in command of the United States iron-clad steamer 'Weehawken,' which led to her capture on June seventeenth, eighteen hundred and sixty-three; and also for the zeal, bravery, and general good conduct shown by this officer on many occasions."

Approved December 23, 1863.

Be it resolved by the Senate and House of Representatives of the United States of America in Congress assembled, That the thanks of Congress are hereby tendered to Commodore Ringgold, the officers, petty officers, and men of the United States ship "Sabine," for the daring and skill displayed in rescuing the crew of the steam transport "Governor," wrecked in a gale on the first day of November, eighteen hundred and sixty-one, having on board a battalion of United States marines under the command of Major John G. Reynolds, and in the search for, and rescue of, the United States line-of-battle ship "Vermont," disabled in a gale upon the twenty-sixth of February last, with her crew and freight.

Sec. 2. And be it further resolved, That the Secretary of the Navy be directed to communicate the foregoing resolution to Commodore Ringgold, and through him to the officers and men under his command.

Approved March 7, 1864.

Be it resolved by the Senate and House of Representatives of the United States of America in Congress assembled, That the thanks of Congress be, and they are hereby, tendered to Admiral David D. Porter, commanding the Mississippi squadron, for the eminent skill, endurance, and gallantry exhibited by him and his squadron, in co-operation with the army, in opening the Mississippi river.

Approved April 19, 1864.

THE SECOND SESSION OF THE THIRTY-EIGHTH CONGRESS

Resolved by the Senate and House of Representatives of the United States of America in Congress assembled, That the thanks of Congress are due, and are hereby tendered, to officers, petty officers, seamen, and marines of the United States steamer Kearsarge, for the skill and gallantry exhibited by him and the officers and men under his command in the brilliant action on the nineteenth of June, eighteen hundred and sixty-four, between that ship and the piratical craft Alabama, a vessel superior to his own in tonnage, in guns, and in the number of her crew.

Approved December 20, 1864.

Resolved by the Senate and House of Representatives of the United States of America in Congress assembled, That the thanks of Congress are due, and are hereby tendered, to Lieutenant William B. Cushing, of the United States navy, and to the officers and men under his command, for the skill and gallantry exhibited by them in the destruction of the rebel iron-clad steamer Albemarle, at Plymouth, North Carolina, on the night of the twenty-seventh of October, eighteen hundred and sixty-four.

Approved December 20, 1864.

Resolved by the Senate and House of Representatives of the United States of America in Congress assembled, That the thanks of Congress are hereby presented to Rear-Admiral David D. Porter, and to the officers, petty officers, seamen, and marines under his command, for the unsurpassed gallantry and skill exhibited by them in the attacks upon Fort Fisher, and the brilliant and decisive victory by which that important work has been captured from the rebel forces and placed in the possession and under the authority of the United States, and for their long and faithful services and unwavering devotion to the cause of the country in the midst of the greatest difficulties and dangers.

Sec. 2. And be it further resolved, That the President of the United States be requested to communicate this resolution to Admiral Porter, and through him to the officers, seamen, and marines under his command.

Approved January 24, 1865.

APPENDIX B

The Demise of the Mississippi Squadron, as Illustrated by the Fate of U. S. S. *Carondelet*

Writers of Civil War history have long been interested in the adventures of the Federal fresh water navy. During the 1960's no less than five volumes pertaining in whole or in part to the Mississippi Squadron, along with numerous journal articles, were produced.[1] Unfortunately, most of these accounts ended with the fall of Vicksburg or the Red River Campaign of 1864. From an operational viewpoint, such finales may be justified; yet, from an administrative stance, the never-logged work of force reduction, in many ways as difficult as the fleet's creation, was still ahead.

The military history of the Civil War was, for all practical purposes, settled by late April, 1865. The warships of the Yankee inland navy saw few heroic days after the December, 1864 Battle of Nashville and were employed mainly as escorts for army convoys or as guardships for various river towns, forts, and crossings. On May 3, Navy Secretary Gideon Welles passed orders for Rear Admiral Samuel P. Lee to commence the reduction of his command. In the weeks ahead, one of the more interesting sagas of our Navy's many demobilizations would unfold.[2]

The Navy Department's directive to its Western admiral left in his hands the formulation of a scenerio for the eventual elimination of the Mississippi Squadron, a force which on May 1 numbered over a hundred vessels.[3] After two and a half weeks, Lee was able to forward to Washington a workable plan for demobilization.

Once the Rebel forces in the Trans-Mississippi formally surrendered, as they were expected to within the month, the admiral foresaw all of the ironclads withdrawn from service. Only a few gunboats of the "tinclad" variety would need to be maintained "until social order is restored."

Once the area was normalized, all of the Northern warships could be laid up. By years end, only a few tugboats were envisaged as still in commission.

In addition to these thoughts, Lee put forth details for disposing of his surplus. Extra men would be discharged or transferred, with unnecessary goods, to the West Gulf Coast Blockading Squadron at New Orleans. The many vessels, at times calculated to give the best advantage to the Federal Government, would be sold in several large auctions. First to go, in anticipation of renewed trade on the rivers of the ex Confederacy, would be the tinclads. After allowing a grace period in which to reconvert these from a war-footing, a sale would be held under the direction of the Navy at the Mound City, Illinois, Naval Station. Advertisements for each event would be placed in the daily papers of such river cities as Cincinnati, Memphis, and St. Louis, specifying terms of purchase, additional items (such as anchors, cable, or armor plate) to be sold, and the time and date of auction.[4] With minor exceptions, Lee's memorandum was accepted as operating procedure by Welles' department.

The process by which the vessels of the squadron were recalled, dismantled, laid in ordinary, and eventually sold can best be illustrated by tracing the career's end of a single vessel, in this case U. S. S. Carondelet. Her fate and the manner of its occurrence represents, in the main, that which befell all of her sisters and, indeed, the entire inland fleet.

While composing his memoirs late in the 1870's, Rear Admiral Henry Walke paused to consider his first ironclad command, the U. S. S. Carondelet. She was "a most successful craft," he recalled. Under half a dozen skippers, the vessel "was in more battles and encounters with the enemy (about fourteen or fifteen times); and under fire, it is believed, longer and oftener than any other vessel in the Navy." From Fort Henry through the siege of Vicksburg and from the Red River Campaign through the December, 1864 defense of Nashville, this ship ran up a record unsurpassed by any other unit of the Union's brown-water navy.[5]

In the century since the conclusion of the Civil War, many have shown an interest in this ship. Unfortunately, most of these questing individuals are modern scholars of the conflict. A useful paper by William Geoghegan of the

Smithsonian Institution's Transportation Division recently followed her career to the end of the war, but uncovering the final saga of what was "possibly the most famous of all the river gunboats of the Civil War" might have proved no easy task. Owing to the seeming lack of records, authors have not previously attempted to tell her post-war story. This is understandable. Added to the probable dullness of it all, they find that contemporary naval officers and rivermen were so unimpressed with the ironclad's future peacetime potential that none thought even to take her lines. [6]

The spring of 1865 found the famous old lady a unit of Lieutenant Commander Robert Boyd's Ninth District of the Mississippi Squadron. This area ran from Mound City down the Tennessee River to the Mussel Shoals. For most of this season, she was tied to the bank at Eastport, Mississippi, where her last skipper, Acting Volunteer Lieutenant John Rogers, served as port commandant.

The ironclad's engines, never noted for their capacity, were in very bad condition after four years service. In February, they had been condemned by survey, necessitating extensive repairs and overhaul. Thus unable to utilize his flagship, Rogers found it necessary to conduct his business aboard the tinclad U. S. S. Naumkeag, leaving the Carondelet's heavy cannon to command the town. The fighting days of the ship, hero-craft at Island Number Ten nearly three years earlier, were now over. While the repairs went forward (and the war closed in the East), she was little more than a floating casemated battery. Still in all, she was a symbol of the might which the inland navy could yet muster for the frustration of any enemy attempt, however unlikely, in that sector. [7]

Toward the end of April, the ship's engineers completed their overhaul. On April 30, Lieutenant Rogers passed the order to raise steam. After rounding to, she churned slowly upstream toward Paducah, Kentucky, arriving two days later. There the crew received its last liberty of the war. [8]

Meanwhile at the Mound City base, Admiral Lee had his May 3 orders to cut costs "in all matters to the lowest possible point" and to retire all but those vessels "as promise to be most useful on the Western Waters." On May 22, Secretary Welles added to them, giving the names of three vessels which he thought should definitely be laid up early. Heading the list was the Carondelet. She, together with the Ozark and Chillicothe, would be retired to the Mound City at the earliest date. A week later, Lee replied in accord and the following day wired Lieutenant Rogers: "Report here with the Carondelet to-morrow, 31st instant."[9]

Shortly after dawn on the last morning of the month, less than a week after the expected surrender of Confederate General E, Kirby Smith in the Trans-Mississippi, Rogers ordered his men to cast off for the final voyage. An hour after noon, the Carondelet arrived at Mound City. Aided in her maneuvers by a pair of steam tugs, the ironclad came to anchor astern of the tinclad U. S. S. St. Clair while the flagship, tinclad Tempest, fired a salute of nine guns.

The Carondelet's commission now had less than three weeks to run. On Friday, June 2, after receiving his instructions, her commander ordered some of his men to begin removing the cannon into a barge alongside. Others were shortly engaged in a complete inventory of the ship's stores. Late in the afternoon, Admiral Lee came aboard to see how the work was progressing. After a brief inspection, he returned to the U. S. S. Tempest assured that the "cost" of this particular ironclad would be reduced in short order.[10]

Within the next few days, all of the great guns and small arms aboard were turned over to the fleet's ordnance department. As there was no suitable place on the base for long-term storage of the large quantity of cannon, small arms, and powder, Rogers learned that those from his ship, as well as other decommissioning craft, would be transported to the army barracks at Jefferson City, Missouri. Meanwhile, the vessels' stores were broken out, and following what was becoming fleet-wide common practice, invoiced, and sent ashore. When these two large tasks were nearly completed, large numbers of the crew were paid off and many of the officers given berths in other ships or sent home to await discharge.

During the afternoon of June 16, a work party reported aboard from the navy yard. These men had orders to effect the few changed necessary to convert the ironclad into an "ordnance boat" or floating ammunition dump. The following day as the carpenters pounded around him, Rogers saluted the flag and went ashore. There he would await the termination of his appointment. Executive Officer Oliver

Donaldson, who came aboard with Captain Walke from the U. S. S. Tyler in 1861 and had served under each succeeding commander, was left in charge.[11]

Sometime in the evening of June 20, Admiral Lee received a large package and letter from Leiutenant Rogers. Opening the communication, he read:

> This vessel is being fitted for an ordnance store ship by authority of Commodore [John W.] Livingstone. I therefore consider her cruise as a gunboat at an end and respectfully forward through you the logbook of this ship to the [Navy] Department.
>
> Allow me, sir, to tender my congratulations to you and the Department on the successful termination of the war, and the many hazardous enterprises this ship has passed through.
>
> Respectfully, Your obedient servant,
>
> John Rogers, Acting Volunteer
> Lieutenant Commanding

From the time Lee received the log, the Carondelet's naval career was finsihed. Much of the mystery which surrounded her eventual fate began at this point. Many of the government's documents, some of which were later printed in the Navy version of the Official Records, shed very little light on the vessel after the first day of summer, 1865.[12]

By August 2, we know that nine ironclads, including Carondelet, were inspected and out of commission ready for mooring in the towhead chutes above the naval station. All were to be laid up "in ordinary," a state requiring only minimum maintenance and not dissimilar from the concept of "moth-balling" presently utilized. At the same time, many of the tinclads and other vessels were being recalled from duty, reconverted to their original peacetime designs, and prepared for sale. The final muster rolls and logbooks of all the retiring ships were forwarded to Washington (where today they rest in the National Archives), while Acting Volunteer Lieutenant George P. Lord, late skipper of the Chillicothe, a few other officers, and a handful of men were assigned to the skeleton crews necessary to keep the ironclads up.[13]

During the second week of August, Admiral Lee reported to Washington that all of the vessels which were to be liquidated had been turned over to Commodore John Livingstone. The fleet ceased to exist on August 14 when the admiral hauled down his flag and returned east, turning the base over to the commodore. Three days later, many of the tinclads, supply, and utility craft were sold at a great auction attended by citizens from all over the nation.[14]

In the months after Lee quit the west, Livingstone continued to sell off the equipment, stores, and vessels of the ex-Mississippi Squadron. The naval base at Memphis was also quietly closed out. During this period, local workmen stripped the ironclads in ordinary. Armor plating and any items which might show a profit if sold seperately were removed. By the middle of November, these vessels were little more than hulks.

The year would be truly profitable for one Daniel Jacobs of St. Louis. Jacobs was a buyer-and-seller of steamboats and their equipment. A competent man by all accounts, he had probably known for some time that Livingstone planned to sell the former ironclads. By November 21, he finally knew for certain; the commodore took out ads in most of the river papers. That morning the St. Louis Daily Missouri Democrat and her rival, the Daily Missouri Republican, both advised the public that some vessels of the late fleet were on the block. The selling would begin promptly at noon on Wednesday, November 29.[15] Livingstone made sure the papers let it be known that all of the remaining boats would be sold to the highest bidder "together with their engines, tackle, and furniture."

We do not know exactly how this particular ship sale progressed. As it was only one of many held around the country in 1865-67 by the Navy and the Army Quartermaster General's Department, no one thought enough of it to write an account either for his diary or the public press.[16] There are, however, a few factors which can be assumed with a fair amount of certainty as based on newspapers and official reports.

As these vessels were known by many of the prospective buyers, it is likely that they had a good idea of their potential functions. Also, since the government was taking rather large losses to be rid of this "surplus," the purchasers probably did not anticipate bidding much for most of it. One thing is certain, Daniel Jacobs and his competitors had to have made their financial arrangements. The advertisements specifically required that each bidder be able to place a five per cent downpayment on each vessel successfully won, the balance to be paid within a few months.[17]

The morning of the appointed day dawned cold in Mound City. Upriver at Cincinnati, ice was reported in the Ohio as well as other tributaries.[18] Daniel Jacobs and the other buyers probably arrived at the station fairly early to inspect the sale items and may even have attended the coal-barge sale the day before.

The chief auctioneer, Solomon A. Silver, doubtless flanked by Commodore Livingstone and his staff, gaveled the sale into session at twelve. With twenty-one vessels and tons of equipment to be sold, a long afternoon was ahead.

At some unknown time during the proceedings, the name of the Carondelet was placed before the buyers. Many there assembled knew her story well--especially the troubles engineer James B. Eads had encountered in finishing her (and the six other craft of the "City Series") and collecting payment from the government back in 1861-1862. When his account was finally closed, the noted riverman had received an average of $101,800 apiece for his warships. Now, after a short period of haggling, Jacobs, the highest bidder, was awarded a bill of sale for his offer of $3,600. Triumphant, he went on to purchase three other ships during the afternoon.[19]

For years after the sale, few people knew or cared what fate now befell the once proud gunboat. In time, her lot became a total mystery which no one writing of her career, even in the "boom" times of the Civil War Centennial, has since gone into.

Some time ago, Mr. William Tippitt of Hernando, Mississippi, while gathering data for a history of Western steamboating, happened to record part of the story. When placed in contact by Mr. Edwin Bearss of the National Park Service, the writer was gratified by the information he so kindly gave. A check of other records and editions soon revealed sufficient material to advance the account of her destiny.[20]

Although Jacobs obtained Carondelet in December 1865, because of the winter weather, nothing was done with her until the following spring. As she still contained some valuable parts, mainly the iron in her hull and the old engines, she was taken to Cincinnati for demolishment in late May. Presumably she was again sold, as upon reaching the Queen City, a voyage incidentally she had never made before, no destruction took place. Until 1873, her owners and the exact whereabouts of her service are unknown. In that year she turned up as a wharfboat at Gallipolis, Ohio, under the ownership of a Captain John Hamilton of that city.[21]

At this point, a mysterious photograph enters the picture. In the files of the famous "River Room" of the Cincinnati Public Library is a scene of the Gallipolis waterfront, taken, notes Frank L. Sibley, former editor of the Gallipolis Tribune, in 1870. In addition to several steamboats, one can see a wharfboat bearing the name Hamilton and Al-____HIRE. While too near the bank for positive identification, and knowing that Captain Hamilton may have owned several such floating storehouses, we suggest, on the other hand, that this vessel, considerably modified in shape from her numerous wartime pictures, may well be the once-notable Carondelet, snapped in her last pose.

In the months following, the ex-warship deteriorated until she could be of no further commercial use, and eventually, she lay in a "sunken condition." By the spring of 1873, Hamilton had decided to scrap her for her remaining iron, "worth several thousand dollars." Before he could execute this plan, nature stepped in and in the spring floods of that year washed her away downstream.[22]

Gallipolis, according to the 1871 edition of James' River Guide, was (and still is) at mile 403 of the Ohio River. The rising waters took the hulk about 130 miles down to mile 273, near Manchester in lower Adams County, Ohio. There she grounded at the head of Manchester Island, bows upstream, deck out of water, and lay "straight up and down the river."

During the last week of April, Hamilton arrived at Manchester, "a thriving village" of about 600, to claim his wreck. Going over to the island, he found her "covered with pirates intent on tearing her to pieces for the old iron." After chasing these sway, he procured the services of a watchman and sent him aboard as guard until the river fell. He would return later to burn her for the ore and what little profit remained in her bones.[23]

We cannot definitely say that the owner destroyed his derelict when the water went down. Historical records and newspapers do not tell. Knowing human nature and the ways of the river, one can be rather sure that he did. Regardless of whether she was consumed in flame or just abandoned, Manchester Island was her deathsite. After twelve years of hard treatment and unflinching service, the Carondelet was no more.

The roster which follows is designed to provide data, for the first time in one place, in so far as is possible, on the post-war fates of the vessels assigned to the Mississippi Squadron on May 1, 1865.[24] In this way, it differs from all of the previously printed lists showing the strengths of the inland fleet.[25]

The arrangement of this section is by class of ship or duty, with the individual vessels, minus the prefix U. S. S., stationed alphabetically under each. Ship specifications, which may be located easily in most of the other published calendars, are not included. In those cases where the words "abandoned," "unknown," or "uncertain," are used to describe a craft's condition after a certain date, one should note simply that records are missing. The vessels may not have totally disappeared. Especially for larger units, they may have continued in service, been converted to wharfboats or barges, or been dismantled. As the writer has done with the Carondelet, those interested in particular ships after 1865 are advised to comb the back files of the river newspapers.[26]

The information for this inventory was gathered from the Official Records... Navies, the "Lytle List," the Navy Department's Dictionary of American Naval Fighting Ships (full reference in the bibliography), and contemporary newspapers.

The Timberclads, 1861[27]

Lexington. Original Cost: $20,666.66. Sold at auction at Mound City, Ill., August 17, 1865 to Thomas Scott & Woodburn for $16,000. Post-1865 fate unknown.

Tyler. Original Cost: $20,666.66. Sold at auction at

Mound City, Ill., August 17, 1865 to David White for $6,000. Post-1865 fate unknown.

The "City Series" Ironclads, 1861[28]

Carondelet. See text of Appendix B.

Cincinnati. Original Cost: $101,800. Sold at auction at New Orleans, La., March 28, 1866 for $7,100. Post-1866 fate unknown.

Louisville. Original Cost: $101,800. Sold at auction at Mound City, Ill., Nov. 29, 1865 to Daniel Jacobs for $3,600. Post-1865 fate unknown.

Mound City. Original Cost: $101,800. Sold at auction at Mound City, Ill., November 29, 1865 to J. E. Burrard for $3,700. Post-1865 fate unknown.

Pittsburg. Original Cost: $101,800. Sold at auction at Mound City, Ill., November 29, 1865 to Cutting & Ellis for $3,100. Post-1865 fate unknown.

The Eads Ironclads, 1861

Benton. Original Cost: uncertain. Sold at auction at Mound City, Ill., November 29, 1865 to Daniel Jacobs for $3,000. Post-1865 fate unknown.

Essex. Original Cost: $20,000. Sold at auction at Mound City, Ill., November 29, 1865 to W. L. Haurbleton for $4,000. Post-1865 fate unknown.

The Eads/Porter Ironclads, 1862

Choctaw. Original Cost: uncertain. Sold at auction at New Orleans, La. March 30, 1866 for $9,272. Post-1866 fate unknown.

Lafayette. Original Cost: uncertain. Sold at auction at New Orleans, La., March 28, 1866. Post-1866 fate unknown.

The Brown Ironclads, 1862-1863

Chillicothe. Original Cost: $92,960. Sold at auction at Mound City, Ill., November 29, 1865 to Cutting & Ellis for $3,000. Post-1865 fate unknown.

Indianola. Original Cost: $182,662.50. Captured and sunk by Confederates below Vicksburg, February 24, 1863. Raised and sold at auction at Mound City, Ill., November 29, 1865 to John Riley for $3,000. Post-1865 fate unknown.

Tuscumbia. Original Cost: $227,669.73. Sold at auction at Mound City, Ill., November 29, 1865 to W. K. Adams for $3,300. Post-1865 fate unknown.

The River Monitors, 1863--[29]

Catawba. Original Cost: $625,905.80. Never commissioned; classed also as a coastal monitor. Sold to Peru on April 2, 1868 by her builder, Alex. Swift and Co. Renamed Atahualpa.

Chickasaw. Original Cost: $389,597.55. Name changed to Sampson, June 15, 1869; to Chickasaw, August 10, 1869. Sold at auction at New Orleans, La., September 12, 1874 to David Campbell for $8,350. Post-1874 fate unknown.

Kickapoo. Original Cost: $394,828.75. Name changed to Cyclops, June 15, 1869; to Kewaydin, August 10, 1869. Sold at auction at New Orleans, La., September 12, 1874 to Schickels, Harrison & Co. for $7,750. Post-1874 fate unknown.

Marietta. Original Cost: $235,039.57. Never commissioned. Completed, December 1865; Accepted by the Navy, April 1866. Name changed to Circe, June 15, 1869; to Marietta, August 10, 1869. Sold at auction at Mound City, Ill., April 12, 1873 to David Campbell for $16,000. Post-1873 fate unknown.

Neosho. Original Cost: $194,757.67. Name changed to Vixen, June 15, 1869; to Osceola, August 10, 1869.

Sold at auction at Mound City, Ill., April 17, 1873 to David Campbell for $13,600. Post-1873 fate unknown.

Osage. Original Cost: $119,678.37. Sunk in the Blakely River, Ala., by torpedo, March 29, 1865. Raised and sold at auction at New Orleans, La., November 22, 1867 in a package with Calhoun and Tennessee for $20,467.10. Post-1867 fate unknown.

Ozark. Original Cost: $215,676.96. Sold at auction at Mound City, Ill., November 29, 1865 to F. B. Ellis & Bros. for $3,000. Post-1865 fate unknown.

Sandusky. Original Cost: $235,039.57. Never commissioned. Completed, December 1865; Accepted by the Navy, April 1866. Sold at auction at Mound City, Ill., April 17, 1873 to David Campbell for $18,000. Post-1873 fate unknown.

Tippecanoe. Original cost: $634,879.79. Never commissioned; classed also as a coastal monitor. Sister ship of Catawba. Completed, December 1865; Accepted by the Navy, February 1866. Name changed to Vesuvius, June 15, 1869; to Wyandotte, August 10, 1869. Post-1869 fate uncertain. Doubtless sold in 1870's.

Winnebago. Original Cost: $381,81[illegible]83. Name changed to Tornado, June 15, 1869; to Winnebago, August 10, 1869. Sold at auction at New Orleans, La., September 12, 1874 to Nathaniel McKay for $7,350. Post-1874 fate unknown.

Ellet Steam Rams, 1862[30]

Dick Fulton. Transferred from War Dept. Sold approximately October 1865. Redocumented as Baltic, January 3, 1866. Exploded at New Orleans on February 2, 1866 with the loss of 4 lives.

Lioness. Transferred from the War Dept. Sold approximately October 1865. Redocumented under her original name, Lioness, October 21, 1865. Abandoned 1870.

Monarch. Transferred from the War Dept. No further data available.

Samson. See the Blacksmith Shop (below).

The Tinclads, 1862[31]

Brilliant. Original Cost: $20,000. Sold at auction at Mound City, Ill., August 17, 1865 to John H. Duffer for $8,000. Redocumented as John S. McCune, October 11, 1865. Lost in 1867.

Cricket. Original Cost: $16,000. Sold at auction at Mound City, Ill., August 17, 1865 to William Thatcher for $5,050. Redocumented as Cricket No. 2, September 25, 1865. Abandoned in 1867.

Curlew. Original Cost: $21,500. Sold at auction at Mound City, Ill., August 17, 1865 to Harvey Darlington for $7,600. Post-1865 fate unknown.

Estrella. Transferred from the War Dept. Sold at auction at New York City, October 9, 1867 for $7,500. Redocumented under her original name, Estrella, December 30, 1867. Abandoned in 1870.

Fairplay. Transferred from the War Dept. Sold at auction at Mound City, Ill., August 17, 1865 to Charles C. Duncan for $5,150. Redocumented as Cotile, October 6, 1865. Abandoned in 1871.

Forest Rose. Original Cost: $22,000. Sold at auction at Mound City, Ill., August 17, 1865 to David White for $8,200. Redocumented as Anna White, October 14, 1865. Smashed by ice at St. Louis, Mo., February 4, 1868.

Great Western. Transferred from the War Dept. Sold at auction at Mound City, Ill., August 17, 1865 to John Riley for $4,300. Post-1865 fate unknown.

Judge Torrence. Transferred from the War Dept. Sold at auction at Mound City, Ill., August 17, 1865 to John A. Williamson for $9,100. Redocumented as Amazon, January 2, 1866. Snagged and lost on Ozark Is., off Napoleon, Ark., February 19, 1868.

Juliet. Original Cost: $16,340.35. Sold at auction at Mound City, Ill., August 17, 1865 to Philip Wallach for $6,150. Redocumented as Goldena, August 17, 1865. Stranded and lost off the White River Cutoff, Ark., December 31, 1865.

Marmora. Original Cost: $21,000. Sold at auction at Mound City, Ill., August 17, 1865 to D. D. Barr for $8,650. Post-1865 fate unknown.

New Era. Original Cost: $14,238.73. Sold at auction at Mound City, Ill., August 17, 1865 to W. S. Mepham for $5,000. Redocumented as Goldfinch, November 27, 1865. Burnt at Ship Is., Evansville, Ind., June 3, 1868.

Prarie Bird. Original Cost: $17,500. Sold at auction at Mound City, Ill., August 17, 1865 to Henry Morton for $8,500. Post-1865 fate unknown.

Romeo. Original Cost: $17,459. Sold at auction at Mound City, Ill., August 17, 1865 to Nathaniel Williams for $7,100. Redocumented under her original name, Romeo, December 23, 1865. Abandoned in 1870.

St. Clair. Original Cost: $19,750. Sold at auction at Mound City, Ill., August 17, 1865 to J. H. Stearn for $9,000. Redocumented under her original name, St. Clair, September 27, 1865. Abandoned in 1869.

Springfield. Original Cost: $13,000. Sold at auction at Mound City, Ill., August 17, 1865 to R. G. Jameson for $4,500. Redocumented as Jennie D., April 1, 1866. Abandoned in 1875.

The Tinclads, 1863[32]

Argosy. Original Cost: uncertain. Sold at auction at Mound City, Ill., August 17, 1865 to U. P. Schenck for $10.000. Redocumented under her original name, Argosy, at an uncertain date. Brunt at Cincinnati, O., on March 7, 1872.

Avenger. Transferred from the War Dept. Sold at auction at Mound City, Ill., August 17, 1865 to Cutting & Ellis for $5,000. Redocumented as Balize, April 16, 1867. Abandoned in 1871.

Champion. Original Cost: $16,000. Sold at auction at Mound City, Ill., November 29, 1865 to Wilder & Wilder for $3,200. Redocumented under her original name, Champion, at an uncertain date. Abandoned in 1868.

Elk. Original Cost: $29,500. Sold at auction at New Orleans, La., August 24, 1865 to Montgomery and Bro. for $9,000. Redocumented under her original name, Countess, September 6, 1865. Abandoned in 1868.

Exchange. Original Cost: $30,000. Sold at auction at Mound City, Ill., August 17, 1865 to W. G. Priest for $7,000. Redocumented as Tennessee, September 4, 1865. Snagged and lost at Decatur, Neb., April 25, 1868.

Fawn. Original Cost: $28,000. Sold at auction at Mound City, Ill., August 17, 1865 to D. Caughlin for $7,300. Redocumented under her original name, Fannie Barker, October 19, 1865. Stranded and lost at St. Joseph, Mo., March 24, 1873.

Fort Hundman. Original Cost: $35,000. Sold at auction at Mound City, Ill., August 17, 1865 to P. Varble for $12,500. Redocumented under her original name, James Thompson, December 5, 1865. Abandoned in 1874.

Gazelle. Original Cost: $30,150. Sold at auction at Mound City, Ill., August 17, 1865 to Henry Scott for $10,350. Redocumented as Plain City, October 23, 1865. Abandoned in 1869.

Hastings. Original Cost: $39,000. Sold at auction at Mound City, Ill., August 17, 1865 to Henry H. Semmes for $12,700. Redocumented at Dora, October 10, 1865. Abandoned in 1872.

Kenwood. Original Cost: $28,000. Sold at auction at Mound City, Ill., August 17, 1865 to W. G. Priest for $10,100. Redocumented as Cumberland, September 15, 1865. Exploded at Shawneetown, Ill., August 14, 1869 with the loss of 18 lives.

Moose. Original Cost: $32,000. Sold at auction at Mound City, Ill., August 17, 1865 to David White for $10,100. Redocumented at Little Rock, October 9, 1865. Burnt at Clarendon, Ark., December 23, 1867.

Nyanza. Original Cost: $33,500. Sold at auction at New Orleans, La., August 12, 1865 to Owen Finnegan for $34,000. Redocumented under her original name, Nyanza, August 26, 1865. Abandoned in 1873.

Paw Paw. Original Cost: $8,000. Sold at auction at Mound City, Ill., August 17, 1865 to Samuel Nancil for $5,850. Post-1865 fate unknown.

Peosta. Original Cost: $22,000. Sold at auction at Mound City, Ill., August 17, 1865 to John W. Waggener for $8,350. Redocumented under her original name, Peosta, December 19, 1865. Abandoned in 1868.

Reindeer. Original Cost: $29,750. Sold at auction at Mound City, Ill., August 17, 1865 to J. A. Williamson for $12,200. Redocumented as Mariner, October 5, 1865. Stranded and lost at Decatur, Ala., May 9, 1867.

Silver Cloud. Original Cost: $33,500. Sold at auction at Mound City, Ill., August 17, 1865 to J. H. Sterritt for $11,000. Redocumented under her original name, Silver Cloud, October 7, 1865. Snagged and lost in Buffalo Bayou, Tex., October 2, 1866.

Stockdale. Original Cost: $32,500. Sold at auction at New Orleans, La., August 24, 1865 to John Smoker & Richard Sinnott for $13,000. Redocumented as Caddo, September 1, 1865. Abandoned in 1871.

Victory. Original Cost: $29,900. Sold to USN before documentation. Sold at auction at Mound City, Ill., August 17, 1865 to W. Thorwegen for $10,900. Documented as Lizzie Tate, October 7, 1865. Converted to a barge in November 1867.

The Tinclads, 1864[33]

Abeona. Original Cost: $37,000. Sold at auction at Mound City, Ill., August 17, 1865 to J. A. Williamson for $13,400. Redocumented under her original name, Abeona, October 17, 1865. Wrecked in June 1867. Recovered, taken to New York City for refitting in November 1867, and as late as 1891 reported to be at the Washington Navy Yard.

Carrabasset. Original Cost: $30,500. Sold at auction at New Orleans, La., August 12, 1865 to E. C. Avery for $18,500. Post-1865 fate unknown.

Collier. Original Cost: $35,500. Sold at auction at

Mound City, Ill., August 17, 1865 to David White for $12,000. Redocumented as Imperial, September 22, 1865. Abandoned in late 1865.

Colossus. Original Cost: $32,900. Sold at auction at Mound City, Ill., August 17, 1865 to R. P. Watts for $9,250. Redocumented as Memphis, September 27, 1865. Snagged and lost off Pine Bluff, Ark., December 17, 1866.

Fairy. Original Cost: $32,000. Sold at auction at Mound City, Ill., August 17, 1865 to J. Kenniston for $9,600. Post-1865 fate unknown.

Gamage. Original Cost: $35,000. Sold at auction at Mound City, Ill., August 17, 1865 to J. R. Griffith for $11,000. Redocumented as Southern Belle, October 4, 1865. Burnt at Plaquemine, La., October 11, 1876 with the loss of 8 lives.

Grossbeak. Original Cost: $33,500. Sold at auction at Mound City, Ill., August 17, 1865 to Robert Keames for $11,000. Redocumented as Mollie Hambleton, October 11, 1865. Foundered off Galveston, Tex., June 9, 1871.

Huntress. Original Cost: $33,000. Sold at auction at Mound City, Ill., August 17, 1865 to Samuel Black for $8,100. Redocumented under her original name, Huntress, October 2, 1865. Stranded and lost at Alexandria, La., December 30, 1865.

Ibex. Original Cost: $41,950. Sold at auction at Mound City, Ill., August 17, 1865 to Thomson Dean for $19,000. Redocumented as Harry Dean, October 5, 1865. Exploded at Gallipolis, O., January 3, 1868 with the loss of 9 lives.

Kate. Original Cost. $37,500. Sold at auction at Mound City, Ill., March 29, 1866 to James H. Trover for $10,350. Redocumented as James H. Trover, April 12, 1866. Stranded and lost 300 mi. below Fort Benton, Mont., June 21, 1867.

Meteor. Original Cost: $34,000. Sold at auction at New Orleans, La., October 5, 1865 to Mitchell, Boardman & Walden for $6,000. Redocumented as DeSoto, October 7, 1865. Abandoned in 1869.

Naiad. Original Cost: $32,400. Sold at auction at Mound City, Ill., August 17, 1865 to B. F. Beasley for $8,100. Redocumented under her original name, Princess, October 21, 1865. Stranded and lost at Napoleon, Mo., June 1, 1868.

Nymph. Original Cost: $32,000. Sold at auction at Mound City, Ill., August 17, 1865 to A. M. Hutchinson for $9,000. Post-1865 fate unknown.

Oriole. Original Cost: $40,000. Sold at auction at Mound City, Ill., August 17, 1865 to Thomas Scott for $17,000. Redocumented as Agnes, October 14, 1865. Snagged and lost at Warrenton, Miss., March 3, 1869.

Peri. Original Cost: $28,000. Sold at auction at Mound City, Ill., August 17, 1865 to Alfred Hoff for $7,200. Redcoumented as Marietta, October 3, 1865. Abandoned in 1868.

Sibyl. Original Cost: $30,000. Sold at auction at Mound City, Ill., August 17, 1865 to R. J. Trunstall for $10,100. Redocumented as Comet, September 28, 1865. Abandoned in 1876.

Siren. Original Cost: $34,500. Sold at auction at Mound City, Ill., August 17, 1865 to E. S. Mills for $9,050. Redocumented under her original name, White Rose, October 3, 1865. Abandoned in 1867.

Tallahatchie. Original Cost: $32,000. Sold at auction at New Orleans, La., August 12, 1865 to S. W. Roberts for $18,500. Redocumented as Coosa, August 25, 1865. Burnt in the Licking River, Ky., September 7, 1869.

Vindicator. Transferred from the War Dept. Sold at auction at Mound City, Ill., November 29, 1865 to W. L. Hambleton for $5,000. Redocumented as New Orleans, February 27, 1866. Abandoned in 1869.

The Tinclads, 1865

Mist. Original Cost: $38,500. Sold at auction at Mound City, Ill., August 17, 1865 to C. C. Hutchinson for $11,500. Redocumented under her original name, Mist, August 31, 1865. Abandoned in 1874.

Tempest. Original Cost: $55,000. Sold at auction at Mound City, Ill., November 29, 1865 to Robert Carns for $12,300. Redocumented under her original name, Tempest, December 11, 1865. Abandoned in 1870.

The Tennessee River Gunboats, 1863-1864

General Burnside. Turned over to the War Dept., June 1, 1865.

General Grant. Turned over to the War Dept., June 1, 1865.

General Sherman. Turned over to the War Dept., June 1, 1865.

General Thomas. Turned over to the War Dept., June 1, 1865.

Captured Confederate Vessels Converted into Union Warships, 1862-1864[34]

Alexandria. Captured at Yazoo City, Miss., July 1863; name changed to U.S.S. St. Mary. Sold at auction at Mound City, Ill., August 17, 1865 to W. Markham for $2,400. Redocumented as Alexandria, October 4, 1865. Abandoned in 1867.

General Bragg. Captured off Memphis, Tenn., June 1862. Sold at auction at Mound City, Ill., August 17, 1865 to David White for $52,100. Redocumented as Mexico, November 6, 1865. Sold aboard in 1870.

General Pillow. Captured off Memphis, Tenn., June 1862. Sold at auction at Mound City, Ill., November 29, 1865 to Wetzel & Hallerberg for $2,000. Post-1865 fate unknown.

General Price. Captured off Memphis, Tenn., June 1862. Sold at auction at Mound City, Ill., October 3, 1865 to W. H. Harrison for $14,000. Post-1865 fate unknown.

Little Rebel. Captured off Memphis, Tenn., June 1862. Sold at auction at Mound City, Ill., November 29, 1865 to Daniel Jacobs for $2,500. Post-1865 fate unknown.

Ouachita. Captured in 1864. Sold at auction at New Orleans, La., September 25, 1865 to Tait, Able, and Gill for $25,000. Redocumented as Vicksburg, November 21, 1865. Abandoned in 1869.

Robb. Captured at Florence, Ala., April 1862. Sold at auction at Mound City, Ill., August 17, 1865 to H. A. Smith for $9,200. Redocumented as Robb, September 9, 1865. Abandoned in 1873.

Tensas. Captured in 1863. Sold at auction at Mound City, Ill., August 17, 1865 to E. B. Trinidad for $6,200. Redocumented as Teche, October 13, 1865. Abandoned in 1869.

Volunteer. Captured in 1864. Sold at auction at Mound City, Ill., November 29, 1865 to B. F. Goodwin for $9,100. Post-1865 fate unknown.

Tennessee. Captured off Mobile, Ala., 1864. Sold at auction at New Orleans, La., November 22, 1867 in a package with Calhoun and Osage for $20,467.10. Post-1867 fate unknown.

Hospital Ship, 1862

Red Rover. Captured in 1862. Sold at auction at Mound City, Ill., November 29, 1865 to A. M. Carpenter for $4,500. Post-1865 fate unknown.

Receiving Ship, 1865

Grampus. Original Cost: $9,750. Sold at Mound City, Ill., September 1, 1868 to D. H. Holliday & Bros. for $450. Post-1868 fate unknown.

Blacksmith Ship, 1863

Samson. Transferred from the War Dept. Sold at auction at Mound City, Ill., August 17, 1865 to J. W. Clark, J. Nixon, et al. for $16,100. Redocumented under her original name, Samson, December 27, 1865. Abandoned in 1869.

Despatch and Supply Ships, 1865

General Lyon. Original Cost: $9,314.28. Sold at auction at Mound City, Ill., August 17, 1865 to H. L. Lee for $26,350. Redocumented under her original name DeSoto, October 22, 1868. Burnt below New Orleans, La., December 31, 1870.

William H. Brown. Transferred from the War Dept. Sold at auction at Mound City, Ill., August 17, 1865 to R. R. Hudson, et al. for $10,700. Redocumented under her original name, William H. Brown, December 18, 1865. Abandoned in late 1865.

Tugboats, 1862--

All of the following were sold at auction at Mound City, Ill., August 17, 1865.

Dahlia. Fate after 1872 unknown.

Daisy. Redocumented as Little Queen. Fate after 1871 unknown.

Fern. Fate after 1877 unknown.

Hyacinth. Redocumented as Rolla. Abandoned in 1884.

Laurel. Abandoned in 1903.

Myrtle. Redocumented as Resolute. Fate after 1865 unknown.

Thistle. Fate after 1865 unknown.

Notes

1. See for example the works of Messers. Bearss, Merrill, and Milligan listed in the bibliography.

2. U.S. Navy Department, Official Records of the Union and Confederate Navies in the War of the Rebellion (31 vols.; Washington: 1897-1922), Series I, Vol. 27, p. 185.

3. Official Records...Navies, Series I, Vol. 27, pp. 172-175.

4. Official Records...Navies, Series I, Vol. 27, pp. 210-212.

5. Henry Walke, Naval Scenes and Reminiscences of the Civil War in the United States.... (New York: 1877), p. 53. In a letter to a Medal of Honor winner and former Carondelet crewman, the ship's first commander confided an interested tidbit on her namesake. Basing his notes on a June, 1795 document sent him by his successor in command, Leiutenant John McLeod Murphy, the admiral stated that she was named for Don Francisco Hector, Baron de Carondelet, the last Spanish governor of Louisiana. The name was given to the village (now part of St. Louis) where James Eads built her in the fall of 1861 and by order of Commodore Andrew H. Foote, she was christened in honor of both. Walke to John Dorman, February 9, 1888 (Library, Ohio Historical Society).

6. E. J. Pratt, Superintendent, Fort Donelson National Military Park to writer, July 12, 1969; William E. Geoghegan, "Study for a Scale-Model of the U. S. S. Carondelet," Nautical Research Journal, XVII (Fall & Winter 1970-1971), 147-163, 231-236; H. Allen Gosnell, Guns on the Western Waters.... (Baton Rouge: 1949), p. i. In 1969, Mr. Geoghegan felt the Carondelet's post-1865 career "conjectural." Geoghegan to writer, June 20, 1969, November 17, 1970.

7. Official Records...Navies, Series I, Vol. 27, pp. 56, 78, 100, 128, 174; Logbook of the U. S. S. Carondelet, February 2-April 15, 1865 (Record Group 45, National Archives) cited hereafter as Logbook. According to the log, the ship's last angry fire was directed furing the Nashville Campaign. Indeed, she fired her cannon only twice more before her retirement and on both occasions, these were warning shots placed across the bows of Union transports disobeying the rules of convoy.

8. Logbook, April 29-May 20, 1865.

9. Official Records. . . Navies, Series I, Vol. 27, pp. 185, 217, 252-255. Lee had replaced the colorful David Dixon Porter as commander of the fleet in the weeks just before the Nashville Campaign. The former boss of the South Atlantic Blockade would be the last war-time chief of the river navy.

10. Logbook, May 31 and June 1, 1865.

11. Official Records. . . Navies, Series I, Vol. 27, pp. 278-279; Logbook, June 9-19, 1865. While Donaldson never rose to captain the vessel, he served a number of times as Executive Officer. To him was given the ship's main battle ensign, presently displayed in the Naval Academy Museum in Annapolis, Maryland. A. B. Donaldson to Secretary of the Navy, June 28, 1929 (Files, U. S. Naval Academy Museum).

12. Logbook, June 20, 1865. This was the final entry in the log.

13. Official Records. . . Navies, Series I, Vol. 27, passim. No further mention is made anywhere of the Carondelet's duty as an ordnance boat. This was probably only a temporary expedient while the guns of the warships coming into Mound City were held prior to transfer to the Jefferson Barracks.

14. Official Records. . . Navies, Series I, Vol. 27, p. 344; St. Louis Daily Missouri Democrat, August 9-20, 1865. While the flotilla was no more, the naval station at Mound City continued to function into the 1870's. Henry Walke served as base commander in 1868-69, his last active duty before retiring. "Rear Admiral Henry Walke, U. S. N." United Service, VII (March 1892), p. 320.

15. The papers also advertised the auction of 5,000 tons of the ex-fleet's coal and a number of coal barges for November 28 and the sale of 250-300 tons of "T" railroad iron--the dismantled ironclad's armor--on November 30.

16. Much of what we know comes from official documents, many of which were reprinted in summary form for example in the annual report of Montgomery Meigs

(for the Quartermaster General's Department) in U.S. War Department, Report of the Secretary of War (Washington, D.C., 1866), pp. 109-110.

17. St. Louis Daily Missouri Democrat, November 21, 1865. This sale was not unlike those which followed other American wars and even now takes place from time to time at various military outlets. For an example of one of these, see the accounts of how the Navy sold the submarines Sailfish and Seadragon in the April 2 and May 4, 1948 issues of the New York Times.

18. Cincinnati Daily Commercial, December 19, 1865.

19. Official Records...Navies, Series II, Vol. 1, p. 52; Edwin C. Bearss, Hardluck Ironclad (Baton Rouge, 1966), p. 177. Jacobs also purchased the ex-gunboats BENTON ($3,300), LOUISVILLE ($3,000), and LITTLE REBEL ($2,500). This last he quickly resold and she was redocumented as the SPY on March 4, 1867; The former flagship TEMPEST, a swift tinclad, was purchased by R. Conner for the best price of the day--$12,000. Two weeks later on December 11 she was redocumented under that name and was soon plying the river as a passenger steamer. St. Louis Daily Missouri Republican, November 30, 1865; William M. Lytle, Merchant Steam Vessels of the United States, 1807-1868; "The Lytle List," edited by Forrest R. Holdcamper (Mystic, Conn: The Steamship Historical Society of America, 1952), pp. 158 and 185.

20. Tippitt to writer, June 8, 1970.

21. Cincinnati Daily Commercial, May 25, 1866; Memphis Public Ledger, April 23, 1873. No further mention is made of her engines and as they were so poor in 1865, one can safely assume they were junked rather than placed in another vessel. A wharfboat is a steamer with upper works removed, a warehouse built on deck, and used to offset the differences in high and low water on the rivers.

22. Cincinnati Daily Commercial, April 18, 1873.

23. Cincinnati Daily Commercial, April 22, 1873; James

River Guide (Cincinnati: 1871), p. 76.

24. On this date, Admiral Lee submitted his last full squadron report prior to receiving Secretary Welles' May 3 order for force reduction. For sentimental reasons, the wartime loss of noted river vessels are indicated by footnote.

25. A poor example is found in Fletcher Pratt, The Civil War on Western Waters (New York: 1956), pp. 231-246. The most useful printed source remains the statistical section in Official Records... Navies, Series II, Vol. 1, pp. 27-246.

26. Thus the previously unnoted sale of the U. S. S. Mound City is made known by the December 3, 1865 issue of the St. Louis Daily Missouri Republican.

27. U. S. S. Conestoga was sunk March 3, 1864 in a collision.

28. U. S. S. Cairo was sunk by torpedo in the Yazoo River, December 4, 1862; U. S. S. St. Louis (later Baron De Kalb) was mined in the same stream in July 1863.

29. U. S. S. Milwaukee was sunk by torpedo in the Blakely River, Ala., March 1865. U. S. S. Manhattan, not technically a river monitor, was released from river duty in mid-1864. Remained on the navy list until 1902.

30. The Lancaster and Switzerland were sunk passing the Vicksburg batteries in early 1863, the Mingo was accidentally sunk off Cape Girardeau, Mo., in November 1862, and the Queen of the West was captured by the Confederates in February 1863 and later destroyed.

31. The flagship Black Hawk was accidentally burnt above Cairo, Ill., April 22, 1865, the Glide was accidentally burnt below Cairo, Ill., in February 1863, the Linden and Betrel were lost in the Yazoo River in the spring of 1864, the Rattler was driven ashore in a storm and abandoned off Grand Gulf, Miss., in December 1864, and the Signal was sunk in the Red River in May 1864.

32. The Covington was sunk in the Red River in May 1864, the Key West and Tawah were destroyed as a result of the November 1864 action at Johnsonville, Tenn., the Queen City was lost off Clarendon, Ark., in June 1864, and the Wave was captured and destroyed by the Confederates at Calcasieu Pass, Tex., in May 1864.

33. The Elfin and Undine were destroyed as a result of the November 1864 action at Johnsonville, Tenn., while the Rodolph was sunk by a torpedo in the Blakely River, Ala., in April 1865.

34. The Eastport was blown up by Federal forces in April 1864 during the Red River Campaign while the Sumter was grounded off Bayou Sara, La., and abandoned in August 1862, later to be burned by the Confederates.

APPENDIX C

Bibliographic Addenda

The following citations, all prior to 1972, came to the attention of the compiler too late to include in the main sequence. None are indexed.

1. Adams, Brooks. "The Seizure of the Laird Rams." Massachusetts Historical Society Proceedings, XLV (December 1911), 243-333.

2. Adams, Charles F. "The Laird Rams." Massachusetts Historical Society Proceedings, 2nd Series XIII (1900), 177-197.

3. Adams, Ephraim. Great Britain and the American Civil War. 2 vols. Gloucester, Mass.: Smith, 1957.

4. Ashcraft, Allan C. "Texas: 1860-1866, The Lone Star State in the Civil War." Unpublished PhD Dissertation, Columbia University, 1960.

5. Baldwin, S. E. "The 'Continuous Voyage' Doctrine During the Civil War, and Now." American Journal of International Law, IX (1915), 793-801.
   A comparison with events afloat before American entry into World War I.

6. Baxter, James P. "Some British Opinions as to Neutral Rights, 1861 to 1865." American Journal of International Law, XXIII (1929), 517-537.
   Includes Admiralty correspondence to the British Commander-in-Chief on the American station.

7. -----., ed. "Papers Relating to Belligerent and Neutral Rights, 1861-1865." American Historical Review, XXXIV (1928), 77-91.
   Reprints documents from the British Admiralty, the U.S. State Department, and the French

Archives de la Marine.

8. Bemis, George. Precedents of American Neutrality, in Reply to the Speech of Sir Roundell Palmer, May 13, 1864. Boston: Little, Brown, 1864. 83p.

9. Bernard, M. Historical Account of the Neutrality of Great Britain During the American Civil War. London: Longmans, 1870. 511p.

10. Birnbaum, Louis. "Ulysses S. Grant Invades France." Mankind, II (December 1969), 40-49.
A comparison of Grant's Vicksburg strategy with the 1944 Allied D-Day plans; ample discussion of naval support.

11. Brent, Robert. "Mahan--Mariner or Misfit?" United States Naval Institute Proceedings, XCII (April 1966), 92-103.
Special emphasis on his Civil War duties.

12. Brooke, St. George T. "The Merrimac-Monitor Battle." Trans-Allegheny Historical Magazine, II (1902), 30-42.

13. Bushnell, Samuel C. The Story of the Monitor and the Merrimac. New Haven: Priv. print, [1924?] 12p.
By the son of one of the Yankee ironclad's builders.

14. Casual Papers upon the Alabama and Kindred Questions and Incidentally, Upon National Amenities. 2nd ed. Hongkong: China Magazine Office, 1869. 86p.

15. Cunningham, Edward C. "Shiloh and the Western Campaign of 1862." Unpublished PhD Dissertation, Louisiana State University, 1966.

16. Curtis, Richard. History of the Famous Battle Between the Iron-Clad Merrimac, C. S. N., and the Iron-Clad Monitor and the Cumberland and Congress of the U. S. Navy, March 8th and 9th, 1862, as Seen by a Man at the Gun. Norfolk, Va.: S. B. Turner, 1907. 17p.
Reprinted, with an additional page, by the Houston Printing and Publishing House of Hampton, Virginia, in 1957.

17. Davis, Doris S., comp. *John Lloyd Broome, 1849-1898*. Manuscript Register Series, no. 6. Quantico, Va.: Marine Corps Museum, n.d. 21p.
This noted leatherneck served aboard U.S.S. *Hartford* during much of the conflict.

18. DeMontmorency, J. E. G. "Sea Policy and the Alabama Claims, 1861-1907." *In* Adolphus Ward and G. P. Gooch, eds. *The Cambridge History of British Foreign Policy, 1783-1918*. 3 vols. New York: Octagon, 1970. III, 54-71.
Reprint of an essay contained in the 1922-1923 edition.

19. Dudley, Thomas H. "Three Critical Periods in Our Diplomatic Relations with England during the Late War: Personal Recollections of Thomas H. Dudley, late United States Consul at Liverpool." *Pennsylvania Magazine of History and Biography*, XVII (1893), 34-54.
Two naval related episodes by "the man who stopped the rams."

20. Ericsson, John. *Contributions to the Centennial Exhibition*. New York: Priv. print. at "The Nation" Press, 1876. 577p.
Several sections on the birth of U.S.S. *Monitor*.

21. Ferris, Norman B. "Tempestuous Mission, 1861-1862: The Early Diplomatic Career of Charles Francis Adams." Unpublished PhD Dissertation, Emory University, 1962.
His handling of such problems as the *Trent* Affair and the British-built Confederate cruisers.

22. Flake, Elijah W. *Battle Between the Merrimac and Monitor, March 9th, 1862*. Polkton, N.C.: The Author, 1914. 12p.
Reminiscences by the last survivor of the *Virginia's* crew.

23. Fuller, Richard F. *Chaplain Fuller: Being a Life Sketch of a New England Clergyman and Army Chaplain*. Boston: Walker, Wise, 1863.
Contains a 22-page account of the *Monitor*/*Virginia* battle by this eyewitness.

24. Gardner, Audrey. "Henry Walke, 1809-1896, Romantic Painter and Naval Hero." Unpublished PhD Dissertation, George Washington University, 1971.

25. Griffin, James D. "Savannah, Georgia, During the Civil War." Unpublished PhD Dissertation, University of Georgia, 1963.

26. Groh, George W. "Sink the Shenandoah." In Alden Price, ed. Sea Raiders: Thrilling True Stories of Daring Naval Exploits in Wartime. North Hollywood, Calif.: Challenge Books, n.d. p. 21-36.

27. Hatcher, Harlan. "Johnson's Island." In his Lake Erie. American Lakes Series. Indianapolis: Bobbs-Merrill, 1945. p. 240-246.
Data on the Rebel plot hatched by John Yates Beall.

28. Hawkins, R. C. "The Coming of the Russian Ships in 1863." North American Review, CLXXVIII (1904), 539-544.

29. Hicken, Victor. "From Vandalis to Vicksburg: the Political and Military Career of John A. McClernand." Unpublished PhD Dissertation, University of Illinois, 1955.
Admiral Porter and General Sherman did not care for this political general's manipulations, especially during the campaign for Arkansas Post.

30. Iles, George. Leading American Inventors. New York: Holt, 1912.
Contains a chapter of John Ericcson.

31. Leeming, Joseph. The Book of American Fighting Ships. New York: Harper, 1939. 283p.
Contains chapters on the Battle of New Orleans, Monitor vs. Virginia, Alabama vs. Kearsarge, and the Battle of Mobile Bay.

32. Long, Edward B. and Barbara. The Civil War Day by Day: An Almanac, 1861-1865. New York: Doubleday, 1971. 1135p.
Not as useful for naval affairs as the Navy's Civil War Naval Chronology, but an important

compendium nevertheless.

33. O'Rourke, Sister Mary M. "The Diplomacy of William H. Seward During the Civil War: His Policies as Related to International Law." Unpublished PhD Dissertation, University of California at Berkeley, 1963.
Much on the blockade and Trent affair.

34. Parrott, Robert P. Ranges of Parrott Guns and Notes for Practice. New York: D. Van Nostrand, 1863.
Many naval vessels were outfitted with such ordnance.

35. Schottenhamel, George C. "Lewis Baldwin Parsons and Civil War Transportation." Unpublished PhD Dissertation, University of Illinois, 1954.
Some attention to river supply routes in the West.

36. Shepard, Frederick J. "The Johnson Island Plot." Publications of the Buffalo Historical Society, VIII (1887), 1-51.
That conceived by J. Y. Beall for the capture of the U.S.S. Michigan and the freeing of Rebel P.O.W.s on the island.

37. Simpson, W. A. C. "Britain and the Blockade: the Blockade--in Theory." Journal of the Confederate Historical Society (Spring 1968), 6-26.

38. Sumner, Charles. The Case of the Florida, Illustrated by Precedents from British History. New York: Young Men's Republican Union, 1864. 19p.

39. United Confederate Veterans. Georgia Division. The Defence of Battery Wagner, July 18, 1863. By Charles C. Jones. Augusta: Chronicle Publishing Co., 1892. 30p.

40. United States of America. Congress. House. Letter from the Secretary of the Treasury in Relation to the Sale of U.S. Vessels, Transports, and Other Vessels, During and Since the Conclusion of the War of the Rebellion. House Ex. doc 113, 41st Cong., 3rd Sess., 1871. 7p.

41. -----. Interior Department. U.S.S. Cairo: The Story of a Civil War Gunboat. Washington: U.S. Government Printing Office, 1971. 56p.

Her sinking and salvage.

42. Warren, Gordon H. "The Trent Affair, 1861-1862." Unpublished PhD Dissertation, Indiana University, 1969.

An important source for the coverage of this controversy.

43. Wegner, Dana M. "Data on Civil War Monitors." Nautical Research Journal, XVIII (Spring 1971), 3-8.

Contains material not dissimilar in arrangement from that in Appendix B of this volume.

INDEX

In this index, a number of abbreviations have been incorporated from the scheme employed by the Naval History Division in its Civil War Naval Chronology.

All officers and men included are drawn from the body of or annotations to numbered references in the bibliography. Most of these may be assumed to have been in the Union (USN) Navy unless otherwise noted. Abbreviations as to service include: USA for the U.S. Army; CSA and CSN for the Confederate Army and Navy; USMC and CSMC for the Marine Corps; RN for British Royal Navy; USRM and USRC for U.S. Revenue Marine (forerunner of the modern U.S. Coast Guard) and U.S. Revenue Cutter; and USCS for U.S. Coast Survey. In general, of course, Am. stands for American (Union) and Conf. for Confederate.

Abbreviations for types of ships include: schnr. for schooner; stmr. for steamer; and b.r. for blockade runner. Rank and, where possible, state names are also shortened, e.g.: Lt. Commander for Lieutenant Commander; Brig. General for Brigadier General; N.C. for North Carolina; N.H. for New Hampshire.

Numerous general categories familiar to many have been inserted, e.g.: Commerce, Strategy, Coast and Harbor Defense. No references are made to the navies or marine corps by name.